Praise for the Book From Across the Different Worlds

FROM THE SOUTHERN WORLD

'The "communiversity" idea is timely. It challenges the dominance of the conventional university. What is even more exciting and appropriate is the fact that this birth is being presided over by Africans, alongside significant others around the world, representing the authentic natural grounding critical for knowledge creation and societal renewal altogether. The communiversity is clearly an answer to a distraught world in which the conventional university has failed to provide solutions. For me, "university" speaks of individualism and selfishness leading to destructive detachment from reality, whereas "Communiversity" speaks of community and teamwork leading to inclusive, transformative development. The time for the communiversity has indeed arrived!'

Douglas Mbowane,
CEO, Econet Wireless, Harare, Zimbabwe.

***

'The very concept of 'communiversity' demonstrates that there are thinkers among us who are rising to the current global systemic and epistemic crisis, characterised not only by uncertainties of knowledge but by the very idea of a university being questioned and universities turning into the key site of struggles. *The Idea of the Communiversity* is a welcome contribution, which transcends seeking to know the world of knowledge and its politics but, courageously and innovatively, offers a way in which to change it. I have nothing but praise for this important book.'

Professor Sabelo J. Ndlovu-Gatsheni,
Author of Epistemic Freedom in Africa: Deprovincialization and Decolonization.
Head of Change Unit, University of South Africa, Pretoria.

i

nomic needs of the 21ˢᵗ century. The need to forge a union between industry and academe, community and economy and revamp the spiritual and moral foundation of society cannot be more pressing than now. The world needs a university model that can reconcile it with nature, community and the environment. I applaud the vision behind the book.'

Professor Ben. E. Aigbokhan,
Vice-Chancellor, Samuel Adegboyega University, Ogwa, Nigeria.

***

'This book is an invitation to reconnect with the healing power of nature: a spiritual, psychological, cultural and technological Renaissance. Theology, Medicine, Law, Technology and the Liberal Arts constitute important issues in the communiversity and related institutions—an era of the social laboratory. The authors clearly expended great energy, enthusiasm, efforts and patience to produce this work.'

Professor Abiodun Falodun,
Rector, Edo State Polytechnic, Nigeria.

***

'A masterpiece. Daring to think differently. A profound work of impeccable scholarship.'

Professor Oluwatoyin Ogundipe,
Vice-Chancellor, University of Lagos, Nigeria

***

FROM THE EASTERN WORLD

'*The Idea of the Communiversity* is a compelling and enlightening read. It is a genuine effort to reap the fruit of integral knowledge. By reinventing terms for this knowledge, the authors are able to coin an authentic definition of learning, where the roots of meaning evolve from communities. Communiversities are live organisms that stem and grow in their unique soils of origin.'

Senator Haifa Hajjar Najjar,
Jordanian Senate House: The Upper House of Jordanian Parliament.

***

'As 'humanity' seems to be less and less of a commodity in our work-places and societies, it is prime time to return human consciousness and a sense of belonging in the world. *The Idea of the Communiversity* offers a new path—an integral approach to learning and being that is rooted in one's self and community, while embracing global knowledge and enter-prise to make a genuine difference in the world we live in.'

Dr Hassib Sahyoun,
Founder and CEO, Medlabs Jordan.

***

'An intellectually stimulating book. It challenges the conventional Eurocentric narrative and puts forth an alternative development ap-proach, nesting together often undermined forces of the community, lo-cal knowledge and spirituality—combined, they present a new paradigm of inclusive development. A unique effort—like a breath of fresh air.'

Dr Amjad Saqib,
Founder of Akhuwat (Integral Finance), Pakistan.

***

FROM THE NORTHERN WORLD

'A truly inspiring text that proposes a visionary and unique approach to community, culture and academia in changing socio-economic times.

The idea of communiversities challenges historic practice and embraces our current local culture with a new mindset and in a new way.'

David E. Jenkins, CEO – The Old Courts Arts & Heritage Trust, Wigan, UK.

***

'Ronnie Lessem is always worth listening to. He challenges the normal and inspires the extraordinary. This book could change your life and our world.'

Dame Jayne-Anne Gadhia,
ex-CEO, Virgin Money, Founder of the Gadhia Group, UK.

***

'The authors argue the urgency of re-situating knowledge/learning communities in historical time and diversity of culture and place. They recall the complex genealogy of Western knowledge institutions (library, monastery and academy, through medieval Republic of Letters, to modern university and laboratory): they insist on the interplay of oral and written forms of knowledge; and on the links between learning, reconciliation, healing and human community. And then, politely, on the challenge to "subvert the epistemological scaffolding" that underpins current Western hegemony (and its discontents)—developing through world examples the proposition that "in the present moment, it is the global south that affords privileged insight into the workings of the world at large". They show that the time has arrived for the resurgence of an intellectual "appropriate technology."'

Professor Martin O'Connor,
Professor of Economics, Université Paris-Saclay, France.

***

'From social innovators in local communities to top leaders of our societies, from rural communities to academia, we urgently need the change of perspective elaborated in this book. In order to release the GEN*E*-ius of Self-Organisation-Community-Society—including Economy—the paradigm shift that these authors advocate includes overcoming the over-emphasis of "Western" and "Northern" perspectives in knowledge creation and sharing. Learning rooted in nature and community, as well as culture and spirituality, are indispensable elements of the "communiversity". The communiversity idea will effectively promote the knowledge-and-institutional transformation needed to address the burning issues of our time.'

Dr Darja Piciga,
Founder of the Citizens' Initiative for Integral Green Slovenia.

***

FROM THE WESTERN WORLD

'In this path-breaking book, Lessem, Adodo and Bradley call for a novel re-conception of the modern techno-centric university. In place of the hierarchical and individualistic university, these scholars propose an institution that is spiritual in purpose, that is communitarian in orientation and that seeks the transformation of the individual and her society. They call this reimagining of the university a "communiversity" and view it as a combination of a community of scholars, engaged in a transformative journey (pilgrimium), that is both an inclusive academy and a functional laboratory. This book is a call to action for educators and activists to create an institution that can work to change concrete societal problems.'

Professor Kenneth B. Nunn,
Professor of Law, University of Florida, USA.

'In *The Idea of the Communiversity*, Lessem, Adodo and Bradley guide us on an epic journey toward reimagining knowledge creation and its application for the purpose of bringing integral transformation to a world in desperate need. Drawing on the historic roots of knowledge creation and transmission, the authors propose a newly integral "communiversity" as an alternative to the now moribund traditional university construct, where one size is supposed to fit all learners. In a world rife with endemic challenges without solutions, the communiversity's core elements of Community, Pilgrimium, Academy and Laboratory offer new hope for the challenges our world faces, by excavating long neglected indigenous knowledge sources that can lead to innovative solutions both local and global. The time has come for the communiversity!'

Dr Sam Rima
Author of Spiritual Capital: A Moral Core for Social and Economic Justice.
Bethel University, Minnesota, USA

About the Authors

PROFESSOR RONNIE SAMANYANGA LESSEM, born in Zimbabwe and now based in the UK, was co-founder, together with Dr Alexander Schieffer of TRANS4M (Hotonnes) which has since evolved, in part, into Trans4m Communiversity Associates (TCA), which together with Trans4m's partner university, Da Vinci Institute in South Africa, founded by Nelson Mandela, focuses on Doctoral Programmes, on the regeneration of particular societies. It is currently mainly active through its emerging Communiversities in Southern Africa (South Africa, Zimbabwe), West Africa (Nigeria), the Middle East (Egypt, Jordan), the Near East (Pakistan) and Europe (Switzerland, Sloveni, UK). Hitherto Ronnie Lessem has launched projects on European management with IMD in Switzerland, European-ness and Innovation with Roland Berger Foundation in Germany, African management, with Wits Graduate Business School in South Africa and Arab as well as Islamic Management with TEAM International in Cairo and Jordan. He studied economics at the University of Zimbabwe, the economics of industry at the London School of Economics, Corporate Planning at Harvard Business School and has since written some 50 books, the most recent, with Anselm Adodo and Tony Bradley, co-founders of TCA together with Aneeqa Malik, on *The Idea of the Communiversity*.

FATHER ANSELM ADODO is a member of the Benedictine order of the Catholic Church. He was ordained a priest in 1997. He is the founder and Director of Nigeria's foremost herbal research institute, the Pax Herbal Clinic and Research Laboratories, popularly called Pax Herbals. He is a prominent advocate of African Herbal medicine research, indigenous knowledge systems, rural community development, health policy reform and transformation of education in Africa. Anselm's approach to research is transdisciplinary and multidisciplinary and this reflects in his publications. He is an adjunct visiting lecturer at the Institute of African

Studies, University of Ibadan, Nigeria, where he teaches African Trans-formation studies and Traditional African Medicine. He is an Adjunct Fellow of the Nigerian Institute of Medical Research, Nigeria, a Fellow of the Nigerian Society of Botanists and a Senior Fellow at Trans4m centre for Integral Development, France.

REVD TONY BRADLEY is Lecturer in Social Economy and Enterprise within Liverpool Hope University Business School, U.K. He has had an unusual career progression, having been, in turn, a university academic, an Anglican priest, a TV and radio producer, a social entrepreneur, a the-atrical producer and director, a professional script-writer and, for a sec-ond time, a university academic. This progression has, itself, modelled an integral journey of four worlds in one life. Although permanently resident in the UK, he has worked on a range of projects in West Africa, South-West Asia and the Middle East. His most recent social innovation work has been in the arts and social economy sphere in NW England. He is Chair of Trustees for The Old Courts, Wigan and co-leader of the team developing Communiversity Liverpool. *The Idea of the Communi-versity* is his ninth book. He lives in the English Lake District with his wife Carol, their two daughters, their partners, two grandchildren and two dogs.

The Idea of the Communiversity

First published in the UK by Beacon Books and Media Ltd
Innospace, Chester Street, Manchester M1 5GD, UK.

First paperback edition published in 2019

www.beaconbooks.net

ISBN 978-1-912356-24-9 Paperback
ISBN 978-1-912356-25-6 Hardback
ISBN 978-1-912356-26-3 eBook

Cataloging-in-Publication record for this book is available from the
British Library

The Idea of the Communiversity

Releasing the Natural, Cultural, Technical and Economic GENE-ius of Societies

Ronnie Lessem, Anselm Adodo, Tony Bradley

Contents

PROLEGOMENA:

UNIVERSITY TO COMMUNIVERSITY

Preamble:
The Stories We Are

The Idea of the Communiversity *was born out of the communal, conscious raising and the conceptual and commercial experiences of three people: Samanyanga Ronnie Lessem, an Afro-European
social philosopher, Father Anselm Adodo, a Nigerian-Benedictine
Monk, priest, philosopher and social scientist and Tony Bradley, a
Celtic-Christian intellectual activist. Each of us, in association with
our academic and commercial organisations and societies, spread altogether over 120 years, has sought to transcend the divide between
industry and academe, the spiritual and the material, community
and economy, one cultural world and another.*

*Each of us has devoted a lifetime to bridging different worlds,
most especially those of community and university, albeit also aligned
with spirituality and with enterprise, spread across the south and the
north, the east and the west. We start then with our own respective
life stories which have led up to* The Idea of the Communiversity,
*an idea that we are currently putting into practice in Africa and in
the Middle East, in Europe and in Asia, as you will see. We begin
with Samanyanga, born and bred in Zimbabwe.*

SAMANYANGA RONNIE LESSEM: BUHERA TO
INTEGRAL KUMUSHA

"There is a saying that 'elephants never forget', as they have extraordinary and highly intelligent memories. They walk the earth's meridians and tune into their vibrations through their sensitive feet. This sensitivity allows them to feel dense energy along the meridians and aid in clearing and opening these channels and pathways. They walk along the 31ˢᵗ meridian, Earth's energetic spine. It's not surprising that their ears are in the hope of the continent of Africa; they represent the ability to hear the very sensitive vibrations of the Earth below, which are tuned into support the opening of the key lines, the flow of energy in the universe."

Carol Mattimore and Linda Star Wolf,
Sacred Messengers of Shamanic Africa

Local Grounding/Learning Community

UCRN: Europe Bereft of Africa

I can vividly remember a pregnant moment whilst studying economics at the University College of Rhodesia (now Zimbabwe) and Nyasaland (now Malawi) based in Salisbury (now Harare),when our lecturer in Applied Economics, Nigel Pearson, fresh from Great Britain, alluded to the ground nuts grown in Nyasaland. That was the one and only time in the three years of our undergraduate degree that the principles of economics touched base with Africa! For the rest of the time, although physically we lived in Southern Africa, epistemologically we were lodged, fair and square, in Western Europe.

Kwajack: Home-and-Workstead

My parents in fact came from eastern (Lithuanian) and central (Austrian) Europe and Rhodesia of course was then a Western European

(English) colony. When my father, Abe Lessem, migrated to Africa at the age of 17, he lived in a small rural town in the centre of the country called Buhera. Together with his brother Jack, he gradually established their rural home-and-workstead there; a large house with a borehole alongside a warehouse, a retail store, a grinding mill and a distribution outlet, altogether called African Trading, which marketed the African produce grown around them. They became part of the place; a trading and learning community. 'Kwajack' in fact, as their home-and-workstead is known today some eight decades later, has become part of local folklore.

Local-Global Emergence: Developmental Pilgrimium

African Trading/European Literature

Gradually the Lessem Family built up some 25 rural stores one after another under the guise of African Trading, until they also established their wholesale clothing business in Salisbury. At the same time Ronnie-becoming-Samanyanga's sophisticated European mother had enticed Abe to leave the African bush and set up home in Salisbury—modern-day Harare. In fact his mother felt as much an alien in Africa as his father felt at home. For in Lithuania, Abraham grew up as a Jew in a foreign land where the locals despised him for who he was. His mother, on the other hand, felt Austrian through and through, until Hitler, a fellow Austrian, came to power. Thereafter she continued to feel very much a central European, an expatriate in Africa.

In the 1930s, Abe Lessem established the wholesaling business in Salisbury while his brother Jack stayed on in the bush as the trader he was and always would be. Jack never came to realise though, that some of his fellow traders were Jews like him, although black rather than white.

5

Samanyanga's African Soul and Ronnie's European Mind

As an impressionable young man and sensitive soul, he empathised with the very people who remained forbidden fruit. Deep inside he felt he was an African and yet was repeatedly told by his mother that Ronnie-becoming-Samanyanga was a European and told by his father that he was a Jew. The irony was that in his twilight years, it was not his Jewish brothers and sisters that brought tears to Abraham's eyes, but the cattle—the *mombis*—as they were called in local Shona African language. He grew to love the land of Rhodesia, including the two farms he had purchased and cared for, as well as the cattle that roamed through them.

Psychology in the Backroom – Economy in the Front/or Vice Versa?

As a seven-year-old, little Ronnie-becoming-Samanyanga can vividly remember walking down the factory floor (African Trading had now been turned into Concorde Clothing, a factory now with a thousand African machinists) and none of them ever smiled.

Ten years afterwards, he can remember retrieving a red London University prospectus from a dusty school library shelf. He turned to a previously untouched page headed 'Industrial Psychology' and told his parents that this was what he wanted to make of his life. Of course nobody in Zimbabwe, including himself, had heard much of such industrial psychology at the time. So Ronnie's parents consulted their trusted friend and then Rhodesian Minister of Finance.

The Minister pronounced emphatically, "Young Lessem, psychology is for back-room boys." Of course, Ronnie did not yet have the self-awareness to fully appreciate why such a course of study was for him, so he instead pursued an undergraduate degree in the Principles of Economics. That was more to his parents' liking. Little did he know then how alienating and yet auspicious, that choice would turn out to be. Indeed it would be the south-eastern 'back-room' communally and spiritually, that would ultimately serve to overturn these 'front-room' epistemological and economic horizons.

Development From Within

Having then completed his economics honours degree, accredited of course by the University of London and not really knowing where to go from there, he decided to move to London, probably due to his mother's pressure for Ronnie to get out of the 'dark continent' of Africa. There he studied financial accounting like an obedient son. In actual fact, his unfulfilled sole cause at the time was to work in economic development in Zambia, which had recently become independent. But Ronnie was not strong-willed enough at the time, in his early twenties, to follow his own chosen course of Ronnie-becoming-Samanyanga. In any case, he had only an intimation of what that would be.

Life as Double Entry

On landing on English shores in the early 60s as a 23-year-old, Ronnie was quickly ushered by a family contact to the veritable Howard Howes and Co., a firm of chartered accountants in the City of London. His most abiding memory was of the black top hats they wore and the very posh accents with which they spoke. He was thrown deep into the English class system. Luckily enough his colonial Rhodesian accent saved the day; he was classless in this rigidly divided (including between north and south) land.

He hated financial accounting with a vengeance and from the outset, could not wait to extricate himself from his position as an 'articled clerk'. However, Ronnie-becoming-Samanyanga became fascinated by the principle of double entry and felt sure that there was much more to such than was revealed by standard accounting. For every asset there is a liability; for every debit there is a credit; for every north there needs to be a south, for every west an east; and the other side of modernity is coloniality! There were, it seemed to Ronnie, profound lessons for life in the offing.

LSE: Academy Bereft of Industry

Nevertheless, after six months Ronnie could not bear to take one more auditing assignment in some remote corner of south-east England and so he escaped to the London School of Economics (LSE) to pursue, as it was called, a Masters degree in the Economics of Industry. In fact, he found the LSE incredibly sterile—your typical 'ivory tower'.

The so-called economics of industry had nothing whatsoever to do with real business and life, at least in the way he had hitherto experienced it in African Trading. Moreover, it was an isolated, total non-experience of English individualism in education to an unhealthy extreme. He also remembered that the star student at LSE was a compatriot from Rhodesia, Stanley Fisher, who would ultimately become Deputy Director of the IMF thirty years later. He was a great devotee of Milton Friedman and the Chicago Boys. The ivory tower had served him well!

Taking stock at the point of completion of his LSE degree and having given up his plans to become a development economist in Zambia, not least because of his continuing 'blood' family influence, he decided to return to his still ambivalent Jewish roots and pay a visit to Israel. Perhaps, he thought to himself, he could play an important part in helping the Israeli economy to develop being closer to home than Africa's Zambia, so his Jewish family persuaded him. He discovered after spending two months in the country that the Israelis were interested in securing their own livelihoods, as well as defending their country from the Arabs, but nobody he met seemed interested in the economic development of the country.

So Ronnie-becoming-Samanyanga gave that emergent vocation a miss and, once again under parental influence, proceeded on to Harvard, no less—the pinnacle of business studies at the time.

HBS: American Academe Disconnected From African Enterprise

HBS was indeed a surprise. Ronnie-becoming-Samanyanga had virtually nothing in common with most of the students there, who were intent on becoming future business moguls, but he did enjoy the intensity and community of the place. Students studied cases day and night in close-knit groups, indeed as small-scale learning communities. That touched his African soul. At the same time he found the American Business School to be as distant from his African 'real world' as the LSE had been. Why should that be?

Firstly, the case studies were on American, if not also European paper and print, not embodied in the African, or indeed the Asian soil. It was easy enough for business school students to decide that the VP of Human Resources, based in Chicago a thousand miles away, needed to be fired, for example, but what if the person was actually sitting there beside him in Boston, if not Bulawayo? How would she or he handle it then? It all seemed quite vacuous. So, after graduating with his Harvard MBA, what then?

Clothestown: Prophet Not for Profit

At his father's request—after all, Abe had sponsored his son's studies—he decided to try his hand at running the family business. It did not take him long to realise he was an absolute fraud.

What did someone of 26, fresh from Harvard in America, know about running a business in the rag trade in South Africa? Ronnie can remember to this day when the merchandising manager came into his office (he had been the so-called MD for 18 months by then) and put a blue baby-grow on the table in front of him. "Feel the cloth, Mr Lessem," she said.

Ronnie-becoming-Samanyanga felt nothing. Nothing at all. He was not a rag trader. His mission in life was not to clothe people, as his father had done for some 25 years. It was rather, as he had come to realise, reinforced by the part-time teaching he had been doing in organisational development, to research, to educate and to transform, to, pretentious as it might sound, become a 'prophet', rather than 'make profit' in his own land—'I think where I am'.

9

On a personal level, meanwhile, within the space of three electrifying days, he had met and married his wife Joey and they are still happily together forty years later. As he was already unhappy in apartheid South Africa and she had a background as a political activist and was therefore pursued oftentimes by the security police, they decided it was time to go. Ronnie then, after his Clothestown experience, wanted to pursue an academic career, so headed to the UK, specifically settling for London's City University Business School. It was there, moreover, that he would inadvertently pursue his PhD, thereby, via such research, linking enterprise and economy, learning and development. Indeed, this would set an overall stage for the rest of his work and life.

PhD: Action Learning for Business Development

His mentor and subsequent PhD examiner would be the redoubtable Reg Revans. "Be ye doers of the word and not hearers only," Revans quoted from the St James Bible. In fact, Revans had been a physicist at Cambridge University (thinking), a deeply religious man (feeling) and an Olympic long jumper (doing). Drawing on all of this, he turned to management development, cognitively, affectively and behaviourally so to speak, starting out in hospitals with the development of nursing management and in the coal mines with the management of miners.

Ronnie, then, was lucky enough to be asked by Revans to write the introduction to his *Biography of Action Learning* (1), the latter's magnum opus in the 1980s. As such, Revans gave him all his previous articles and correspondence as relevant background. What a treasure trove! Revans was in fact at war with the management academic establishment. For Reg, as for Ronnie, management had become colonised by the analytically based 'professional' American approach to business administration, as per the umpteen MBA programs that proliferated now around the world. As kindred spirits, at the time, Revans became Ronnie's mentor. Another of Revans's famous sayings was: "You learn more from comrades in adversity than you do from teachers on high."

As he had no need to position himself as such a teacher on high, in his planned entrepreneurship development programme, Ronnie did not need to be an expert himself. Instead he became a facilitator, of 'learning sets' or small groups, in action learning jargon, of budding entrepreneurs who met on a fortnightly basis, at the same time they were setting up their businesses. This became the basis for his PhD thesis on 'Action Learning for Business Development'. At the same time, as co-founder of Urban and Economic Development (URBED) he undertook a major project within the inner cities on *Centres of Knowledge: The College and the Community* (2).

CUBS Management MBA: Self, Organisational and Communal Transformation

Meanwhile at City University Business School (CUBS) where he was still based, he newly shared an office with an effervescent young woman, who had become involved in setting up a new project-based Management MBA with an old colleague of Ronnie's, now a Professor of Export Marketing at CUBS.

Moreover, it did not take long for Ronnie to realise that what they were engaging in, implicitly if not explicitly, with large companies such as Ford Motors, the London Stock Exchange, American Express, Virgin Money and Sainsbury's supermarkets, was organisational, as well as managerial transformation. In fact, Anglian Water, having come to the same conclusion, decided to involve one of their own management developers with Ronnie in running a 'Transformation Journey', involving 3,000 of their staff, ranging from their road diggers to the CEO, extended over an 18 month period. For Ronnie, the transformation was less overtly that from public to private, about which he had significant misgivings, but instead from an engineering-based utility to a knowledge-creating company.

Meanwhile, the City University based Management MBA had been spreading its wings, teaming up with TEAM International, a major Arab consultancy based in Cairo, to offer the Management MBA all across the Arab world, from Egypt and Lebanon to the West Bank and Gaza, as well as in Jordan, where, in Amman, the programme most prolifically took off. For Ronnie this was an opportunity to get close to the Arab world, again reaching across to 'the other', this time as a Jew, while also brushing up on his knowledge of Islam. Sadly his university, CUBS, decided to pull the plug on this 'unprofitable' programme. So Ronnie-becoming-Samanyanga decided to leave a university with which he had been associated for 28 years. Meanwhile, something that was even more significant had been happening in the wings.

Newly Global Navigation: Trans4m Research Academy

Out of Africa: Body, Mind, Heart and Soul

In 1981, Rhodesia had gained its independence having become Zimbabwe and Ronnie-to-become-Samanyanga began to make it known to students coming to CUBS from that country that it was time for him to come 'home'. He then started to read books about southern African philosophy and spirituality, initially that of Laurens van der Post. One passage from Van der Post's *Dark Eye of Africa* (3) stuck out in his mind:

> *"European man walked into Africa by and large totally incapable of understanding it, let alone of appreciating the raw material of mind and spirit with which this granary of fate, this ancient treasure house of the lost original way of life, was so richly filled. He had, it is true, an insatiable appetite for the riches in the rocks, diamonds and gold ... but not for the precious metal ringing true in the deep toned laughter of the indigenous people around him."*

Those words rang in his ears as he prepared for his return after 15 years, whereby Rhodesia-becoming-Zimbabwe now matched Ronnie-becoming-Samanyanga and inspired the first of his own works, subsequently with his Trans4m partner Alexander Schieffer, on *The Soul of Business* (4). In a subsequent article for the academic journal Long Range

Planning, entitled *Managing in Four Worlds* (5), he wrote some twenty years ago:

> *"For the past 150 years and most particularly during the course of this (twentieth) century, global politics and economics has been marked by two sets of politically and economically divisive, rather than culturally and psychologically integrative, forces—the East/West mutually antagonistic divide of communism/capitalism and the North/South chasm of wealth and poverty."*

More specifically then, taking on from where Jung himself left off with his psychology of 'individuation', this is what he further wrote:

> *"While the reality of 'communist' East and 'capitalist' West, if not also 'rich' North and 'poor' South, in political and ideological terms, have proved altogether divisive rather than mutually supportive, their symbolical importance in cultural and psychological terms is what is key to the 'four worlds'."*

What was clearly apparent then, is that Ronnie-becoming-Gatsheni had reconnected with the Rhodesian Minister of Finance's pronouncement, that 'psychology was for back-room boys' and brought that back-room to the forefront of business and economics.

MMBA to MTM to MSET: Masters in Transformation Management in Jordan

Meanwhile, Ronnie moved on from City to Buckingham University because of the close connections he had with a longstanding colleague who had originally brought him out to India. In fact, it was this colleague, who having been active in the field of organisational transformation, was instrumental when Ronnie moved the former Management MBA to the University of Buckingham (UB), in renaming it a 'Masters in Transformation Management.' When the head of Team International in Jordan heard Ronnie-becoming-Abu al-Tahawal ('father of transformation' in Arabic) had moved from City, she immediately contacted him with a view to resurrecting the masters programme in Amman. One of the first to join this programme was Manar al-Nimer, now Dr Manar, as a graduate of Trans4m and Vice President of Medlabs.

In drawing on the Transformation masters, now based at UB, to enable Medlabs in Jordan to be transformed from a centralised and hierarchical to a 'self-organising', decentralised group of medical laboratories, she would be paving the way for others to follow, at the interface, now in Jordan, between industry and academe.

MTM to MSET: Masters in Social and Economic Transformation in South Africa

In the new millennium, Lovemore Mbigi cropped up again in Ronnie-becoming-Samanyanga's life, when they met on a workshop in Amsterdam on African management. He suggested they might want to run a new masters programme together in social and economic transformation (MSET) in South Africa, accredited by Buckingham University where Ronnie was based. This would be for a new kind of South African University with which he was closely associated; CIDA – Community and Individual Development Association.

Two Zimbabweans on the MSET program in particular were able to take part in the transformative occasion and attend dramatically to their own individual, organisational and communal needs, ultimately serving to promote food security for some 3,000 villages in and around Chinyika, some of whom had hitherto been starving. In fact such a development paved the way, as a further evolution of the masters, for a subsequent PhD program with Trans4m (Geneva), which by now had been co-evolved by Ronnie Lessem and Alexander Schieffer and the Da Vinci Institute in South Africa, originally co-founded by Nelson Mandela. Now we turn more fully to Trans4m.

PhD/PHD: Global – Local Effect: Trans4m Life/Communiversity

Trans4m Life: Home for Humanity

Trans4m then developed a new doctoral programme, emerging out of the old transformational masters programmes, now based on their newly constituted *integral research* (6) and *development* (7) focused on *integral enterprise* (8) and *integral economics* (9). That altogether constituted Trans4m Life, spanning education and development, organisation and community, if not also each and every particular society as a whole. In Trans4m's 'Home for Humanity', based in the French mountains near Geneva, each of these 4 I's are embodied, spanning each of the above four fields.

Communiversity: Learning Community to Socioeconomic Laboratory

As Ronnie reviewed the course of his life and work so far, he was made aware of one overarching theme; that of the interchange (or more often the lack of interchange) between university and community—that is, in the latter respect, both the social (as well as ecological) and the business communities. Such a disconnect has pervaded his life and work all over the world; hence the need for the development of what we have termed a *communiversity,* in my case journeying all the way from Buhera to what we now term, in the indigenous Shona language, an integral *kumusha*, bringing the university back home.

In fact it was in his work on *Integral Dynamics: Cultural Dynamics, Political Economy and the Future of the University* (10) that we first paid elaborate attention to such, thereby further enriched through their work on *Integral Development* (11). Now and for the first time, *The Idea of the Communiversity* (12) emerged, whereby we shall devote a whole volume to the subject, drawing on our experiences in Africa (South – Zimbabwe, South Africa, Nigeria) and Europe (North – UK, Slovenia), the Middle (Egypt, Jordan) and the Near East (Pakistan) and to a lesser extent on North America (West). Co-authors Anselm Adodo in Nigeria, hereafter and Tony Bradley in the UK thereafter, take the story on from here, starting with *Nature Power* and, thence, reflecting on *Four Worlds in One Life*.

ANSELM ADODO: NATURE POWER TO COMMUNIVERSITY

My African Context

I was born in a serene environment of a modern government hospital in Akure, the capital of Ondo State, Western Nigeria. No fuss, no complication; just the normal birth of an ordinary child on an ordinary day. I read about the birth of a child named Jesus, who was born in Bethlehem of Judea. According to the biblical story of his birth, angels were flying everywhere and a whole multitude of angelic hosts were singing '*allelu-ia*' at his birth. Well, nothing close to such happened upon my birth. I asked my teacher in nursery school why no angels were flying around when I was born. She replied that the angels were probably too busy preventing genocides and civil wars in many African countries, including Nigeria, rather than hover over a tiny little thing like me.

My childhood experience was a pleasant experience of growing up in a family where I cultivated the habit of reading and studying early in life. My family context did not put me in a situation where I learnt the English language as a tool of oppression or suppression, nor did I feel that I had been deprived of something by learning a second language. Rather, I was fascinated by the beauty and magic of words in both English and the Yoruba language. While we communicated in my native Yoruba language in my father's household, we also discussed in English, listened to news and music, watched movies and read literature and newspapers in both languages. My grandmother used to tell me that there is more to language than spoken words and that wisdom consists in drilling beyond the surface of words to discover the deeper meanings.

The Yoruba worldview in which I was immersed as a child is a world of relationships between the living and the dead; between human beings, animals and spirits; between this world and the beyond; between the physical and the metaphysical; the indigenous and the exogenous. Growing up as a city boy in the 1970s also meant that I did not experience the often stereotyped village life of half-naked African children sitting in the open courtyard at moonlight listening to folk tales at night or begging for food to eat during the day. At night, I watched the television, listened to highlife music or immersed myself in books. However, from time to time and when the situation permitted it, my grandmother told me stories of the spirits, of ancestors and family traditions, while my mother was away at church and my father was engaged in his laboratory work.

In Love with Learning

My father was a school principal and lecturer and my mother, too, was a school headteacher—so it was that I grew up not surrounded by the mythical African thick bush, mysterious forests, wild animals or rich vegetation of the stereotyped African life. Life in Africa is, in fact, more complex and varied than that. I grew up in my father's library, which was a forest of books. My father was an avid reader of books and never missed the daily newspapers. The most frequent visitor to our house at that time was Tunji, the newspaper vendor who used to deliver fresh newspapers to our house every morning. By the age of 14, I had read *The Brothers Karamazov* by F. M. Dostoyevsky, *The Prophet* by Khalil Gibran, *Siddhartha* by Herman Hesse, *Animal Farm* by George Orwell, *Gulliver's Travels* by Jonathan Swift, *The Pilgrim's Progress* by John Bunyan, *Alice in Wonderland* by Lewis Carroll, *The Old Man and the Sea* by Ernest Hemingway and many others. I had also read most of the plays of William Shakespeare (my favourite being *Romeo and Juliet*) and other classics.

I also immersed myself in the works of Yoruba authors and read Yoruba classics such as Fagunwa's *Igbo Olodumare* (*The Forest of God*,

1949), *Ireke Onibudo* (*The Sugarcane of the Guardian*, 1949), *Irinkerindo ninu Igbo Elegbeje* (*Wanderings in the Forest of Elegbeje*, 1954) and *Adiitu Olodumare* (*The Secret of the Almighty*, 1961). Daniel Fagunwa was a famous Yoruba author who pioneered the Yoruba language novel (13). In 1938, Fagunwa wrote his first novel, *Ogboju Ode ninu Igbo Irunmale*, arguably the first novel ever written in the Yoruba language and one of the first to be written in any African language (14). In 1968, Wole Soyinka, a Nigeria novelist who later won a Nobel Prize in Literature, translated the book into the English language as *The Forest of a Thousand Daemons*, published by Random House (15). Fagunwa was awarded the Margaret Wrong Prize in 1955 (16). He died in 1963, but remains the most widely read Yoruba-language author and a major influence on such contemporary writers as Amos Tutuola, Ben Okri, Gabriel Okara and a host of other Nigerian novelists.

Fagunwa's works (17) portray the Yoruba worldview; a world in which spirits, human beings and animals relate, where the line between the visible world and the invisible world is very thin and one can easily move from one realm to the other. In such a world, spirits take on human forms to carry out different assignments, while human beings, especially hunters, diviners and herbalists, borrow animal bodies to carry out different functions as well as search for information about nature, spirits and the supernatural. Fagunwa's works are rich in picturesque fairy tales containing many folklore elements: spirits, monsters, gods, magic and witchcraft.

Encounter with 'School'

I went to school because I had to. My school was a Catholic boys' college, famed for discipline, high academic standards and excellence in sports. My father wanted me to become a scientist and I showed flashes of becoming one. I excelled in mathematics, physics, chemistry, agriculture and the sciences. However, I had always lived in many worlds; the many worlds that also existed in the household in which I grew up. The world of an exogenous, scientific, non-religious father; a holistic-minded, Christian mother; an indigenous grandmother who believed in traditional knowledge systems; a grandfather who was an Ifa Oracle devotee, a firm believer in traditional religions who later became a Christian convert, without throwing away the traditional Yoruba values. It was within this multifaceted worldview of science, nature, tradition and culture that I grew up. I felt at home being alone in the gardens and the forest pathways as well as in the forest of books that was my father's library.

As I grew up I learned a lot from my grandmother, who told me stories about the moon, the stars and the spirits. My grandmother used to tell me that the palm trees, the mango trees, the baobab trees, the Iroko trees and the forest can talk (18). I asked, "How can the palm trees, the mango trees and the Iroko trees talk? Are they human beings?" She would smile and reply, "There is more to hearing than what you hear; there is more to seeing than what you see; there is more to life than being awake."

Something within me revolted against schooling, despite doing well in the subjects. I mastered the art of writing examinations and giving my school teachers the answers they wanted from me. However, there was no subject on how to admire the moon, the stars and the forest. There was no subject on aloneness (19) or listening.

Searching for Holistic Knowledge

The world of biology, chemistry, mathematics and physics fascinated me. I cannot but marvel at the intricate complexity of the single-celled amoeba, the sophistication of the human heart and its incessant rhythm, the intricate complexity of the human brain and the laws of physics and chemistry. I also wondered at the audacity with which these laws were stated as if they were infallible church dogmas. In later years, I came across this quotation from Robert L. Weber (20), an American scientist: "It is disconcerting to reflect on the number of students we have flunked in chemistry for not knowing what we later found out to be untrue." Weber was expressing the reservation I had about the so-called unquestionable claims of science. It turned out that, after all, those laws of physics and chemistry were not written in stone!

The invention of the microscope was a big step forward in the human search for knowledge, as hitherto unseen microbes, bacteria and viruses, invisible to the naked human eye, could now be seen, studied and examined. Is it possible that one day, human beings will invent a machine that can penetrate the world of the spirits and expose the invisible world? The impact of the microscope was immediately felt in the field of medicine as it led to the discovery of new drugs such as antibiotics. Could this invisible world of bacteria, microbes and viruses be the invisible world that my grandmother was referring to when she said that there is more to things than what the eyes could see? I was determined to know more about this invisible world.

I devoured books on Eastern religion and spirituality such as the Bhagavad Gita, the Upanishads and a series of Vedic literature. I read the complete works of Lopstang Rampa, the *Epic of Gilgamesh* and many others. From the African literature category, I read the works of Gabriel Okara, Wole Soyinka, Amos Tutuola, Ayi Kwei Armah, Chinua Achebe, Ngugi Wathiongo, Peter Abraham, Mongo Beti, Kamara Laye, Cyprian Ekwensi, Nelson Mandela, Ali Mazrui, Christopher Okigbo, Flora Nwapa, John Munonye, Lenrie Peters, L.S. Senghor and a host of others. I was in fact torn between the world of 'school' and the world of creativity; between the rigid world of teaching knowledge and the dynamic world of imbibing wisdom. I was searching for holistic knowledge.

Nature Power: Healing as Transformation of Worldview

In 1997 I started a small herbal garden. From the herbs that grew in the garden, I prepared some herbal mixtures for malaria, coughs and other common ailments. My office was a bamboo tent. Six months later, I was able to construct a 3-room wooden shaft with a loan of $200. A young man from the village came to join me. The herbal remedies we prepared were based on local medical knowledge. The villagers who took the cough syrups and malaria medicine came back with very positive results. Before long, the news had spread around the village, which comprises of Christians, Muslims and traditional religion practitioners in a balanced proportion. The 3-room clinic was called Pax Herbals centre.

By the year 2008, Pax Herbal Clinic and Research Laboratories, as the herbal centre is now called, had become one of the biggest, best-equipped, best-organised and most modern herbal research centres in Africa, with fully computerised research and clinical laboratories, rated among the best in Africa. Within a record five years, over 35 of the herbal supplements produced were approved by the National Agency for Food Drug Administration and Control (NAFDAC).

My experiment with the idea of a communiversity started in the year 2000 when I published my book, *Nature Power* (21). The aim was to document and preserve African indigenous knowledge. At that time, the practice of herbal medicine in Nigeria and most parts of Africa was conflated with witchcraft, sorcery, ritualism and all sorts of fetish practices. Because herbal medicine was associated with paganism, many African Christians secretly patronised traditional healers and the educated elite and religious figures did not want to be associated in any way with traditional African medicine. *Nature Power*, like a lonely voice in the wilderness, was written to correct the misconception that African herbal medicine is synonymous with paganism, ritualism and fetishism.

Since its publication, *Nature Power* has been reprinted and revised more than eight times. It has contributed immensely in changing the attitudes of both the government and other stakeholders towards the practice of herbal medicine. *Nature Power* has also helped to show that health is more than an absence of disease. Health is wholeness of mind, soul and body. It is said that knowledge is power. True enough. But knowledge is power only when it is relevant and makes a difference in the lives of people. For me, then, education is what takes place in the daily life of people, a communiversity where knowledge is translated into capabilities and capabilities into knowledge.

The Idea of the Communiversity: All Knowledge is Local

In my 2017 book, *Integral Community Enterprise in Africa: Communitalism as an Alternative to Capitalism* (22), I described how Pax Herbals grew from a small cottage industry to one of the biggest phytomedicine research centres in Africa. On the one hand, the book described how Pax Herbals got to its present state; the challenges and the philosophy (and spirituality) behind its business model. On the other, it explored how the business, community health and social innovation being actualised by Pax Herbals can be systematised, conceptualised and documented (from tacit to explicit knowledge) in such a way that it can lead to the development of a community university in Edo State Nigeria, that serves to recognise and release individual and communal potentials. In other words, how can Pax Herbals be a model for synergy between culture, spirituality, science, economy and enterprise in the context of the global world?

In my interactions with local healers, I observed how they applied local music and rhythms to treat depression and madness. I sat down with elderly local healers, traditional midwives, local bonesetters (orthopaedic specialists), local psychiatrists and psychotherapists in different parts of Nigeria to observe different methods of traditional medical treatment. There were also professional counsellors and diviners who applied divination systems to proffer solutions to personal problems, success in business, protection against witchcraft etc.

Meanwhile, the traditional healers had become an endangered species, as many of them died due to old age without passing on their knowledge and expertise to their children. The children migrated to the cities to attend modern universities and acquired degrees in modern medicine, business administration, banking, architecture, geography, criminology, engineering and a host of others. Some became fire-spitting evangelists, pastors and Christian crusaders who declared 'war' on traditional medical practices and branded their parents as idol-worshippers and pagans. Modern Christian education and Western education managed to brainwash children to turn against their traditions, their traditional families and their culture.

In 1999, I witnessed a moving display of misdirected evangelical piety as a young man who had just graduated from a Pentecostal college in a nearby city returned to the village and discovered that his father, a renowned traditional healer, had died at age 90 two days earlier. The young pastor brought out all the religious paraphernalia in his father's 'laboratory', the cooking pots and concoction jars and, with the King James version of the Bible in one hand and a made-in-England firelighter in another, set the whole collection ablaze. Thus, a whole library of medical knowledge was destroyed. In some other parts of the world, if a library was set ablaze, it would be seen as arson, an offence punishable by law. In Africa, with every old person that dies, a library of books and a body of knowledge is lost forever.

Today, Africa is faced with the challenge of re-understanding, re-inventing and re-expressing ancient knowledge (indigenous) in the light of modern scientific knowledge (exogenous). This requires a synergy of both systems. In order to become global, one must first be *local*. While the indigenous needs the exogenous to rise to global integrity, the fact remains that the exogenous loses its substance and transformative power without the indigenous. When there is no proper synergy between the indigenous and exogenous, education becomes artificial and insubstantial.

The world is heading back to the south, to its roots. The planet and its people are living in times of major change. Our very survival is dependent on raising the collective consciousness of humanity, on shifting from conflict and war to love and compassion. In order to do this, we need to unite the old with the new, north with south, indigenous with exogenous. We need to look at the past to learn lessons that will help us to face the future with stronger hope, not to be stuck in the past. The richness of the ages must be drawn together to create a synergy that utilises the accumulated knowledge of ancient tradition, religion and science, while also embracing modern exogenous knowledge. As we evolve, rather than dismiss that which went before, respect must be cultivated for traditions that have stood the test of time. The ability to form a creative synergy between doing and being, thinking and doing, science and spirituality, business and ecology, nature and culture, is the hallmark of the university of tomorrow: our communiversity.

TONY BRADLEY: FOUR WORLDS IN ONE LIFE

"A vocation is always a call from a social reality that is deemed greater than the mere individual self... a call may be a course of action in a struggle for an inclusive social good, as in variants of the 'activist' life. The call is to participate in social movements working to reconstruct society in a way that better serves its members. Or again, the call may be to a mode of daily life that enriches otherwise mundane activities." (23)

Cycles of Vocation

The idea of calling—especially for those who have accepted a role involving the pursuit of social transformation—rarely proceeds in the sort of smooth *linear* progression that might be interpreted from many models of social change. As Matthew Fox has observed:

"Leadership... calls on the strength and wisdom of the ancestors as it operates as a cyclical, not a linear, process. It requires spiritual practices, including vision quests, rites of passage and deep grieving" (24).

It may be noted that Fox presents his reading of vocation in a four-fold way. This is by no means accidental. Through his exhaustive research into the lives of Christian mystics, Fox concluded that there are four paths to the vocation of leadership, through what he calls "creation spirituality" (25). These are the Via Positiva, Via Negativa, Via Creativa and Via Transformativa. This pattern of stages, forming the core aspect of the human psyche as a fundamental structure of consciousness, was termed the "quaternity archetype" by C.G. Jung (26).

In presenting life journeys in this way Fox adopts an indigenous, cyclical understanding, recognising that we weave our ways through life, as might be represented in Celtic Christian knot-work or Islamic calligraphy. There may be progression, but it often happens as we return to earlier stages, at regular points, before 'moving on'. As we might seek to identify both the specificity of practices and the cyclical dynamics out of which my (or anyone else's) vocation has emerged, it is important to recognise certain features.

'Inner calling' and 'outer challenge' don't link in a pattern of causation. They are more akin to a dialectic and reciprocal inter-dependence. Call and challenge are mutually conditioned by the dynamics of context and cycle. As such, reflecting on my own pattern of personal transformation I have discovered a cyclical process that had been working its way, in respect of my engagement in community transformation in Liverpool, for over forty years.

Community Grounding: In my Liverpool Home

My early life was spent in a cyclic journey around university cities in England, as my father took us from our home in Liverpool to postgraduate work in Bristol, his first lecturing job in Exeter and thence to Cambridge, where he lectured in Criminology until his premature death at the age of 39. After that, my mother moved us back to Liverpool, in something of a poor state and to one of the most deprived inner city neighbourhoods in Britain, 'Liverpool 8'. It was the area that gained notoriety in 1981 for the so-called Toxteth Riots, when the city reached boiling-point as a result of the perceived racist targeting of black youths, under the police policy in Margaret Thatcher's first government of 'stop-and-search'.

But it was there as a teenager that I had my first brush with 'community development' work. It was 1972 and that phrase had not percolated into the popular consciousness, although it would after the Toxteth Riots a decade later, through the Conservative patrician-politician, Michael Heseltine. He had become Secretary of State for the Environment and, following the riots, commissioned Britain's first series of Community Development Projects (CDPs). In the most unlikely conjoining Heseltine had fallen in love with Liverpool and its people, at a time when Thatcher's Chancellor of the Exchequer had sent a private memo to the Prime Minister saying "Let Liverpool rot".

For me, however, my experience as a teenager was to work with one of the most inspirational, tireless and committed people, one Des McConachie. His name is all but forgotten in Liverpool, as I discovered thirty-five years later. But Des founded the Shelter Neighbourhood Action Project (SNAP) in Granby Ward, Liverpool 8, as a housing and urban regeneration project. It was transformative for the area, the people and for me and the other volunteers, who learned the power of concerted action to change lives by helping local people to help themselves. Des wrote up his experiences quietly to government and was instrumental in helping to frame Heseltine's plan.

Then, more than three decades later, I returned to the city and was asked to do a series of short radio broadcasts for BBC Radio Merseyside about a Scouse kid returning home. In the second of these I mentioned Des by name. A few days later I received a phone call from an octogenarian with a frail voice. I wondered who it was. The voice said, "You spoke about SNAP and Des McConachie on the radio the other day. I haven't heard his name mentioned in many years." I was intrigued. "Who is this calling?" I asked. "My name is Des McConachie," was the reply. I heard his voice cracking with emotion and imagined the tears rolling down his cheeks. I had not forgotten his inspirational work or his pivotal role in transforming British community development practice.

Nor was this a singular moment of cyclical serendipity. I have experienced many such incidents of worlds colliding in time; what Jung referred to as 'synchronicity'. From Liverpool I went to London University to study environmental science and later, rural sociology, before going on to engage in academic research. At one point in my early research career in 1979, I visited Exeter University and met with John Dunford, one of the lecturers there. When I sat in a chair in the Department of Agricultural Economics I saw him go white as a sheet. I was told that I was sitting in the exact same chair at the same desk in Exeter, which my father had occupied some 20 years earlier. I had had no prior idea about my dad even being in that department, as I'd been very young. It alerted me to the fact that we do not always choose our own paths, even if we consider ourselves to be 'free agents'. As such, I suspect that a considerable part of my early vision was shaped by the interventions of others in my formation.

My parents were both active socialists involved in the British Labour Party, especially through its CPGB roots, the Trades Union Movement and WEA. My mother had worked as a secretary in Barcelona during the Spanish Civil War. My father had been an active *kibbutzim* member in Israel, during the period of the partition of Palestine and the formation of the nation-state of Israel in 1948. They had met in Liverpool, grounding me in that community. With this background it was hard not to be committed to social justice and an improvement of the conditions of the working-class in Britain, even if I'd chosen a more entrepreneurial route to achieving this burning desire.

Emerging Pilgrimium: The Psychic Road to Personal Integration

In order to delve deeper into the way in which my inner, burning desire has been shaped it is worth a brief reflection on the more formal process of my professional development.

After my first research projects, I worked for the UK Department of Environment on their Deprivation and Welfare in Rural Areas reports with Brian P. McLoughlin. The vision for transformed communities continued to burn within me, always 'local' (27). But the concern for local social change was scarcely credible for me if I hadn't, in prior experience, undergone a significant inner transformation that could pave the way for an outer manifestation of a changed set of relationships. As such, it was at the time of my research for the DoE that I began to see some of the core connections that it is possible to read from the hierarchy of functions pattern in a Jungian type profile.

At the heart of Jung's theory of personality (28) is the axiom that each of us changes over time. We are not a static 'type' but a dynamic flux of relationships between the functions we express. It is even possible that our core type profile may change at the margins, although it is much more common that we each learn how to display different 'faces' as we grow. Often these are because we have shifted to a different life stage and, consequently, have reached a point of *enantiodromia,* where a previously unconscious aspect of our psyche surfaces.

My ENTJ type in the 1980s was unconsciously searching for its shadow introverted feelings (Fi) side to surface. Jung seemed to consider that the different functions within the dynamic hierarchy were most likely to emerge at certain significant life transitions. Whilst the dominant function would most likely rule in childhood, adolescence could offer a point of emergence for the auxiliary function; in this case, introverted intuition (Ni). Throughout my teenage years I kept on attempting to write, but it wasn't until I reached university that I discovered that I could write poetry and drama. Even so, although I had some small amateur plays staged, it would be another thirty years before I had my first major professional theatrical production as a playwright.

In mid-life there is a time for integrating some of the tertiary function and I discovered a need to play golf and go mountain climbing; two obviously extraverted sensing function expressions. Yet at the point that is often called the 'mid-life crisis', I found that I was suddenly attracted to examining my own feelings, a side of my life that I'd always been deeply suspicious of hitherto.

We can fast forward a few years to the period of young adulthood. I had been ordained as an Anglican priest after a few years working in a university department, at exactly the point that Levinson suggests for transition: aged 30. But, what connected each period of ministry—in locations as diverse as down-market seaside Essex, Coventry city centre, or well-heeled, leafy, suburban Warwickshire—was my significant engagement with supporting community transformation, which Levinson refers to as 'orientation'.

In Southend-on-Sea this had been through the local homelessness centre. Coventry saw my involvement in inter-church work, networking with several hundred other leaders to establish a broad movement for trans-denominational education, training and Christian mobilisation. Additionally, I had worked strenuously—at some times alongside the current Archbishop of Canterbury, The Most Revd Justin Welby and Canon Andrew White, the well-known 'Vicar of Baghdad'—in reconciliation work, in areas of Israel-Palestine, most notably with the establishment of a new school in Beit Jala, Bethlehem, through Coventry Cathedral's Cross of Nails community. Then, in my final parish, before a life-changing event in 2004, we established two social enterprises in our small Warwickshire village; one as a Fairtrade café-shop and distribution centre, the other as a children's nursery. Again, the vocation to community development was reflected both in the regular pattern of pastoral and teaching ministry and in the specific projects that I gave my energies to.

Various life circumstances came along, including a serious spinal problem and the need to give up my role as a parish priest, which brought me into formal counselling and therapy. In this situation the themes that had attracted me theoretically suddenly began to mean something to me at a deeply personal level. Many friends commented on how I had changed, some with deeply anxious looks on their faces. Whereas, for myself, I recognised that much to my surprise, the Jungian principle of equivalence was actually taking shape in me before my very eyes!

There is within every ENTJ a latent introverted idealist (NiFi). This developing contact with 'the shadow side' of the personality can come as something of a revelation. For someone who is very good at seeing the big picture and acting decisively on it, discovering that empathy, compassion and being kind, even to oneself, are important aspects of life, is a shock. However, the introverted feelings function can readily team up with the introverted intuition in mid-life to condition a very different way of being. And, of course, such changes are of profound spiritual significance in terms of the pathways of discipleship that we follow.

As I look back, I can see the transitions I've just described in alternative ways, if I choose to use the language of spirituality. The very vocal and extraverted child, who converted from Judaism at the age of eight, started to want to see the meaning in the Bible during his teenage years. It wasn't that I simply wanted to read the Bible; I wanted to know what it *all* meant. The intuition side of the NT personality came strongly to the fore in my days at college. The early experiences of a Jewish boy came back to the surface—almost visibly rising from my personal unconscious—as I learned to connect the symbols of Judaism with the message of Jesus Christ.

Navigating through a Personal Academy: Shaped for the Journey

Now I can see that the Jungian principles behind the process of individuation are part of God's work in shaping a vocation for the journey. The Lord who knows me from the inside and who formed me in the womb was guiding my steps towards wholeness, *shalom* and realisation of the archetypal self. Even so, this raised within me the further question: how does this connect to the person who was increasingly becoming focused on local social change and transformation? What was taking place in me was a profound experience of communiversity academy, although I couldn't name it as such at the time.

My life experiences had helped to explain, at least to my satisfaction, something of the apparently contradictory teaching of the Second (New) Testament concerning my personal freedom (Galatians 2:4, 5:1, Colossians 2:6) and the predestination that I have in Christ (Romans 8:29–30, Ephesians 1:5–11). Although God has chosen me in His image, with the personality and psyche that I have—which has a certain ideal destiny and path attached to it—the freedom that I display means that the precise road I follow will not perfectly mirror the divinely appointed path at every point.

I would need to change; to reflect within myself some of the transformations that I was longing to see in the objective world of my action research engagement. The one could not take place without the other. Moreover, I needed to understand that this shaping was never a solitary and isolated process; it was always a collaborative process with others, in an academy of the mind and spirit.

My wife Carol had a mature career as an intensive care nurse and I had a reasonably successful career as a CofE minister. At the time, in 2004, there came a major moment for entering onto the Via Negativa, in Matthew Fox's terms. I had a serious spinal event that left me paralysed for a time, only partially recovering slowly over the next two years, at which point I was 'invited' to retire from practical ministry on health grounds. Then, after moving home, family and life across several hundred miles, I was remarkably healed. Carol took on a new career, I set up my own business and was then 'called' back to the academy and our personal lives were turned upside-down again.

The point of my recounting this aspect of my personal history is to emphasise the radical discontinuities—or recursions, as we describe them later—that frequently occur along the progressive route from vision to legacy. This is why I find Fox's cyclical model of smaller cycles within larger ones far more helpful than a linear model of sequential progression. The re-emergence of my inner call to community transformation, within the context of a new academic and action-research career in my mid-50s, was not an aberrant version of a linear progression. It was more a natural consequence of a cyclical and technical interpretation of social structures that were currently taking place, linked to my own personal circumstances.

Effecting Co-Laboratory: The Outcomes of Four Worlds in a Single Life

In Table 1 I present a summary of how the four worlds have worked out in my own personal life. It points to the way that I see my life as having been on an Eastern Path of Renewal. It has integrated the Four Worlds (29) (see Ronnie Lessem's journey above), with its realms in Community/Nature, Spirituality/Self-hood, Systems/Methods and Enterprise/Political Engagement. Equally, I can see that I have also followed my way circling through the four rounds of Self, Organisational, Social and Cultural life and at each round of the realms, within each world of the entire Renewal Path, I've had my own particular experiences, peculiar to me, but reflecting aspects that are common to many.

Taken together, these experiences have resulted in a series of enterprises, innovations and experiments, shared with others, which lead towards an experience of co-laboratory effects. I have seen this work in community development and environmental social action, through my work as a writer/producer in musical theatre and, most recently, in the early stage development of a communiversity in Liverpool. So, strangely, or possibly not, I have found myself 'returned to the place from which I first started' and, as T.S. Eliot puts in the *Four Quartets*, "seeing it, as if for the first time". This should not surprise me, for all our lives are spent circling around the four worlds.

The questions are: how can we bring these circles together? And what will it look like when we do? Throughout this book we introduce a variety of cases that reflect the principles of the communiversity. You will meet some of the same and other, different cases, in different guises, repeatedly. In this way we present the spiralling processes of the four

worlds and dynamic GEN*E*, worked-out in very diverse cultures. Together, as we explore them in some depth across the pages that follow,
we open up the idea of the communiversity.

Table 1 Fields of Individual and Collective Experience within the Eastern Path of Renewal

Eastern Path of Renewal	Integral World	Integral Realm	Integral Rounds	Integral Experience
ORIGINATION **Narrative Method**	SOUTH	Community/ Nature	SELF	1.Shifting homes/ locality
			ORGANISATION	*2.Local Churches*
			SOCIETY	3.<u>Community development</u>
			CULTURE	*4.Social environmentalism*
	EAST	Spirituality/ Self-hood	SELF	5. Christian/ with Jewish background
			ORGANISATION	*6. Evangelical/ charismatic (biblical focus) groupings*
			SOCIETY	7. Church Ministry
			CULTURE	*8. Creative Arts world*
	NORTH	Systems/ Methods	SELF	9. Environmental/ social justice
			ORGANISATION	*10. Universities*
			SOCIETY	11. Political economy theory/ artistic method
			CULTURE	*12. Scientific and artistic societies/ Trans4M/ Initiatives of Change*
	WEST	Enterprise/ political engagement	SELF	13. Artistic change agency
			ORGANISATION	*14. Social enterprises*
			SOCIETY	15. Societal animateurism
			CULTURE	*16. Media/ Arts Production*

REFERENCES

1 Lessem R (1997) *A Biography of Action Learning.* Ex Pedlar M (ed) *Action Learning in Practice.* Farnham. Gower Publishing

2 Lessem R and Tarran H (1978) *Centres of Knowledge: Linking College and Community.* Journal of Further and Higher Education. Volume 2. Issue 3

3 Van der Post L (1956) *The Dark Eye of Africa.* Cape Town. Lowery.

4 Lessem R (1987) *The Soul of Business.* London. Prentice Hall/Pearson

5 Lessem R (2001) *Managing in Four Worlds: Culture, Strategy and Transformation.* Long Range Planning. Volume 34. Number 1

6 Lessem R and Schieffer A (2010) *Integral Research and Innovation.* Farnham. Gower Publishing.

7 Schieffer A and Lessem R (2012) *Integral Development: Self, Organizational and Societal Development.* Farnham. Gower Publishing

8 Lessem R and Schieffer A (2009) *Transformation Management: Toward the Integral Enterprise.* Farnham. Gower Publishing.

9 Lessem R and Schieffer A (2010) *Integral Economics : Releasing the Economic Genius of your Society.* Farnham. Gower Publishing.

10 Lessem R et al (2013) *Integral Dynamics: Cultural Dynamics, Political Economy and the Future of the University.* Abingdon. Routledge.

11 Schieffer A and Lessem R (2014) op cit.

12 Lessem R, Adodo A and Bradley T (2019) *The Idea of the Communiversity.* Manchester. Beacon Academic.

13 Fagunwa, D O (1949) *Ireke Onibudo.* Ibadan: Printmarks Ventures.

14 Fagunwa, D O (1954) *Irinerindo Ninu Igbo Elegbeje.* Ibadan: Printmarks Ventures.

15 Soyinka, W (1968*) The Forest of a Thousand Daemons.* London: Random House.

16 Fagunwa, D O (1939) *Ogboju Ode Ninu Igbo Irunmale*. Ibadan: Solar Offset Ltd.

17 Fagunwa, D O (1961) *Adiitu Olodumare*. Ibadan: Printmarks Ventures.

18 Ilesanmi, T M (1989) *Ise Isenbaye*. Ibadan: Claverianum Press.

19 Kosemanii, S (1987) *Owe ati Asayan oro Yoruba*. Ibadan: Vantage Publishers

20 Weber, R (1992) *Science with a Smile*. Bristol, UK: Institute of Publishing INC.

21 Adodo, A (2000) *Nature Power: A Christian approach to Herbal Medicine*. Akure: Don Bosco Press.

22 Adodo, A (2017) op. cit.

23 Weigert A J and Blasi A J (2007) Vocation. Chapter 1 in Guiseppe Giordan (Ed.), *Vocation & Social Context*. Leuwen. Brill.

24 Fox M (2011) *Leadership as a Spiritual Practice*. [Available at: http://www.matthewfox.org/blog/leadership-as-a-spiritual-practice].

25 Fox M (1991) *Creation Spirituality: Liberating gifts for the peoples of the Earth*. San Francisco. HarperCollins.

26 Jung C G (1969) *The Archetypes of the Collective Unconscious*. Princeton. University Press.

27 Bradley T and Lowe P D (Eds.) (1984) *Locality and Rurality: economy and society in rural regions*. Norwich. Geo Books.

28 Jung C G (1971) *Psychological Types, The Collected Works of C G Jung, Volume 6*. London. Routledge & Kegan Paul.

29 Lessem R and Schieffer A (2010) op.cit.

Chapter 1

The Idea of the University

IN THE CELTIC WAY OF JOHN HENRY NEWMAN

*We can split the atom, find cures for the most terrible diseases, con-
duct surveys of whole populations and produce massive dictionaries
of lost languages—but we cannot generate a modest program of
general education for undergraduate students. This is the parable
of our time.*

Harold Bloom, *The Closing of the American Mind*

1.1. INTRODUCTION

1.1.1. A Reflection on the Nature of Education

On our way to our so-called 'communiversity' we begin at the beginning, so to speak—that is, with *The Idea of a University*. For although our idea departs from such conventional wisdom, we still need to signal our point of departure.

The source from which this book flows will not be lost on anyone who has even a passing acquaintance with the writing that has shaped the creation of modern universities. John Henry Newman's original 1852 lectures, which later became collected with other works as *The Idea of a University* (1)[1], stands as a masterpiece of literature and is a reflection on the nature of education that is grounded in spirituality and the principle of a scholarly collegium. However, to modern ears, it is a deeply troubling book. It is often contradictory, fully earthed in the alien soil of Victorian England, riddled with the arcane controversies of the Church of England and its prejudices for and against differing religious traditions, perplexing in many of its contentions, deeply bigoted in the values it reflects and, in some respects, antithetic to liberal business-minded universities of the 21st century Western world.

It is precisely for these reasons that it is important to return to this source text and its author, if we are sincere in the quest for a new type of university for our own age. Although we will not agree with many of Newman's particular campaigns and his thorough-going advocacy of the Tractarian Movement, within and later without the Church of England, his fundamental commitment to seeking truth that connects to community needs is part of the inspiration behind this present volume. Indeed, whilst the idea of a communiversity would have sounded peculiar to

---

1 All references to and quotes from *The Idea of a University* refer to pages in the 1996 Yale University version, edited by Frank M Turner.

Newman, his life and work sketched out several of the themes which we articulate throughout this text.

1.1.2. Following the GENEalogy Pattern

As such, in this chapter we introduce some of our core themes, illustrating them from Newman's own journey and through the themes of the various essays that were compiled into *The Idea of a University* (1891/1996). The dominant refrains of this book cover what we term the GENEalogy, from which develops the GENE-ius that each culture needs to (re-)discover, if it is to be released from the shackles of monocultural, monopolistic, monochrome capitalist society. Equally, the three authors of this book, with their roots in Africa and Europe, their spirits in Jewish and Christian (Protestant and Roman Catholic) as well as in indigenous faiths, their heads in the theories of Southern and Northern worlds and their hands in activating enterprises inspired by Western approaches, have discovered, in very diverse ways, that such a genealogical perspective is vital as we enter more deeply into the 21st century.

We live in an age of unprecedented challenge for the human species and spirit. At the same time, we sense that this is an age of integrality, when the principles and practices of the four worlds—of South, East, North and West—are able to be integrated in cyclical and spiral sequence beginning from the South, to generate such genealogical dynamism. Consequently, the structure of this book follows the GENEalogy pattern. In doing so, we outline four key themes of vital significance for the idea of what we term a communiversity. These are:

- The solidaristic principle of communitalism (as opposed to both capitalism and socialism) for **G**rounding community engagement.
- The spiritual principle of pilgrimium (as opposed to doctrinally static faiths) for **E**merging human well-being.
- The *scientia/sapientia* principles of academy (as opposed to fragmented, disciplinary departments) for **N**avigating towards the emancipation of cultural knowledge.

- The societal principle of (co-)laboratory working (as opposed to solo, 'heroic', individualistic and profit-maximising entrepreneurship) for *E*ffecting new learning-based, research-to-innovation enterprises.

In respect of these themes, we also follow the pattern of considering the developmental, research, enterprise and economic aspects of each. Whilst these four approaches do not precisely map to the GEN*E*alogy or the four worlds (SENW) they represent the dynamic dimensions that are required for activation at each stage of the communiversity's genealogical life. Each needs to be developed in order to benefit from the value of research, which will mobilise the academy for bringing into effect the co-creative fruit of the communiversity's laboratory. As such, in the latter sections of the book, we introduce some of the cases where such communiversities are taking shape across the world. But at the outset, we begin by drawing a sketch of how some of Newman's own writing and life journey reflected these principles, albeit in a different time and with a different language. We preface this with a note about the words we are using, something that Newman did through his *Nine Discourses on the University*, which developed from the original Dublin lectures of 1852.

1.1.3. The Language of the Communi-versity

Language is important. And we make no *apologia*[2] for coining a range of terms which are unfamiliar neologisms. The problem is that conventional language points in entirely wrong directions, so far as we are concerned. As such, we have needed to create some new words to express the meaning we are introducing. Above, we mentioned the over-arching GEN*E*alogy. The next of these is the concept of the 'communiversity' itself.

---

2 Newman's most famous text was his *Apologia pro Vita Sua* (1864), which deliberately used Catholic Latin to challenge many of the doctrines of the English Church and engendered a thunderous response from the Anglican cleric and children's author Charles Kingsley, accusing Newman and the Tractarians of theological dishonesty.

There are at least two ways of hearing this composite noun. One is to speak about the comm-university, which sounds simple enough as a 'community-based university'. But that is not what we mean. Another way into this complex is to speak of the communi-versity. The prefix connects the ideas of community to communion, whilst the suffix derives from the Latin *vertere*, meaning to turn. We are speaking of a turning that takes place in communion.

1.1.4. *Vertere*: Turning Against to Turning Into

Usually, English words derived from *vertere* have the meaning of turning against e.g. *versus* is often abbreviated to 'vs' or even 'v'. In the area of the world where one of us (Bradley) is an ardent supporter of The Reds (Liverpool FC) we will note in our diary certain fixtures dates as red-letter days, such as Liverpool v Manchester United. This is a convention for describing sporting fixtures and events. However, this is to miss the richness of the term.

Equally, it can mean contrast or alternative, rather than simply adversarial opposition. For example, we might say that 'we studied well-being in economics versus studying only profit maximisation'. Indeed, the fuller meaning of *vertere* is related to change as transformation. We might think of a caterpillar, as it *vertere* into a butterfly, as a result of the changes that take place in the chrysalis. Therein hidden conversions occur. A body undergoes transformative metamorphoses that at first sight seem quite baffling, almost miraculous, to the casual observer, who doesn't know or understand that caterpillars are an earlier stage of butterflies. We might question what capitalism or the conventional Mode 1 universities are earlier stages of? Indeed, in relation to Newman, his roles in the Church of England and at Oriel College, Oxford, were the caterpillar stages before his butterfly form within the Roman Catholic church and the Catholic University of Ireland, although this is being written by the one of us who is an Anglican priest, from a moderately Evangelical background (exactly as Newman was).

Another derivative from *vertere* directly connected to the idea of the university, is that of the suffix *varsity*. This also has an interesting etymology, in that it became associated with sporting contests between the medieval English universities of Oxford and Cambridge. Subsequently, it has been applied to all such university and collegial contests, so that inter-varsity events are termed 'varsity matches'. The team element, representative of their institution, is vital to the meaning of varsity. However, if we connect the meanings derived from *vertere*, we can see that the Western perspective, which focuses on turning against in an oppositional contest, is only one set of meanings. We shouldn't be surprised at this as the Western world is the home of legal and political adversarial contests. Alternatively, we can talk about '*versity*' as a place of turning into, changing and transformation, not as an individual, but as a community.

1.1.5. Education Beyond the Individual

Thus, *the communiversity is a place of transformative change, for a group or community, where contrasts are worked out in communion.* While this might seem uncontroversial, it challenges the current idea of the university at its core. Universities have become places for privatised learning, where the pinnacle is the personal achievement of a PhD. Yet, the doctorate can be a corrosive concept. It elevates some at the expense of others. I have personally experienced this over many years. Those without the doctorate or the masters or the graduation certificate are made to feel inferior—through the exercise of many subtle and some not-so-subtle power relations—to those who have achieved such.

Now, of course, in talks at graduation events, the emphasis is always placed on the wonderful achievements of those who have reached that momentous day. And rightly so, in the conventional university! As a university teacher myself, I get a lump in my throat as I stand with my colleagues applauding the ranks of graduates who pick their way self-consciously down the steps of one of our two great cathedrals in Liverpool each summer. But, there is no getting away from the fact that the celebrations in such contexts are *versus* the experience of those who are non-graduates, masters or new doctors. I have looked into the eyes of countless parents, siblings, grandparents, friends and acquaintances and seen the mixture of pride, deference and nervousness, when faced with all the ranks of gowns, mortarboards, caps and hoods parading in front of them. Every time, I feel the urge to shout: "We're all part of the same communion—no distinctions!"

From their Western heights, our Mode 1 universities miss the richness of what the communiversity can be. The Western privatisation of education is profoundly opposed to the African idea of *ubuntu*, meaning 'I am because we are', emphasising the participation of the individual in the community, or the Eastern one of enlightenment, emphasising the surrender of the individual into the eternal. To be enlightened is to be like a city set on a hill, a lamp on a stand, giving light to the entire house (Matthew 5:15, Second Testament). In this understanding, education is an experience of communal transformation, changed together, from one measure of glory to another.

1.1.6. Learning on the Journey

Additionally, in this book, alongside genealogy and the communiversity, we add a third new word: that of *pilgrimium*. When we come to the pilgrimium we arrive, as it were, like a communal caterpillar entering into a corporate chrysalis. It is a place of change, from which we thereafter incorporate the dimension of journeying together. If the communi-butterfly is to emerge, it will first need to have undertaken the communal hero's journey.

Two of the great Oxford writers of the mid-20th century who were both members of The Inklings—Celtic Christian and C.S. Lewis—each employed the metaphor of epic journey to explain the great transformation. Whereas Tolkien's *The Hobbit* and *The Lord of the Rings* journeys were solo, made by little Bilbo and Frodo Baggins respectively, in Lewis' *The Chronicles of Narnia*, the journey is always shared, amongst the four

Pevensie children, even when Edmund sometimes turns the wrong way. Admittedly, there is a great team supporting Frodo Baggins; but it is he alone, who must complete the heroic solo journey, to plunge the immortal ring into the volcanic mouth of Mount Doom, under the all-seeing eye of Sauron.

In other words, Lewis understood the power of communal journeying (see the chapter on Pilgrimium Theory, in relation to Luke-Acts). For Tolkien, the communion of saints was that great cloud of witnesses (Hebrews 12:1) who look on at the individual heroic spiritual disciple, as she makes her way through the treacherous paths of life. Instead, Lewis seemed to understand the Celtic Christian idea of *peregrinatio*, or 'white sacrifice', a principle that has stayed with me since I first encountered it, together with the history of those remarkable Christian saints, of the 5th–8th centuries CE, some thirty-five years ago.

Why mention the Celts? Well, of course, Newman's journey was akin to that of his great forebear St Patrick—who was raised in what is now Cumbria, on the Solway coast—who left England for Ireland and, once there, discovered the Celtic way. Actually, this is stretching Newman's history, in that the Catholicism that he embraced in Ireland was about as far from the spirituality of Patrick and the Celtic saints as it is possible to travel, whilst remaining within the Church. Nevertheless, the journey to Ireland, as part of the Celtic way, was Newman's own journey. Moreover, in a very important way, as we reflect on further below, Newman was intensely involved in a *peregrinatio*.

The pilgrimium, then, is the place in which we as a community-in-communion journey towards our transformative experience of the academy and, ultimately, embark on new innovations within our co-laboratory spaces. We will return to the Celtic way of *peregrinatio* when we discuss Newman's connection with pilgrimium. At this point, we turn to consider Newman's connection to the first of our four phases of the communiversity process: development in community as a form of community development.

1.2. NEWMAN AND THE IDEA OF COMMUNITALISM

1.2.1. A Model of the Collegium of Scholars

For the first half of his adult intellectual life, Newman was a fellow of Oriel College, Oxford, and the keenest of devotees to that place of elite learning, which was regarded as the pinnacle of the Oxford colleges at the time. He became a fellow in 1822. It was the most particular academic grove, quintessentially English, upper-class and the epitome of a community for the privileged. In that sense it represented, for Newman, a model of the collegium of scholars, surrounded by students and support staff, mirroring the sacred panoply of chapter 5 in the Book of Revelation, where the saints, martyrs and company of the heavenly host gather around the throne of God for worship. That would have been his idea of the academic community. Yet Newman left the fellowship and comfortable confines of Oriel and Oxford in 1845, when he 'converted' to Catholicism.

Whilst we may find it hard to understand what this meant in the mid-19th century, we can recognise that his concept of the academic community was necessarily subservient to his view of universal truth. Community was, for Newman, founded in something beyond the particular; even that represented by the embodiment of intellectual standing, as at Oriel, Oxford. The true academic and intellectual life required commitment to a community that sought to enshrine universal truth. It should be community writ large and founded in something far greater than the specificity of culture and place.

1.2.2. A Patron Saint for Communitalism

As such, there is in the writings of Newman a universalism, but one that is fundamentally bounded. He was a religious writer at the time of Darwin and Huxley, when the conflicts between evolutionary theory and creationism were at their height in the 19th century. In Dublin after

1851, he was an English intellectual cleric amongst an Irish pragmatic laity. Newman was an Englishman promoting an Irish university, but speaking to many who were deeply suspicious of a Catholic education, preferring to identify themselves with an English-style Oxbridge over the Irish Sea at Trinity College, Dublin. He was a convert to Catholicism lecturing indigenous Roman Catholics from the standpoint of one who had led a radical oppositional movement within the Church of England. Consequently, although appearing to be a profoundly conservative figure, Newman was, in retrospect, a champion of the rights of minorities, who were to be incorporated into a wider academic community in the idea of a university. In this respect, he can be claimed as a patron saint[3] for communitalism.

This is the idea coined by one of us (Adodo) to describe an African and Southern world form of political economy. It grounds the possibility of a culture-centric university that is open to all within the indigenous population, eschewing the narrower participation of conventional Mode 1 universities. Communitalism emerges from the philosophy of *ubuntu* and the surrender of the self into the sea of the tribe, clan, group or community. However, the point of communitalism is to suggest that there is a distinctively African 'third way' between the locked-together titans of capitalism and socialism. Of course, there are many other 'third ways' in the West and across the globe, but communitalism has an African indigeneity and necessary boundary, in order to protect itself from the 'acids of Western modernity and individualism'.

Equally, in his own day, because of his intense desire to privilege Catholic teaching, Newman was also aware of the eroding effects of post-Enlightenment thinking. This led to a cultural boundary in Newman, which is confusing and paradoxical, in that he wants to protect Catholic dogma and at the same time expose students to 'universal truth'. Of course, given that Catholic can mean 'universal', he has a get-

---

3 Indeed, Newman is about to be canonised, as we write in 2019, by Pope Francis, after decades of advocacy on his behalf.

out-of-jail card, so far as the university curriculum is concerned. However, Newman was sufficiently intellectually competent to recognise the inherent contradictions in his position, which he circles around repeatedly in his lectures.

Castro-Klaren (2) mounts a trenchant criticism of Newman as a defender of elites, an opponent of free speech and a pernicious advocate of illiberality. For her, Newman is one to stoke the flames of repressive multiculturalism or, even, parallel development and apartheid. But this is to miss the point that Newman, in his advocacy of a university that sought the 'universal truth' of Catholic doctrine as its foundation, was, in fact, arguing for an epistemology that could be grounded in local soil, without descending into a sterile and meaningless relativism. Rather, he saw the possibility for a university that was established on the basis of a particular community, with its own authenticity and distinctive approach to learning, research and inculturation; one which, nevertheless, stood for universal values.

Of course, there are dangers in this educational philosophy but he did, at least, recognise that there is a debate surrounding the search for knowledge and the need to foster cultural identity and what we term communitalism. Nor was this a peculiar dilemma for his age. The self-same issues of bounded rationality exist in the contemporary Western Mode 1 university. In the same breath—taken to speak out about academic freedom and liberal open-ness—we hear of curriculums created that preference particular epistemologies of science against faith and deny platforms to speakers who, however odious their views, need to be listened to, if only to be opposed. Newman, in fact, reserved some of his most outspoken criticisms for Protestants, whom he regarded as inspired by feelings and emotion rather than revealed Truth. Whilst he was indisputably wrong in his analysis, his intention to foster a collegium where truth could emerge in community was, arguably, a noble aim.

Furthermore, his larger point, which we can recognise despite his peculiar prejudices, is that the accumulation of a body of learning depends on initiation into a corporate community of scholarship, avoiding the inimical practices of private, independent study. Knowledge, community mobilisation and activation run together. This is a vital principle for our understanding of the communiversity that is based in communitalism. The gathered collegium is the community in which learning is to take place, which is activated around the search for universal truth, as understood within its own bounded culture.

There is little place for the atomised self, the lone scholar ploughing a solitary furrow of intellectual and research endeavour. By contrast, learning is as much a matter of socialisation and inculturation. Of course, there are grave dangers of this becoming associated with a form of totalitarianism and awareness of this is equally a vital aspect of communitalism. Nevertheless, we can take serious issue with Newman's view, given that it undergirds what many have identified as the 'culture wars' of today's Western university campuses (3). There is no doubt that Newman adopts a politically conservative standpoint in respect of intellectual freedom and 'free speech'. His understanding of education is transmissive rather than transformative; indeed, we may shudder when we read Newman's views on Chinese or 'Hindoo' civilisations. However, we should not only read him in the context of his racist and colonial times; we need to reflect that he was making a case for knowledge and learning to proceed from culture.

Of course, viewed from the standpoint of looking back at the bloody history of 20th century apartheid and 'separate development', we cringe at Newman's view of white English supremacy. Even so, it was his fear of culturally and communally created interpretations of knowledge and the need for the Catholic University to oppose other cultural interpretations that reveals his depth of understanding. We should dismiss Newman's conclusions, but at the same time, we may marvel at his considerable interpretation of the power of cultures to generate their own epistemologies and knowledge creation. He had a powerful political insight, even if it was one that we may see as antithetic to the idea of the communiversity.

Overall, Newman's view of the self is hostile to that of the university. He opposes the rationality of Kant and the personal development understanding of 19th century Romanticism. Equally, he is dismissive of mere readers compared to the writers of books. The former are passive recipients, the latter active creators. He would not have understood reader-response theory. And yet, there is in his desire for the collegiality of a learning institution, the seeds for germinating communitalism.

In this sense he was both behind and ahead of his times, appearing to favour medieval scholasticism but, in effect, grounding the possibility of distinctive cultural learning institutions. Where we, of course, take issue with Newman is in his desire to universalise one culture against another. Where we share his view is in recognising that 'universal truth' needs to be exposed to alternative cultural reinterpretations. We should not raise the barricades of culture wars; however, we can identify that different communitalist universities can ground their distinctive, regional epistemologies and then engage in a spiral of development, research, enterprise and economic output that releases the knowledge genius of distinctive cultures, when acting together, in concert, to produce integral truth.

1.2.3. Newman and the Idea of the Pilgrimium

Every life is a journey. But some can be regarded as a more purposeful journey, even a pilgrimage. Newman's life was such a pilgrimage, which took him away from the security of English, Anglican Oxford to the relative obscurity of Irish, Catholic Dublin and the founding of the Oratory of St Philip Neri, which became housed in Edgbaston, Birmingham. In this respect, whatever we may think about the idiosyncrasy of his life voyage, we can appreciate the degree to which his pilgrimage of faithful commitment involved surrender, sacrifice and some personal change of identity.

Newman proclaimed many of the inclusive values of the Celtic missionary saints of the 5th–8th centuries CE. As such, his travel from England to Ireland, the home of the Celtic world, to modern ears mirrors that of St Patrick, taken 1400 years earlier. As we shall reflect in more detail in later chapters, the Celtic Christians had a very particular understanding of pilgrimage, which connects to Newman. It embraced the idea of 'white sacrifice' or *peregrinatio*—the journey that takes you across the sea from which you never return. We can hear the painful recollection of Newman, written in his *Apologia pro Vita Sua* (4), on leaving Oxford and his personal tutor.

> *"Like him I took leave of my first college, Trinity, which was so dear to me and which held on its foundation so many who had been kind to me both when I was a boy and all through my Oxford life. Trinity had never been unkind to me. There used to be much snap-dragon growing on the walls opposite my freshman's rooms there and I had for years taken it as an emblem of my perpetual residence even unto death in my University. On the morning of the 22nd [February, 1846] I left the Observatory. I have never seen Oxford since, excepting its spires as they are seen from the railway."* (ibid, p. 213)

Newman did return to Oxford briefly in 1860, but even then it was as an exile and someone who had maintained their *peregrinatio*, at much personal cost. *Peregrinatio*, along the Celtic path of sacrificial journeying, offers an important model for the emergence of the communiversity, in that it signifies that when we enter into the cultural-spiritual (Eastern) aspect, we are not seeking this experience as a point-of-arrival, as if we have entered a place of settled ritual. Indeed, as we discuss in the section following, it may seem peculiar that we connect a communiversity experience to a journey of faith, spirituality or indeed, religious commitment in any sense. But, beyond the secularised Western world, such connections are understood as vital to a rounded life.

That said, in a conventional religious vein many traditions look to a particular 'holy place' as their 'sanctuary'. But, equally, all faith traditions recognise the need for pilgrimage and the journey of faith. Even outside of conventional faith it is not unusual to hear people speak of the 'road less travelled' (5), which is a latter-day meditation on *peregrinatio*. Indeed, within some traditions, such as the Lukan and Markan traditions of the biblical Second Testament, the entire definition of faith is connoted around the practice of a spiritual journey. On that basis, in this volume on the communiversity, we have sought to bring together these two traditions—the constructivist/Sanctuary and the organic/Pilgrimage—into the neologism of 'pilgrimium' (See Chapter 6).

For Newman, the painful journey from his spiritual homeland to his own 'promised land', as a type of Abrahamic pilgrim's progress, was conducted as a road to the university that he envisaged, beyond the dreaming spires of Oxford's establishment. But, as Gerald O'Collins (6) indicates, Newman's life reflects a classic case of 'the second journey'. He reflects on the incident of Newman becoming seriously ill with typhus in Sicily in 1833. O'Collins points to six characteristics of second journeys, in that they are:

- sudden, unexpected and triggered by a particular event
- typified by a sense of crisis or *kairos*
- characterised by an outer journey that expresses the more significant inward journey
- associated with a search for new meaning, values and commitment to goals
- lonely, involving travelling beyond the liminal boundaries of a community's conventions and
- ended with a (quiet) awareness of deeper wisdom and having secured a new equanimity.

Those familiar with the writings of Carl Gustav Jung on the nature of the psyche and the cyclical progression of personality development will recognise this model. Jung borrowed the term *enantiodromia* from Heraclitus, meaning 'rushing to the opposite', to characterise the mid-life search for personal integration. Many of us discover the need to integrate missing aspects of the fourfold pattern of personality when we are in mid-life, from the ages of thirty to sixty and beyond. O'Collins points to the way in which Newman's Sicilian illness triggered this need at the age of 32, after which he returned to Oxford, determined to set out on the Tractarian cause, which eventually led to his own *peregrinatio* to Dublin, Birmingham and becoming a refugee from English Anglicanism.

Within our understanding of the communiversity, the one distinction to make from O'Collins' depiction of the second journey, in respect of our understanding of pilgrimium, is that it is not a journey along the road less travelled that is made alone. This is a vital reinterpretation of the Jungian fourfold model. We are not talking about the isolated individual's enantiodromic adventure. Rather, it is one for a *pilgrim people*, as for the ancient Jews. As we show in later chapters, it is one that is definitively biblical and familiar to many other spiritual traditions. The journey in a 'place' of pilgrimage, towards a new goal of awakening consciousness to learning afresh, is a shared journey. Indeed, it must be, if it is to have meaning in the communiversity, because the entire community needs to participate in the collective *peregrinatio*, towards emerging a new understanding of its communal purpose and goal.

On his return from Palermo, Newman wrote his most intensely personal poem, which has become known as the hymn *Lead, Kindly Light*, taking up the opening line of the first stanza.

> *"Lead, kindly Light, amid the encircling gloom, Lead Thou me on!*
> *The night is dark and I am far from home—Lead Thou me on!*
> *Keep Thou my feet; I do not ask to see*
> *The distant scene—one step enough for me."*

That sense of the next step being enough to see is a vital aspect of the pilgrimium within the communiversity. The pilgrim people—on their learning journey of awakening consciousness for what the community may become—will not know even the outline of the distant shore. But to take the next step and the next and the next together, in their place of *peregrinatio*, is a shared aspect which Newman sought to lead others into and which reflects the communiversity's spirit.

1.2.4. Newman and the Idea of the Academy

To modern ears Newman's principles for the university's knowledge curriculum sound as if they point in opposite directions. His understanding of the quest for knowledge was predicated on two premises. On the one hand, he asserted that theology should be at the heart of the curriculum, whilst on the other, he believed that a university should teach universal knowledge as its fundamental end. The problem rests, for contemporary university scholars, with his definition of universal knowledge, which meant the dogmatic truths of the Roman Catholic faith.

In respect of the communiversity we see Newman's viewpoint as a strength rather than a weakness. Most sympathetic commentators on Newman gently ignore his perspective that theology is 'the queen of sciences', *pace* Thomas Aquinas. But, there are some arguments to be made for connecting what elsewhere (7) we have identified as the need to conjoin *scientia* and *sapientia* (science and wisdom) in the contemporary curriculum.

The Catholic apologist and philosopher Bernard Lonergan (8) argues that the integration of the humanities is to be found in theology rather than philosophy. In making this point he is echoing Newman's historiography, which conceived of 'natural or secular history' as existing within the wider framework of 'sacred history'. This is a debate that has resurfaced through the writings of Wolfhart Pannenberg (9), amongst others, who bemoans the tendency of modernist scholars to restrict theological insights to the realm of existentialism, neglecting to recognise that faith has a history beyond the individual's personal commitment.

Equally, Pannenberg castigates conservative theology for creating a dualism between biblical history and general history. Such theology fails to recognise that God is in all things (*ta panta*) and so, whilst there is a special biblical revelation, it is not distinct from the revelation of God in universal history. Arguably, this is close to Newman's view and explains why he conceived of the university curriculum as requiring theology at its centre.

For us, in respect of the communiversity, this has resonance when we come to the third of the four dimensions—that of the academy. Research is as much a matter of understanding the community's widest context, including his faithing history, as it is in undertaking detailed empirical science. This is not to argue against empirical investigation, although Newman was profoundly disinterested in the university's research agenda. Rather, it is to recognise that once the consciousness of the mobilised community has been raised, its research focus will often be on interpreting its own history, within the framework of all history, which is the history of God, humanity and the world. In a time of global ecological catastrophe, such a perspective is especially valuable.

This does, however, immediately raise the issue of theodicy; the problem of suffering and evil and how this is to be addressed within the communiversity. When we turn to examine the pilgrimium in more detail, we consider the fourfold nature of salvation history and the recognition of Fall as a recursive aspect of the GENEalogy. If salvation history can be identified as the fourfold process of Creation, Fall, Redemption and Salvation, connected to the four stages of the dynamic GENE, then emergence of an activated consciousness doesn't always follow from the mobilisation of a grounded community. Instead of turning from South to East, the community will often 'follow the money and the material' and attempt to turn West, before it recognises its error and seeks a recursion by returning to its inner moral core.

In other words, the research academy will often focus on interpreting the community's history of fall, recursion and redemption. As it does so it will, necessarily, identify the aspects of a 'fallen world', sin, evil and suffering that have been manifest in the community's journey towards releasing its GENE-ius. The university, as Newman understood it, could only pertain to addressing these issues if it was anchored to the Church. Whilst we regard that as unhelpful in today's context, where we do side with Newman is in connecting the university to the faithing of the community, as we shall see for one of us (Adodo) in relation to the Benedictine Order. The academy develops from the pilgrimium and adds to it a research framework which takes evil, fall and suffering seriously.

Whilst the Western liberal tradition believes that through institutional transformation, including the activities of the university, suffering can be eradicated, Newman regarded such liberalism as fundamentally misguided and foolishly optimistic about the human condition. Even so, it was the legitimate place of the university to teach the extent of the problem, including human depravity, which he had no desire to shy away from. Similarly, we regard the communiversity's academy as the correct place for investigating the nature of innovation to transform communities, whilst at the same time, recognising the limitations of such transformation.

Where we profoundly take issue with Newman is that he had little interest in knowledge-creation. By contrast, we see the communiversity's academy as the most vital place for research-to-innovation, generating fresh insights, understanding and even facts about the community's history, situation and potential. Newman saw little value in useful knowledge. Indeed, as Frank Turner (10) puts it:

> *"[Newman] made the distinguishing value of the university its apparent* uselessness *(his emphasis). The usefulness, indeed the higher calling, of the university was its very direct lack of social and economic utility."*

Alternatively, we place the communiversity's emphasis in a very different direction. There is, undoubtedly, an important value in detaching the communiversity from utilitarian requirements. Yet the mobilised community on its pilgrimium journey will want to understand its social, technical and economic position, so that it can enter into new models of transformation, through research that leads to innovation. Even so, that research will pertain as much to the conventional fields of history, literature, anthropology and psychology as to business, finance, politics and engineering.

We conceive of a curriculum wherein these disciplinary boundaries become erased in trans-disciplinary, trans-cultural and trans-historical studies. In this respect we are not so far from Newman's vision, although we would see theology and spirituality in a wider sphere than his narrower Catholic religious outlook. In a vital dimension we are far closer to Newman than most modern universities, which talk of knowledge-creation for its own sake but focus on the bottom-line of profit-maximisation. Our communiversity vision is, certainly, one where knowledge is useful; but it is the definition of usefulness that is contested, as we conceive use-value in releasing cultural genius, rather than appeasing the gods of capitalist society.

In terms of the precise focus of the communiversity's academy we are, furthermore, with Newman in his ambiguous and even vague, depiction of the curriculum. He took "into account the nature and importance of each [area of knowledge]" (1, p.223). By this turn of phrase he indicated his understanding that spheres of knowledge would change and that the balances between disciplines would shift. And, even if he was disinterested in research-based knowledge-generation, he recognised that the institutions needed to be shaped by the interests of the collegium. We regard this as vital, in respect of the communities in which the communiversities are located and to which they act as loci of articulation and mobilisation. It is worth quoting him in this respect, although it is important to divest ourselves as we do so of his fondness for speaking about the solo learner, especially one who is male, white and privileged:

> "... for the sake of the students; and though they cannot pursue every subject open to them, they will be the gainers by living among those and under those who represent the whole circle... They learn to respect, to consult, to aid each other... A habit of mind is formed

*which lasts through life, of which the attributes are, freedom, eq-
uitableness, calmness, moderation and wisdom... a philosophical
habit."* (1, p.77)

For the writers of this volume, the academy is important because it
focuses the value-in-research of 'the whole circle'. This has a very particular meaning for us, in respect of the GEN*E*. But, equally, it reminds
us that the life of an individual communiversity academy, in whichever
cultural enclave of the four worlds of South, East, North and West it is
manifest, needs to reflect the distinctive journey of that community and,
vitally, its contribution to the whole circle of all the communiversities,
in a way that encourages it to 'think local and act global'.

1.2.5. Newman and the Idea of the Laboratory

It is certainly in respect of the fourth and final point on our genealogical circuit that our communiversity most diverges from the idea of
Newman's university. This relates to that of the effective co-laboratory,
wherein new knowledge is tested out, to the benefit of the community. When Newman wrote, laboratories for science were only beginning
to become established. Now, as we write, the concept of co-laboratory
hubs and working spaces for digital creatives, writers, artists, engineers,
technologists and enterprise innovators are the standard fare of 'artisan
quarters' across the globe. Furthermore, it is at this point, which reflects
the utility of Western culture, that we see each round of the communiversity's 'whole circle' coming to its conclusion and in which Newman
had almost no interest.

There is, however, another aspect of Newman's life-work which holds
surprising resonance for the principle of the co-working space, in which
effective enterprises are forged, reflecting the out-working of the laboratory. Newman was a member of the congregation of the Oratory of St
Philip Neri. Indeed, he concludes his final Discourse IX of the original
Dublin lectures with what is, in effect, a dedication of the work to St
Philip, from whom his inspiration for the university had derived.

57

Filippo Romolo Neri was a 16ᵗʰ century Roman lay-worker and later priest, who became known as the 'third Apostle of Rome', after SS Peter and Paul. He was a near contemporary of St Ignatius Loyola, founder of the Jesuits, St Francis Xavier, missionary to India and Charles Borromeo (also canonised) and a close friend of the eminent musician and composer Giovanni Palestrina. However, he is most famous for founding a society of 'secular priests' which he termed the 'Oratory.' The idea of the secular priests was that they would stay closer to 'the world' than 'the Church', in order to be practised in speaking, teaching and discoursing on the faith with lay people, using language drawn from everyday life.

To an extent, the need for such a society was testament to how far from the teaching style of Jesus of Nazareth, as recorded in the Gospels, the Church had drifted. It had become clericalised, aloof and disconnected from the community it served, as shown in St Philip's mission to create a society, rather in the manner that Francis had done in Assisi some three centuries earlier. Philip Neri's Oratory was the latest in a line of radical attempts to bring the Church to the people, which would result in the Reformation, the work of Protestant leaders such as John Wesley and many of the evangelical revival movements of the 19ᵗʰ and 20ᵗʰ centuries. But, the distinctive nature of Neri's society was its evening meetings in a hall (or Oratory). These were large-scale gatherings, often with a concert form which Palestrina would play at, in which music (oratorios), theatre, art and lecture would be mixed, along with theological discourse, readings from scripture and the Fathers, together with some Christian worship. The principle was that the teaching of the church would be effective on the streets. At the time, the idea of preaching sermons in a range of churches or in secular gatherings was hardly practised in Rome; something that would surprise the regular church congregation today, when biblical preaching is so much a part of Church practice.

The Oratory was, therefore, a considerable innovation in the life of the 16ᵗʰ century Church. Indeed, whilst contemporary congregations are used to a variety of evening meetings, the mixing of styles which Philip Neri initiated would be regarded as unusual even today. Inevitably, the informality of the Oratory meetings gave way to institutionalisation when, in 1575, a community of secular priests, the Congregation of the Oratory, was established and housed in its own building. Even then, however, Philip Neri declined the title of Superior General for the rapidly increasing number of Oratory houses, preferring to remain attached to the original Oratory, indicating that all other communities retain their own autonomy, governance and independence.

John Henry Newman had become a member of the Congregation of the Oratory of St Philip Neri and established one of its houses in Edgbaston, Birmingham, which is now dedicated to the memory of Newman. In turn, Newman was clearly devoted to the memory of Philip Neri, perhaps because he was so unlike his devotee, renowned, as Newman was, for his austere and serious demeanour. It is poignant to read Newman's quoting of Bacci's life of Philip, which suggests a longing for his own transformatory 'third journey' (see above):

> "... he was all things to all men. He suited himself to noble and ignoble, young and old, subjects and prelates, learned and ignorant... When he was called upon to be merry he was so; if there was a demand upon his sympathy he was equally ready... so that his room went by the agreeable nickname of the Home of Christian mirth."
> (1, p.163)

It could be a depiction of the Dickensian character Samuel Pickwick, Esq. The point is that there is—in this pattern of the Oratory—an image of the communiversity co-laboratory. A laboratory is a place for work and the diverse range of activities that innovate in the bringing together of arts, science, technologies, makers, do-ers and creatives. It is distinct from the academy in being less a place of formal learning and research and more the site of practice and specific experimentation with community-based innovation. However, it shares some of the features of Philip

Neri's GEN*E*-ius in establishing its activity in the midst of the public square and mixing work, culture, leisure and innovation.

1.3. CONCLUSION: IN SERVICE OF THE COMMUNITY

The communiversity co-laboratory, in Western guise, builds on the rest. It exists in service of the community. It emerges out of the pilgrimium experience of the community's journey towards transformation. Its activities are a direct result of the research-to-innovation systems, processes and technologies that have been learned in the academy. Moreover, it is a co-operative space, in which a wide range of practitioners meet to co-create their works, geared towards a transformation of the community—its people and locale—but crucially connected to other communiversity laboratories, from which it draws inspiration and to which it contributes practice and expertise.

For those of us who have been engaged in such co-laboratory spaces across the Trans4m Communiversity worlds, we've seen the development of new centres for plant-based healing in West Africa; structures for teaching and practice micro-finance initiatives in Islamic Pakistan; bio-dynamic agriculture, utilising the principles of Rudolf Steiner, in North Africa; the greening of manufacturing industry in Slovenia; and the creation of new works of musical theatre and cultural regeneration in the UK. There is no prototype laboratory. How could there be, given the immense variation that there is across the globe, between communities that are establishing communiversities for transformation?

In the chapters that follow we trace the four elements of the communiversity—from community, through pilgrimium, to academy and laboratory—in a range of different settings, as well as through the writings of a range of scholars who have assisted in shaping our thinking on the idea of the communiversity. At each point we consider the connection to four themes: development, research, economy and enterprise. This is by no means the last word or work on the communiversity, although it may be one of the first. Nor is it particularly attuned to the rarified and elitist idea of a university as exemplified by John Henry Newman. But, as we close this baseline chapter we do give Newman the last word, at least at this point, to state his views on the integral nature of knowledge; a fitting preamble to the idea of a communiversity:

> "... I lay it down that all knowledge forms one whole, because its subject-matter is one; for the universe in its length and breadth is so intimately knit together, that we cannot separate off portion from portion and operation from operation, except by a mental abstraction... they all belong to one and the same circle of objects, they are one and all connected together." (1, p.45)

We now turn to our current day and age, in the 21st as opposed to the 19th century, where, as we shall see, de-coloniality has come to the fore, providing a somewhat different university-communiversity context to that in Newman's time and place.

1.4. REFERENCES

1 Newman J H(1996) *The Idea of a University* (Ed. Frank M Turner). New Haven. Yale University Press.

2 Castro-Klaren S (1996) The Paradox of Self in The Idea of a University, contributory article in Frank M Turner (Ed.) edition of *The Idea of a University*. New Haven. Yale University Press.

3 Sugarman J and Martin J (2018) Campus culture wars, psychology and the victimization of persons. *The Humanistic Psychologist*, 46, 4, 320-32.

4 Newman J H (1994) *Apologia pro Vita Sua* (Ed. Ian Ker). London. Penguin Classics.

5 Scott Peck M (1983) *The Road Less-Travelled*. London. Hutchinson & Co.

6 O'Collins G (2007) *The Second Journey of John Henry Newman*. The Way [Available at: https://www.theway.org.uk/back/462OCollins.pdf].

7 Lessem R and Bradley T (2018) *Evolving Work – employing self and community*. Abingdon. Routledge.

8 Lonergan B (1967) The Role of the Catholic University in the Modern World, in F. E. Crewe SJ, (Ed.) *Collection – papers by Bernard Lonergan*. St Louis. Herder & Herder.

9 Pannenberg W (1968) *Revelation as History*. New York. The MacMillan Company.

10 Turner F M (1996) Newman's University and Ours, contributory article in Frank M Turner (Ed.) edition of *The Idea of a University*. New Haven. Yale University Press.

Chapter 2

De-Colonising the University

TOWARDS A KNOWLEDGE ECOLOGY

Decolonial thinking and doing aim to delink from the epistemic assumptions common to all areas of knowledge established in the Western world since the European Renaissance and through the European Enlightenment. Re-existence follows up delinking... the sustained effort to reorient our human communal praxis of living by enacting it in the academy...

Walter Mignolo W and Christine Walsh,
Decoloniality: Concepts, Analytics, Praxis

2.1. INTRODUCTION: UNIVERSITY TO COMMUNIVERSITY

2.1.1. The Original Idea of the University

Giving Enlargement and Sobriety to the Ideas of the Age

We now carry on specifically from where Cardinal Newman, with his 'western' idea of the university left off. In fact, since its publication almost 150 years ago, *The Idea of a University* (latterly termed 'Mode 1 university') has had an extraordinary influence on the shaping and goals of higher education. In fact, for us, this 'western' influence is as strong as the effect of liberal democracy, politically and capitalism, economically, on the world at large. The role of our communiversity, as we shall see, is to counteract that monolithic and ultimately destructive, influence.

The issues that Newman (1) raised in Britain—the place of religion and moral values in the university setting, the competing claims of liberal and professional education, the character of the academic community, the cultural role of literature, the relation of religion and science—have provoked discussion from Newman's time to our own. It is only in the new millennium, though, that they are coming fundamentally into question, leading us to the idea of the communiversity. At the same time, as we shall see, the 'idea of the communiversity' is very old.

For Newman, then, as revealed in the last chapter:

> *"A University training aims at raising the intellectual tone of society, at cultivating the public mind, at purifying the national taste, at supplying true principles to popular enthusiasm, at giving enlargement and sobriety to the ideas of the age, at facilitating the exercise of political power and refining the intercourse of public life. It shows man how to accommodate himself to others, how to throw himself into their state of mind, how to influence them, how to come to an understanding with them."*

Newman Displayed a Wholehearted Ethnocentricity

Like most other leading Victorian writers, Newman—for Frank Turner, the Professor of History at Yale University, who supplemented his above text on *The Idea of a University* with pertinent commentaries—assumed the unity of truth. He thereby rejected the early inroads of moral and cultural relativism and the pervasive angst and doubt they would later foster. Newman also displayed a wholehearted ethnocentricity:

> *"'Civilization' for him rarely extended beyond the lands and cultures of the Mediterranean world. Along with others of his generation, he unhesitatingly embraced the metaphors of imperialism, proudly portraying the university as a vast 'imperial intellect'."*

2.1.2. The Integral Idea of the Communiversity

Our—myself, Ronnie Samanyanga Lessem as the Afro-European Zimbabwean, Anselm Adodo as the Nigerian African and Liverpudlian Tony Bradley in the UK in Europe—idea of the communiversity (see next chapter) then takes on, in 21st century pluriverse guise, from where Newman has left off. Inspired by our pluriverse of "four worlds" (2), spanning 'south' and 'east', 'north' and 'west', we transcend the idea of a duly westernised 'uni-versity', accordingly.

In the process and as we shall see, we develop the notion of an 'inter-institutional pluriversity', if you like, altogether spanning a learning *community* (embodying the south), a developmental *pilgrimium* (inspired by the east), a research *academy* (informed by the north) and a socio-economic *laboratory* (energised by the west). We start, as such, with the current move to 'de-colonise the university', which is presently gaining significant ground, especially in South America and in South, if not also West, Africa.

2.1.3. The University at a Crossroads

In 2012, a full volume published by the journal *Human Architecture: Journal of the Sociology of Self-Knowledge* (3) was released entitled '*Decolonizing the University: Practising Pluriversity.*' One of its most noted contributors, Boaventura de Souza Santos, an intellectual leader behind the World Social Forum based in Port Alegre in Brazil, Professor of Sociology and Director of the Centre for Social Studies at the School of Economics, University of Coimbra (Portugal) states:

> *"We can assert, in general, that the university is undergoing—as much as the rest of contemporary societies—a period of paradigmatic transition. This transition can be characterized in the following way: we face modern problems for which there are no modern solutions."*

He then goes on to provide some 'strong questions' facing the university at the beginning of the 21st century. Firstly, given the fact that it was part and parcel of the building of the modern nation state, *how should it now function in a globalised world?* Secondly, he asks, *what is the place of the specificity of the university as a centre of knowledge production and diffusion in a society now with many other centres of production and diffusion of knowledge?* Thirdly, can we still call a university an institution that *only produces competent conformists and never competent rebels and that only regards knowledge as a commodity and never as a public good?* Fourthly, *is there a contradiction between our emphasis on cultural and social development* and the emphasis of some European politicians and powerful think-tanks on economic development *and the university's contribution to global competitiveness?* Fifthly, while the modern European university started in Bologna as a civil society initiative, *is it now problematic that in the last three decades the market has taken the lead in structuring university life?* Finally, is the university prepared to recognise that the understanding of the world by far exceeds the Western understanding of the world? *Is the university today equipped to enter the debate on models of development and civilisational paradigms,* or rather to serve a-critically to reinforce one dominant model? This brings us on to what is indeed a major movement of our time: de-coloniality.

2.2. DE-COLONIALITY AND INTEGRALITY

2.2.1. Belief in One Sustainable System of Knowledge is Pernicious

The initial idea for the book by Argentinian born Walter Mignolo, Director of the Centre for Global Studies and Humanities, at Duke University in the U.S., *The Darker Side of Western Modernity: Global Futures, Decolonial Options* (4), was to show that the belief in one sustainable system of knowledge is pernicious to the well-being of both the human being and life on the planet.

Such a system of knowledge, referred to as the 'Western code', serves not all of humanity, but only a small proportion. This code has in fact, for him, been preserved in a security box since the Renaissance in modern European languages—that is, Italian, Spanish, Portuguese, French, German and English. Decolonisation then is the horizon of thinking that originated as a response to such. For us, moreover, de-coloniality is the other side of the integral coin, as per de-coloniality/integrality.

While European modernity should be admired for its many virtues, its imperial bent to 'save the world' by making the world an extended Euro-America, is, for Mignolo, unacceptable. The problems of the present and future will be played out between a successful European-American modernity that is taken as a model and the 'rest of the world' which refuses to be told what to do.

2.2.2. The Significance of Knowledge and Subjectivity

Quijano and the Colonial Matrix of Power

Mignolo's initial focus, then, is on the unity of what has been termed the 'colonial matrix of power' (CMP), of which the rhetoric of modernity and the logic of coloniality are its two sides: one constantly named and celebrated (progress, development, growth) and the other silenced or named as problems to be solved by the former (poverty, misery, inequity, injustice, corruption). The de-colonial then confronts all of Western civilisation, which includes liberal capitalism and Marxism. In its original formulation by the Peruvian sociologist Anibal Quijano (5) in the 1980s, the *patron colonial de poder* (colonial matrix of power), he described as four interrelated domains, the last one, knowledge/subjectivity, being the most critical:

- Control of the economy
- Political authority
- Gender and sexuality
- Knowledge and subjectivity

These are altogether underpinned by:

- Theology/secular philosophy
- Patriarchy

In the final analysis, for Quijano and for Mignolo, *imperium* has run its course and global futures are being built in which many trajectories and options will be available; however, there will be no place for one option, he says, to pretend to be *the* option, ontologically and epistemologically as embodied in the conventional university, as well as politically and economically, lodged within the conventional enterprise, economy and all round polity.

Zero Point Epistemology Is Not the Ultimate Grounding of Knowledge

Basically, from a conventional, universal-university perspective, what Mignolo calls 'zero point epistemology' is the ultimate grounding of knowledge, which is paradoxically ungrounded. It is grounding without grounding; it is in the mind and not in the brain and heart. Every way of knowing and sensing (feeling) that does not conform to the epistemology of the 'westernised' zero point are cast behind as myth, folklore, local knowledge or the like. Since the zero point is always in the presence of time and centre of space, *it hides its own local knowledge universally projected.*

While for example, historically, Arabic remained crucial locally, it lost its global influence once the modern/European language—derived from Greek and Latin—became the language of universal knowledge, disavowing the epistemic insights of non-European languages. "I am where I think" sets the stage then for epistemic affirmations which have been disavowed. Only the European epistemology was built on the premise "I think therefore I am", wherever I am. By way of this strategy, scientific knowledge positions itself as the only valid way of producing knowledge and Europe acquires an *epistemological hegemony* over all other cultures of the world. "I am where I think", in de-colonial guise, legitimises all ways of thinking and de-legitimises the pretence of one singular version.

As such, de-colonising knowledge is not rejecting Western epistemic contributions to the world. On the contrary, it de-chains these from their imperial designs.

"I Am Where I Think" – Sociogeny: Learning Community

The first step in de-colonial thinking is to accept the interconnection between geo-history and epistemology and between bio-graphy and epistemology, that has been kept hidden by linear global thinking and the hubris of the zero point in their making of colonial and imperial differences. That is, the first step is to assume the legitimacy of "I think" and not be afraid of inquisitorial corporate and post-modern thinkers. As such and as we shall see, our communiversity is grounded in a particular learning community, as per "I am where I think".

In the late 19th century in fact, Sigmund Freud insisted that the individual factor of alienation be taken into account through psychoanalysis. Frantz Fanon in the mid-20th century substituted an ontogenetic perspective (6). It will be seen that the black man's alienation is not an individual one; thereby he referred to sociogeny. The implication for Fanon here is that an overall societal psyche transcends the individual one. Mignolo's Southern African de-colonial colleague, Sabelo Ndlovu-Gatsheni (7) takes the argument on from here, in contemporary African guise.

2.3. EPISTEMIC FREEDOM

2.3.1. De-colonising Education and the University in Africa

The Universities Promised Freedom of Thought Only to Stifle It

Newman's modern 'North-Westernised' university has played a central role in the invention and universalisation of what Ndlovu-Gatsheni alludes to as "coloniser's model of the world". In fact it was the Arabic/Muslim civilisation as well as pre-colonial African civilisation that enabled universities to emerge from indigenous cultural soil. But these non-European universities, just like African religion, were not hegemonic and imperial in character. This partly explains why they were easily overtaken by the North-Westernised model of the university. And it is this modern university, at least in South Africa where Ndlovu-Gatsheni is based, that is facing its worst systemic, epistemic and institutional crisis today. Why is this?

Firstly, it is the universities that promised freedom of thought only to stifle it through religiously adhering to a Eurocentric epistemology and Western-centric cultures and practices. Secondly, the university has the highest concentration of young people eager to understand, at least in

South Africa, why the institution is still maintaining alienating Eurocentric cultures and is not considering the cultural and practical relevance of what it delivers. Thirdly, despite the institutional constraints, the university is still the place where ideas are explored.

Creating the African Developmental University

A 1972 AAU (Association of African Universities) workshop called 'Creating the African University: Emerging Issues in the 1970s' demonstrated that the struggle for the university was continuing even as African economies were collapsing. In line with de-colonial thinking, six functions of the African university were delineated:

Table 2: CORE FUNCTIONS OF AN AFRICAN UNIVERSITY IN THE 1970s	
Function	Explanation
Pursuit, promotion and dissemination of knowledge	Practical, immediately useful to the ordinary people and locally-oriented
Research	Research priority given to local problems and improvement of rural life of ordinary people
Provision of intellectual leadership	Cutting edge leadership capable of leading government, society and commerce in devising and implementing meaningful economic and social development
Manpower development	Relevant skilled graduates capable of playing a leading role in the social revolution and production
Promotion of social and economic modernisation	Breaking the chain of tradition that inhibits African genius capable of advancing social and economic development
Promotion of intercontinental unity and international understanding	Responsibility to emancipate the African continent from isolation, marginality and pursuit of Pan-Africanism

The Corporate University and the Commodification of Knowledge

In fact, the struggle for an African University failed in the 1960s and 1970s. The late 1980s and 1990s witnessed the rise of the 'corporate university', characterised by the invasion of the university by business models. The corporate university, for Ndlovu-Gatsheni, is a product of the triumph of the Washington Consensus, which routinised the neoliberal dispensation. Within this, the marketplace evaluation of scholarship is through the principles of quantification and annual reports.

But what has really plunged the corporate university into violent crisis is its commodification of education, which has reduced students to customers and the professoriate to an academic proletariat. Higher education has been turned into a marketable product, rated, bought and sold by standardised units, measured by mechanical tests. The pegging of higher education at a commercial value has not only closed out poorer students but has also burdened those who have gone through the corporate university with huge debts. This brings us to, at least in the South African context, 'Rhodes Must Fall'.

Resurgent Struggles for a Decolonised University

The South African students then who spearheaded the 'Rhodes Must Fall' and 'Fees Must Fall' movements must be understood broadly as heirs to the longstanding struggle for an African university and the wider decolonisation of Africa, because what was gained in 1994, according to Ndlovu-Gatsheni, was democracy without decolonisation.

What these two movements have successfully brought to the fore, therefore, are longstanding, unresolved issues of opening the doors of learning and education to everyone, as promised by the ANC and Freedom Charter of 1955.

This involves:

- Rescuing the university from capture by neoliberal market forces and repositioning it as a public good.
- Rethinking and redefining the university as a truly African institution serving African communities.
- Rethinking and rearticulating the broader philosophical foundations of higher education in Africa.
- Financing and funding higher education to enable access; decolonizing the epistemology, curricula and alienating institutional

cultures of the university.
- Democratizing student-staff relations to enhance learning; using indigenous languages for learning and teaching.
- Ending the dehumanising outsourcing of black workers; as well as the de-patriarchalization, de-racialization and de-westernisation of universities.

The paradoxical structural situation bequeathed on Africa by colonialism is that a modern education produced a people who were deeply alienated from themselves, their cultures, their languages, ancestors and knowledges, but were at the same time eager to end colonial rule. It is therefore not surprising that these very Africans whose minds were deeply invaded by epistemological colonialism have continued to reproduce cultural colonialism. Consequently, the struggle to decolonise the 'university in Africa' is still on course in the 21st century.

Strategising About Epistemic Freedom Rather than Shallow Academic Freedom

For Ndlovu-Gatsheni, the 2007 financial crisis was also an epistemological crisis. This crisis of Euro-North American-centric thought is both a challenge and an opportunity. It means that Africans, not to mention the Arabs or Pakistanis with whom we are also directly involved, must take advantage of leveraging their thoughts together with those of the rest of the Global South. A space for another reason, logic, thought and epistemology is open, capable of enabling autonomy from traditional Eurocentric thought and epistemology that enables global coloniality.

Only a decolonised being can appreciate the value of indigenous and exogenous knowledge as ideas for the creation of African futures. As such and in our conversations, strategising about epistemic freedom rather than shallow academic freedom must be top of our list. Epistemic freedom enables a tapping into the rich and inexhaustible wisdom and knowledge of the world as we break away from Eurocentrism.

However, what Ndlovu-Gatsheni, Mignolo, or indeed all those advocating for decolonising the university miss out on is the actual structure, over and above the content of such a university, or indeed 'pluriversity'. As such, we now turn to an evolved 'northern' notion of a 'Mode 2' university (the more basic 'western' version will be reviewed in chapter 9), duly accompanied by *Rethinking Science,* especially as advocated by Austrian social philosopher Helga Nowotny. In fact, our own Trans4m Communiversity has been established in partnership with the Da Vinci Institute in South Africa, a Mode 2 University co-founded by Nelson Mandela, which follows more of a 'western' Anglo-Saxon course.

2.4. MODE 1 TO MODE 2 UNIVERSITY

2.4.1. Rethinking Science

Four Conceptual Pillars

Austrian social philosopher Helga Nowotny (8), until recently, was President of the European Research Council and a leading figure in the field of science and society. From the outset she and her English colleagues, Peter Scott (who was recently Vice Chancellor of Kingston University in the UK and Michael Gibbons, Secretary General of the Association of Commonwealth Universities) sought to develop and open a dynamic framework for re-thinking science. It was based on four conceptual pillars: firstly, the nature of a so-called *Mode 2 society;* secondly, the *contextualisation of knowledge* in a new public space, called the *agora;* thirdly, the development of *conditions for socially robust knowledge;* and fourthly, the emergence of *socially distributed expertise.*

Under so-called Mode 2 conditions, science and society, for Nowotny, are subject to co-evolution. What are the historical underpinnings of such?

Transformation of Society: Mode 1 to Mode 2

Hitherto, the clock and later the machine, became the arbiters of production. They became the guiding, so-called Mode 1 metaphor and the dominant iconography of the political order. At first regarded as the worldly embodiment of a cosmic order, later this political order was reflected in and also celebrated, the machine-like operation and technocratic efficiency of welfare-state capitalism and liberal democracy. In its smooth and predictable functioning, the process of modernisation in the highly industrialised Western countries reached its climax during the quarter century after 1945. Moreover, modernisation was no longer attributed to the 'hidden hand' of the market or other apparently impersonal forces; instead it was publicly on display for all to see, a powerful affirmation of man's control over nature and society.

The rise of so-called post-industrialism and post-modernism as such, represents a crisis of both social legitimisation and of methodical, epistemological and even normative authority—although some would prefer to talk of opportunity rather than crisis. Not only has the received canon of knowledge been questioned, but increasingly, the limits inherent to scientific knowledge and the knowable have also been probed. It is in this sense that a Mode 2 society, Mode 2 science and Mode 2 university, for Nowotny in contemporary 'northern' guise, are inextricably bound together.

Social Change and Knowledge Production

The growth of the 'know-how' industries has not only led to an increase in 'knowledge' workers and proliferation of sites of production, but has also eroded the demarcation between traditional knowledge institutions such as universities and research institutes and other kinds of organisations. However, an even more radical change is underway; many, perhaps most, organisations in a knowledge society have to become learning organisations in order to develop their human and intellectual capital.

75

In reductionist science—still the Mode 1 to which many scientists aspire—it is necessary to establish clear boundaries that form the scientific arena and distinguish science from non-science. Mode 2 knowledge production, in contrast, takes place within and between open and shifting boundaries. It consists of the re-configuration of knowledge and people, whereby a new kind of integration with the context is made possible.

It is in this sense that Nowotny talks of the contextualisation of science, as an enlargement of its scope and enrichment of its potential. The increasing emphasis on diversity and pluralism in fact tends to confirm the preference for our integral brand of 'research' with its multiple paths and trajectories. Rhetorically, if not actually, science attempts to unify, but there can be no unity in research; it is diverse and heterogeneous, as borne out in the author's own work on *Integral Research and Innovation* (9). Mode 2 knowledge production as such occurs in many different sites and in many heterogeneous contexts of applications. The knowledge production system—industrial research, laboratories, government research establishments, research councils, universities—has been caught up in this whirlwind of transformation.

2.4.2. The Role of Universities in Mode 2 Knowledge Production

The University as a Scientific and Social Mode 1 Institution

During the course of the 20th century the university, then, became the key knowledge-producing institution—in large parts of Europe and North America at any rate. Under the regime of so-called Mode 1 science, for Nowotny, the universities exercised scientific hegemony through their production of 'pure' research that was the foundation on which society's capacity for innovation and the economy's ability to exploit technological advances, ultimately depended. On the other hand, stimulating 'knowledgeability' was the key task of an elite system of education. The university played a leadership role through its formation of future elites—social and technical. Scientific literacy (and perhaps also cultural authority) would allegedly trickle down.

There historically existed a tension between the university's aim to reproduce a cultivated elite, often associated with antiscientific (or at any rate anti-positivistic) notions of liberal education or *Bildung* and its scientific development. This tension took the form of 'culture wars' (for example, England during the 1880s between Huxley and Arnold; Germany with the originally higher status of the humanities which came to be later challenged by the natural sciences).

Mode 1 versus Mode 2 Universities: An Elaboration

While it was (and is) possible to contain Mode 1 science as 'objective' and disinterested and thereby de-contextualised, within a restricted number of elite institutions, dominated by equally restricted scientific communities, it is however not possible to contain Mode 2 knowledge production in the same way. Firstly, Mode 2 knowledge production transcends disciplinary boundaries. Secondly, it expands the number of research actors. Thirdly, by shifting the focus from Mode 2 science to Mode 2 society, the emergence of a knowledge society means that a much wider range of social, economic and even cultural activities now have 'research' components.

Under Mode 2 conditions, moreover, the distinction between research and teaching tends to break down. The reflexivity of Mode 2 knowledge production as such, transforms relatively closed communities of scientists into open communities of 'knowledgeable' people. A 'knowledge economy' depends on dissemination and popularisation; on not only PhD training but also 'research activism'.

Reliable Knowledge to Socially Robust Knowledge

The increasing emphasis on the contribution of science to wealth creation (and social improvement), the growing deference to so-called 'user' perspectives and the great weight now attached to ethical and environmental considerations are all examples of the intensification of what Nowotny calls contextualisation.

Reliable knowledge, then, produced by a wider network of collaborators working under Mode 2 conditions is reliable in terms of a wider consensuality (as per a learning community as we shall see in the next chapter); it is outer-directed. It is reliable in terms of the problem relevance of the context in which it arose and which continues to influence it (as we shall see reflected in Part 4: Socioeconomic Laboratory). To suggest that reliable knowledge must engage the social world more openly and directly is not to seek to diminish but to enhance its status and validity, by arguing that reliable knowledge—to remain reliable—has to also be socially robust knowledge.

A more nuanced and more sociologically sensitive epistemology is needed which incorporates the 'soft' individual, social and cultural visions of science as well as a 'hard' body of knowledge. Within the wider environment in which science will have to work in the future, which Nowotny calls the *agora*, a disembedded and self-organising science striving to discover invariant rules and accumulate knowledge will need to be complemented by a new vision of science, richly contextualised, socially robust and epistemologically eclectic.

Rethinking Science

The argument of Nowotny's, together with her colleagues, is thus organised around the description of four interrelated processes. First, it is contended that the emergence of more open systems of knowledge production—Mode 2 science and the growth of complexity and uncertainty—in a Mode 2 society are phenomena linked in a co-evolutionary process. The implication is that not only does science speak to society, but society speaks to science. Second, the process of reverse communication is transforming science and this, in its simplest terms is what is meant by contextualisation. Thirdly, the process of contextualisation moves science beyond merely reliable knowledge to socially robust knowledge.

Neither state nor market, neither exclusively public or private, the *agora* is the space in which scientific and societal problems are framed and defined and where what will be accepted as a 'solution' is negotiated. Fourthly, the range of perspectives found in the *agora*, together with the ability of their proponents to articulate their wishes and concerns as well as to mobilise resources for research activities, implies a more complex role for scientific and technical expertise in the production of socially robust knowledge. The novel factor is that the role of scientific and technical expertise is changing as it becomes more socially distributed.

These four processes—*the co-evolution of science and society* (we would incorporate in the former the natural sciences and in the latter the humanities and the social sciences) in a Mode 2 direction, *contextualisation*, the *production of socially robust knowledge* and the *construction of narratives of expertise*—are interrelated and will be brought together, often in conflictual forms, in the *agora*. However, they can also form the main elements of a framework for re-thinking science. Though the process of rethinking science has barely begun, Nowotny highlights five of these:

- *Uncertainties, rather than being progressively eradicated, will proliferate;* uncertainties are generated by two forces—the success of science in provoking novelty and the insatiable demand in society for innovation.
- *The challenge now is how to cope with these uncertainties;* coping with uncertainties has two dimensions. The first is the demand for new social—and not only scientific and technical—innovations to enable individuals and groups to cope with ever encroaching uncertainties. The second is the growth of multi-disciplinary identities and the development of multi-task teams.
- *The emergence of Mode 2 society raises acute issues of social justice, economic equality and the further democratisation of knowledge;* without broadly based 'ownership' of, or access to, knowledge—the virtuous—circle of innovation-uncertainty-innovation will be replaced by a vicious circle.
- *Universities will need to be adaptable organisations (and*

comprehensive institutions) rather than specialised organisations; first, universities may be unable to react rapidly and creatively to future demands if they are constrained within either a historically determined or a bureaucratically imposed division of institutional labour; secondly, universities, as successful generators of uncertainties, may have peculiar capacity for accommodating these uncertainties, at any rate in the research domain.

• *A variety of knowledge traditions is needed to constantly replenish the epistemological core;* openness to a great variety of knowledge traditions is a way of constantly re-activating the creativity of the core. These riches allow us to constantly re-configure knowledge.

2.5. CONCLUSION: ROBBEN ISLAND AS AN EMERGENT COMMUNIVERSITY

2.5.1. Learning Community to Socioeconomic Laboratory

University to Communiversity

In conclusion, as a bridge between the perspectives provided by De Sousa Santos (De-colonising the University), Mignolo (De-coloniality) and Ndlovu-Gatsheni (Epistemic Freedom) in the 'Global South', on the one hand and Nowotny, Scott and Gibbons in the 'Global North' (Mode 2 University) on the other, we turn to the so-called 'Robben Island University'. In the freedom struggle in fact, in apartheid South Africa, Robben Island was known as such. This was not only because of what Nelson Mandela and his fellow inmates learned from books, or because prisoners studied English, Afrikaans, art, geography and mathematics, or because so many of the men earned multiple degrees. Robben Island was known as the 'university'—we would call it an embryonic 'communiversity'—because of what they learned from each other. Prisoners became their own faculty, with their own curriculum and their own courses.

Learning the History of the ANC: Engaging in a Regenerative African Pilgrimium

They then made a distinction between academic studies, which were official, and political studies, which were not. The 'university' grew up, moreover, at least partly out of necessity. As young men came to the island, they realised that they knew very little about the history of the ANC (African National Congress). Walter Sisulu, perhaps the greatest living historian of the ANC, began to tell them about the organisation in its early days. Gradually this informal history grew into a full course of study which became known as Syllabus A, involving two years of lectures on the ANC and on the liberation struggle. Syllabus A also included a course on 'A History of the Indian Struggle'. Another comrade added a history of the coloured people. Mac Maharaj, who had studied in the German Democratic Republic, added a course on Marxism. The style of teaching was Socratic in nature; ideas and theories were elucidated through the course leaders asking and answering questions.

Engaging in Learning Communities: Education for the Real World

As the courses became known in the general section of the prison, they began to get inquiries from men on the other side. This started what became a kind of correspondence course with the prisoners from the general section. The teachers would smuggle lectures over to them and they would respond with questions and comments. This was beneficial for teachers and students alike, as they were all learning from each other. These men had little formal education but great knowledge of the hardships of the world. Their concerns tended to be practical rather than philosophical. "If I have land and no money and my friend has money and no land, who is in greater need?"

Emergent Research Academy: Towards the Most Advanced Stage of Economic Life

For a number of years, Mandela himself taught a course in political economy. In this course he attempted to trace the evolution of economic man from the earliest times to the present, sketching out the path from ancient communal societies to feudalism to capitalism and socialism. He was by no means a scholar and claims to have been not much of a teacher, so he generally preferred to ask questions than to lecture. His approach was not ideological, but was biased in favour of socialism, which he saw as the most advanced stage of economic life then evolved by man. In addition to his formal studies, his legal work continued. He sometimes considered hanging his name plate on his cell. He spent many hours a week preparing judicial appeals for prisoners. He enjoyed keeping his legal skills sharp. In some cases, sentences were reduced or overturned.

Socioeconomic Laboratory: How to Keep the Idea of the Struggle Before the People

Meanwhile, one of the issues that always concerned them was how to keep the idea of the struggle before the people. One day, Ahmed Kathrada (Kathy), Walter Sisulu and Nelson Mandela were talking in the courtyard when they suggested that Mandela ought to write his memoirs, which would ultimately turn out to be his book called *The Long Walk to Freedom* (10). When he decided to do something he would start immediately and he threw himself into this project. They created an assembly line to process the manuscript. Each day he passed what he wrote to Kathy, who reviewed it and then sent it to Walter—Kathy then wrote his comments in the margins. This marked-up manuscript was then given to Laloo Chiba, who spent the next night transferring Mandela's writing to his almost microscopic shorthand, reducing ten pages of foolscap to a single small piece of paper. It would be Mac Maharaj's job to smuggle the manuscript to the outside world. At the end, they had to dispose of the manuscript, so they buried it in the garden.

In the Wake of a Misconceived Robben Island Communiversity: Rhodes Must Fall

It is saddening that from the 1990s onwards, there was no concerted attempt to turn Robben Island University into a formalised, communiversity equivalent. Instead the conventional universities, as Ndlovu-Gatsheni has pointed out, continued to function largely 'Mode 1 like' as before, albeit opening their doors now to the South African student population as a whole. The end result, at least in the second decade of the new millennium, was the two movements: 'Rhodes Must Fall' and 'Fees Must Fall', both arguably the outcome of a failure to recreate Robben Island Communiversity, retrospectively and a fully fledged communiversity, prospectively, as is now being co-evolved by one of us in Nigeria (11), alongside emergent others. We now turn to the Trans4m version of a communiversity specifically, by way of an introduction.

2.6. BIBLIOGRAPHY

1 Newman J (1996) *The Idea of the University : Rethinking the Western Tradition.* New Haven. Yale University Press (Turner F ed)

2 Schieffer A and Lessem R (2014) *Realising the Transformative Potential of Individual, Organisation and Society.* Abingdon. Routledge

3 Tamdgidi M (ed) Human Architecture: Journal of the Sociology of Self-Knowledge. *Decolonizing the University: Practising Pluriversity.* Issue 1. Winter 2012. Volume X

4 Mignolo W (2011) *The Darker Side of Western Modernity: Global Futures, Decolonial Options.* Durham, North Carolina. Duke University Press

5 Quijano A (1972) *Nationalism and Capitalism in Peru: A Study in Neo-Imperialism.* New York. Monthly Review Press

6 Ndlovu-Gatsheni S (2018) *Epistemic Freedom in Africa: Deprovincialisation and Decolonisation.* Abingdon. Routledge

7 Fanon F (2007) *Black Skin White Masks.* New York. Grove Press.

8 Nowotny H, Scott P and Gibbons M (2001) *Re-Thinking Science: Knowledge & the Public in the Age of Uncertainty.* Cambridge. Polity.

9 Lessem R and Schieffer A (2010) *Integral Research and Innovation: Transforming Enterprise and Society.* Abingdon. Routledge

10 Mandela N (1994) *The Long Walk to Freedom.* London. Abacus

11 Adodo A (2017) *Integral Community Enterprise in Africa: Communitalism as an Alternative to Capitalism.* Abingdon. Routledge

Chapter 3

The Idea of Trans4m Communiversity

COMMUNITY – PILGRIMIUM – ACADEMY – LABORATORY

... knowledge has been fundamentally reinvented a number of times in the history of the West. In each case one new institution has replaced the knowledge based institution that preceded it ... Today the laboratory and the research university still stand as the most evolved and overlapping intermeshed institutions of knowledge. But since the central dynamic in the history of knowledge has been for a single institution to supersede its predecessor, the time is ripe for reinvention.

McNeely and Wolverton, *Reinventing Knowledge*

3.1. INTRODUCTION: STRUCTURE AND AGENCY

3.1.1. Genealogy and Communiversity

As we saw in the last chapter, the contemporary university is ripe for evolution, whether following in the footsteps of de-coloniality/pluriversity, the so-called Mode 2 university, or indeed what we have coined 'Robben Island Communiversity' (termed Robben Island University by Mandela himself). Moreover and as such, it has become apparent, as revealed by the great French post-modernist Michel Foucault, as cited by Prado (1) through his *Introduction to Genealogy*, that something is glaringly missing in the world of knowledge.

> *"The impetus to genealogy is feeling something is amiss ... We need a historical awareness of our present circumstance. That awareness problematises current truths by tracing their descent and emergence and by uncovering alternatives ... the role of the intellectual is to question, therefore, what is postulated as self-evident, to disturb people's mental habits, the way they do and think things, to dissipate what is familiar and accepted and to re-examine rules and institutions."*

Most universities as well as research laboratories and management consultancies are Eurocentric (including Euro-America) in nature and scope. As such there is no overall global integrity, authenticity, or indeed 'alternity' in the 'scientific' education that a Zimbabwean, a Nigerian, an Arab or a Pakistani receives—in their cases inevitably French or English in origin—or in the kind of research they undertake, which is more likely to be American in its empirical, or more likely pseudo-empirical, orientation. Secondly, therefore, when it comes to the development, or unfolding, of a particular country or community, what we call the release of its 'GENE-ius', again there is no obvious place to start. The West (in fact for us 'north-west') predominates over the rest.

The Eurocentric or US-centric research agenda, or educational curriculum is firstly, then, alien from where non-Europeans (that is most of the world) individually and societally are. Consultants and research laboratories, secondly, deal with the development of products, services and organisations, inevitably constrained by 'western' macro forces, notably those of the 'Washington Consensus', that are invariably beyond their control. Community developers, thirdly, seem to have faded into oblivion in the wake of methodical individualism and all-pervasive individual leaders and entrepreneurs—now social as well as business ones—have become the order of our day.

Finally and altogether as a result, the social and economic transformation of whole societies seems to be on the one hand left locally and largely to chance, notwithstanding the sincere (or indeed insincere) efforts of public policy makers to deal with such. On the other hand and globally, most societies are at the mercy of the Washington Consensus (as of the time of writing in October 2018, Pakistan has just joined that long list), if not also the parochial 'north-western' knowledge consensus that underlies such. As a result, moreover, a newly emergent Zimbabwe, for example, is now also open for business.

3.1.2. Modern Myopia and the Contemporary University

The mess we see around us today, whether in Zimbabwe, in Pakistan or indeed in Britain or America, from the transformative perspective adopted here, is, at least in significant part, a creation of the modern university, duly embodied in the 'universality' of especially social, 'scientific' knowledge. In our integral or 'four world' terms, such knowledge, in the natural and social sciences at least, is inevitably 'north-western'. In geographical and cultural terms that means Western Europe and America; in temporal terms it means the 'modern' era, particularly that of the past two hundred and fifty years. In both instances as such it lacks the overall cyclical, spiralling, non-linear dynamic embodied in a pre-modern/modern/post-modern/trans-modern trajectory.

Michel Foucault indeed was a post-modern philosopher and social activist, set against the reality of the modern university. In fact, whereas it is obviously apparent that technologically, post-modernity is rampantly upon us, bringing with it the information society and knowledge economy as per Facebook, Twitter, Google and Microsoft, as opposed to mass production and distribution as per Ford, General Motors and Toyota, in other social and cultural respects, modernity continues to prevail. The university pre-eminent amongst such modern institutions promotes mass education, that is an empirically based, one size fits all, 'scientific' approach and a so-called 'international curriculum' that remains, as we saw in the last chapter, invariably Eurocentric. The same of course applies to universally standardised approaches to invariably 'empirical' research.

By way of contrast, we start out by recognising and drawing upon the particular Grounding of a community, organisation or society. This befits our GEN*E*, as we, at Trans4m Centre for Integral Development then based in Geneva, first articulated in our *Integral Dynamics: Cultural Dynamics, Political Economy and the Future of the University* (2). After local **G**rounding, dynamically speaking, comes local-global **E**mergence, newly global **N**avigation and global-local *E*ffect—though not necessarily in that order—if you like GEN*E*alogy of a different kind. However, Foucault (see quote by Prado above), for all his philosophical genius, never attempted to create the kind of institution that would reflect his genealogical orientation.

The question then is what kind of new genealogical agency, in our case the so-called Trans4m Communiversity as different from a conventional university starting from a particular communal ground up, can put this into effect? We now turn to American cultural historians McNeely and Wolverton to take our story on, historically, if not also prospectively.

3.2. COMMUNITY, 'MONASTERY' REVISITED, ACADEMY, LABORATORY

3.2.1. The Organisation of Knowledge: Structure Building and Structure Changing

Two Oregon University based historians of knowledge, husband and wife partnership Ian McNeely and Lisa Wolverton, wrote a seminal book in the first decade of the new millennium on *Reinventing Knowledge: Alexandria to the Internet* (3). In it they introduce six institutions which, for them, have served to build up the knowledge that we all have today. Three of these—the monastery (which we now term a 'pilgrimium' to avoid any particular religious and also purely human, devoid of natural, connotations), the academy and laboratory—are structure-building constituents of our transformative perspective.

The other three as we shall see—the library, the so-called 'Republic of Letters' and the disciplines—for us, though not necessarily for them, constitute intermediate, transitional or structure changing categories. We now turn to their way of organising knowledge. Underlying all of this, for us, is the learning *community* as opposed to the individual student. This is key to the de-colonisation of the typically 'north-western' university.

Together, for McNeely and Wolverton, their six above-mentioned institutions have safeguarded knowledge through the ages by acting as interfaces between scholars and the rest of society:

> *"Each was formed to organise the totality of knowledge at the time. Each coalesced in reaction to sweeping historical changes that discredited its predecessor or exposed its limitations. And each arose out of dissatisfaction and disillusionment with existing ways of knowing into an all-encompassing new ideology legitimating its mission for the outside world."*

In times of stability, these institutions carried the torch of learning. In times of upheaval, individuals and small communities reinvented knowledge, as we are attempting to do now because of our dissatisfaction with the status quo, in founding new institutions. It is time for us then, in the social scientific arena if not in the natural sciences, for a newly genealogical reinvention and as such for a newly integral dynamic to underpin knowledge creation and societal renewal.

3.2.2. Consciously Evolving Education, Training or Consultancy

In fact, we all too easily lose sight of the fact that the organisation of knowledge has been mediated, in the past and the present, by specific institutions and that we will need to continue to create and re-create these, including specifically here, in relation to the universities (if not also schools), in the present and future. So for us, accordingly, there is a need to combine a *learning community* (local grounding in nature and community); *developmental pilgrimium* (local-global emergence through culture and spirituality); *research academy* (newly global navigation through science and technology); and *socio-economic laboratory* (global-local effect through economy and enterprise). This will take place, as we shall see, within an overall inter-institutional 'communi-versity', to promote such knowledge-and-institutional transformation.

With a view to such, we start, integrally and transformatively speaking, with nature and community, which provides the grounding for our so-called communiversity, with a view to McNeely's reinvention of knowledge.

3.3. GROUNDING IN ORAL COMMUNITY: HEALING POWER ALIGNED WITH SOCRATIC METHOD

3.3.1. The Healing Power of Nature

Nature, in fact, for Burkina Faso-born California-based African philosopher, Malidoma Some (4) is the foundation of indigenous life. For Pax Herbals in Nigeria as for the Chinyika rural community in Zimbabwe (see chapter 5), it is the basis for food security, as well as for spiritual sustenance. Without nature, concepts of community, purpose and healing would be meaningless. In other words, every tree, plant, hill, mountain, rock, speaks for itself as it were and as such vibrates with a subtle energy that has healing power whether we know it or not. Nature, then, for some, is the indigenous knowledge source, indeed the primal university of life, for those who care to study it and the storehouse of remedies for human ills. Indeed for co-author Anselm Adodo (5), founder of Pax Herbals and co-evolver of a Nigerian Communiversity:

> *"Nature Power is inviting the world to come down to earth so as to regain our health. The earth is the primary source of our creativity, intelligence and humanness. Before we set out to calculate, to create, to invent, to fabricate, the earth already was. The African Universe is a world of relationships, of interactions between the living and the dead, between the natural and the supernatural. A community is not just a place where human beings dwell. The African community comprises plants, animals, human beings, the spirit and the ancestors. Trees are more than trees: the sky is more than we see. There is more to plants and animals than we see with our eyes. Everything in the universe is a language of Life and an expression of Life. Therefore they are sacred and holy."*

For some, ritual, community and healing—related to the *rapoko* crop in Chinyika, for example—are so intertwined in the indigenous world that to speak of one of them is to speak of them all. Ritual, communally designed, helps the individual remember his or her purpose and such remembering brings healing both to the individual and the community. *The community exists, in part, to safeguard the purpose of each person within it and to awaken the memory of that purpose by recognising the unique gifts each brings to the world.* Healing comes when the individual remembers his or her identity—purpose chosen in the world of ancestral wisdom—and reconnects with that world of Spirit.

Such a combined process of natural healing and communal learning needs to be resurrected and juxtaposed with spiritual contemplation, academic scholarship and organisational knowledge creation from the outset. Interestingly enough, there are parallels to such in ancient Greece, as we shall now see.

3.3.2. Revisiting the Orally Based Socratic Method

Socrates in ancient Greece, for McNeely and Wolverton again—like elders and villagers in Africa, indigenous America and rural China today—hearkened back to the living, verbal bonds among men and to the oral pedagogy founded on the productive interchange between masters and students, through the 'Socratic method' of robust question and answer. This also reflected Socrates' belief that the interchange of speech leads to truth. The written word, by contrast, is untrustworthy and corrupting because it is detached from the actions, honour and character of whomever uttered it.

Institutionally, moreover, what Plato and his followers subsequently created through their dialogues and what later imitators copied, was the philosophical school—a brotherhood of scholars constituted in an Athenian grove, which can be likened to membership in a pilgrimium—that ranged freely over what has since come to be known as 'academic knowledge'. Aristotle, conversely, anticipated what was to follow in medieval and modern times thereafter and was able to ground his scholarship in writing.

Before we turn from orality (our Grounding) to literacy (our Navigation), we focus on Emergent scripture.

3.4. EMERGING THROUGH SCRIPTURAL MONASTERY-PILGRIMIUM

3.4.1. Spiritual and Psychological Confessions

If a particular local community (in Chinyika in Zimbabwe, for example) serves subsequently locally-globally, to scripturally evolve learning and knowledge creation, through what we term a developmental 'pilgrimium' (in Chinyika the African Jews embodying such were termed the Baremba), knowledge is developed from the scriptures, together with local community experience. We now turn to the influence of the sacred.

Thanks in no small part to Augustine's *Confessions* in the 4th century AD, based on what is now Algeria, Christian scripture finally, for McNeely, began to displace Roman rhetoric most specifically in the *emergence of personal character and values.* Similar texts were developed by Hindu, Buddhist, Jewish and Muslim scholars over time. The emphasis now for us, in all of such, was not only on service to the community, naturally and socially, but also on self-realisation, on wholeness or on holiness.

Unfortunately, somewhat dogmatic immersion in religion, as opposed to the original Latin meaning of *re-ligere* (literally a continual re-visiting and renewal of our origins), all too often conceals this e-ducative and e-mergent aspect of such culture and spirituality.

3.4.2. Islamic Cultural and Spiritual Renaissance

From the 9th to the 13th century, as McNeely and Wolverton maintain, there was an Islamic Renaissance, in which the *madrassahs* (Islamic schools)—starting out in Morocco in the 9th century—played a leading part in Muslim prayer, contemplation and learning, prior to the formation of the universities in the Middle East and Europe. Indeed, Baghdad had followed in the footsteps of the Great Library of Alexandria in Egypt. Its House of Wisdom, founded around 800 BC, gathered a multi-cultural scholarly community to translate all known exemplars of 'foreign wisdom' into Arabic. In fact, the Islamic mosque today, at least in some notable cases, remains a place of learning as well as prayer and as we shall see in the case of Akhuwat (see chapter 7) in Pakistan, for Saqib and Malik (6) is a source of socioeconomic mobilisation and ultimately, 'soulidarity'.

We now turn, guided by McNeely and Wolverton, to the pursuit of scientific knowledge *per se*, as well as the humanities, via the original 'universitas', the subsequently so-called Republic of Letters and ultimately the research university and its constituent disciplines. Altogether then, community, pilgrimium and academy constitute a formidable, transformative force, to be followed by the laboratory, if purposefully combined in a particular context. How then did the original universities actually get started?

3.5. NAVIGATING VIA PRINT: UNIVERSITY, SCIENCE AND TECHNOLOGY

3.5.1. The Communal Universitas

Starting with the earliest forms of European university (universities in China, India and the Middle East having been established centuries before), the earliest universities, in the 9th century in Baghdad and the 12th and 13th centuries in Bologna and Paris, were not deliberately founded; they simply *coalesced spontaneously around networks of students and teachers, as nodes at the thickest in these networks*. Universitas, for McNeely and Wolverton, as such, was a concept in ancient Roman law referring to a sworn society of individuals—that is, to a group of people, not a physical space. As such the early universities retained some of the communal attributes of pre-modern oral cultures and of ancient times. They also had, from the outset, strongly theological, scriptural overtones.

3.5.2. Initial Schools or Faculties: Theology, Medicine, Law, Liberal Arts

McNeely and Wolverton went on to say that by the year 1200, Paris had become known as the international centre for theology. Other scholarly pilgrimage sites developed academic schools or 'faculties': law in Bologna, medicine in Salerno and much later the liberal arts in Prague. The revival of Roman law, in fact, marked one of the great intellectual movements of the 12th century. Whereas Roman law was rational yet individualistic, German custom, however fuzzily, was much more imbued with community spirit. In their synthesis lies the origin of the universitas as a legal concept and social reality.

We now turn from the early academic schools as separate entities to the newly emerging scientific communities that served to link, as a means of navigation, in our integral dynamic terms so to speak, one with the other. Here we have a scientific—rather than religious—vocation, source of scholarship and communal learning, now internationally as well as nationally and locally oriented, coming together for the first time.

3.5.3. Academic Disciplines and the Emergence of the Research Academy

Research Academy Aimed to Reshape the Inner Person

Europe's and indeed America's leading universities in modern times, according to McNeely and Wolverton—that is, in the late 18th and early 19th centuries—counted among the last places most Enlightenment figures looked to rejuvenate knowledge. The same might apply today, arguably for us, at least in the social sciences! Oxford and Cambridge, for example, were best known for polishing the manners of young gentlemen rather than sending them on to more serious pursuits. The story of how

95

Germany led the world into the age of modern scholarship therefore counts among the most stunning reversals in the history of knowledge.

Founded initially in 1738 and as a predecessor to such a research university, the seminar approach to pedagogy, launched at the University of Gottingen in Germany, aimed to reshape the inner person, not to fashion cookie-cutter gentlemen by drilling them, as was hitherto customary in the prestigious universities, to ape Cicero or Pericles in their outward manners and speech. Instead, they instilled in their students an internalised sense of what it meant to *think* like a Cicero. The hierarchy of the medieval disputation, where masters often literally stood on platforms above their students, gave way to 'circular disputation', where discussants sat around a table together as equals. Beyond how Cicero spoke, beyond what Jesus said, beyond what Homer sang, for McNeely and Wolverton, students and their professors reflected on how cultures think, collectively and creatively, through the study of philology.

Scholarship had finally replaced scripture as the ultimate source of human knowledge. This marks the birth of what we term a *research academy.*

From Scholarship to the Promotion of Ideas: The Case of Karl Marx

At the same time, academic entrepreneurs with a taste for risk could throw in their lot with profit-driven, or indeed socially motivated, publishing ventures. This was the career path chosen, ironically enough, by Karl Marx, for example. He began as a typical academic, writing a dissertation on Greek natural philosophy at the University of Berlin, but his politics forced him out of Berlin's conservative establishment as editor and contributor to a series of radical newspapers.

Today the equivalent of Karl Marx might be a public intellectual such as Pakistani-born Ziauddin Sardar, Chair of the Muslim Institute in London, known for his work on Islamic future studies (7). We now turn from academy to laboratory.

3.6. LABORATORY EFFECT:
NASA, COUNTERCULTURE, WORLDWIDE WEB

3.6.1. The World as Laboratory

Starting out in the natural sciences in the 19th century, laboratory scientists McNeely and Wolverton, after learning to control nature within the four walls of their experimental domains, capitalised on their methods to change the way people lived in homes, neighbourhoods and even whole countries.

Louis Pasteur, for example, as a prominent exemplar in France (1822–1895), began his research life as a chemist. Microbes became his research speciality. Today the simple technique of pasteurisation, today known as the flash-heating of milk to kill bacteria and delay their return at cooler temperatures, applies Pasteurian microbiology to every household refrigerator. *In reshaping our domestic environment, Pasteur's science literally made the world into a laboratory*. Starting in 1910, Pasteur Institutes began to be established throughout France's overseas colonies (in Tunis, Tangiers, Casablanca, Saigon and Dakar) and beyond (in Sao Paulo, Shanghai, Tehran and Bangkok). These laboratories made imperial France's medical science a key component of its 'civilising' mission abroad.

Pasteurian science proved once and for all the social utility of the laboratory and the very real ways in which it could improve human life, as would be the case a century later for the exploration of outer space, ultimately leading to the late President Kennedy's giant step forward for mankind.

3.6.2. NASA Space Agency: A Giant Step Forward for Mankind

At the height of the Cold War in 1969, NASA director James Webb published *Space Age Management,* heralding the application of social-scientific techniques to the one space still unconquered by the laboratory:

the cosmos itself. Within five years the NASA workforce had grown to 420,000 people, dispersed in scores of universities, laboratories, government agencies and industrial contractors. The craftsman's workshop had given way to adaptive problem solving, diverse specialists linked together by coordinating processes in organic flux. Lamentably, in integral dynamic terms, nothing like this exists in the social sciences, which is why Hoppers and Richards, concerned with *Rethinking Thinking* (8), argue:

> *"In today's world there is a tragic contrast between intractable problems and a knowledge explosion. The sheer quantity of knowledge available is mind-boggling and increases exponentially every day. And yet most of the problems are getting worse, not better."*

These problems range from financial crises to unemployment, from crime to civil war and from air pollution to the exhaustion of fossil fuels.

3.6.3. Scientific Management: Efficiency Experts on the Factory Floor

Big factories, big bureaucracies, big machines and big science, according to McNeely and Wolverton, were all novel features of the landscape of late 19th century capitalism and have today spread prolifically beyond. Self-styled efficiency experts faced with the onset of such, stepped forward with their stopwatches and clipboard in hand, ready to make the industrial system run like a well-oiled machine. Frederick Winslow Taylor (1856–1915) became the guru of what his followers called 'scientific management'. Though Taylor would be subsequently reviled in most 'human relations' circles for his mechanistic approach, his overall objective was to apply science to work, albeit in his case more for 'social engineering' than social emancipation.

By 1933, when the Great Depression had finally shut down the Hawthorne experiments, the academic discipline of human relations was born. The crucial figure in this development was Harvard's Elton Mayo and the further evolution of human relations, as we shall see, into more tangibly based 'sensitivity training' and 'group dynamics', would take place via Kurt Lewin. First, though, we turn to America's Jane Addams and then to her compatriot John Dewey, predecessor and kindred spirit of Kurt Lewin (see also chapter 10).

3.6.4. Science, Philanthropy and the Advent of the Social Laboratory

In the early 1900s, Jane Addams' Hull-House in downtown Chicago combined Christian charity and noblesse oblige with a rare opportunity for elite women to live intimately with the poor. Addams (1860–1935) financed Hull-House herself. An art gallery and concerts, a library and bookshops, a night school for adults and public lectures given by the likes of John Dewey, famed subsequently for his action research approach, made cultural and educational outreach an integral, not just incidental, aspect of its mission. Much more than a community centre, Hull-House became a centre for knowledge production.

In fact, it was in that very period that the American business schools, as superbly documented by Harvard sociologist Rakesh Khurana (9), were born. Indeed the second Dean of the Harvard Business School— the selfsame institution that one of us, Ronnie Lessem, attended in the 1960s and which today has become a training ground for future leaders at best and financial engineers at worst—Wallace Donham, had a strong sense of the business executive as a trustee of society's material resources:

"Discontent with the existing condition of things is perhaps more widespread than ever before in history [Donham was writing in the 1920s]. *The nation is full of idealists, yet our civilisation is essentially materialistic. On all sides, complicated social, political and economic problems press for solution, while leaders competent to solve these problems are strangely missing. These conditions are transforming the world for better or worse and they compel a complete reappraisal of the significance of business in the scheme of things."*

As such, business schools such as Harvard (HBS) were intended to be veritable healers of communities, research universities with a sacred mission and laboratories of applied social sciences, to address societal problems. How things have changed today, now that HBS has arguably become more of a school for financial engineers!

For prominent American business journalist Duff Macdonald (10), in fact, in his recent book *The Golden Passport: Harvard Business School, Limits of Capitalism and the Moral Failure of the MBA Elite*:

> *"In the 1980s, HBS graduates were heading for Wall Street. By then the School had abandoned its three-quarter century mission of trying to educate an enlightened managerial class and threw its lot in with Wall Street as it went about dismantling the edifice of American industry that HBS had helped to build. HBS had nurtured the professional manager from the time of his birth and then it helped to kill him."*

3.6.5. Social Labs

Going back fifty years in America, Kurt Lewin, a social scientist who had emigrated in the 1930s from Nazi Germany to America like Dewey and Addams before him, advanced the notion that *the attempt to change the individual was futile unless it also led to a change in the group in which the individual participated.* He reasoned that because the individual is to the group as the part is to the whole, a change in the dynamics of the group will invariably lead to a change in the way in which individuals in the group behave and act. This realisation led Lewin to the field of group dynamics and experiments with new models of psycho-social interaction and so-called 'sensitivity training' or 'T-Groups'. Lewin firstly founded a laboratory for group dynamics in Bethel, Maine and was also, as such, the founder of so-called 'action research', whereby social research and social action were deemed as mutually reinforcing rather than, as hitherto for most, mutually exclusive.

We now turn from *Reinventing Knowledge,* as per the seminal work of McNeely and Wolverton, to our own communiversity, now revisited institutionally, further to and indeed serving to ultimately differentiate and integrate a particular community, pilgrimium, academy and laboratory.

3.7. BEYOND THE UNIVERSITY: COMMUNIVERSITY AS AGENCY

3.7.1. Learning Community to Socioeconomic Laboratory

Today, epochal historical events—most recently climate change and economic crises—have determined that the laboratory, not the university, for McNeely and Wolverton, will continue to exercise a strong influence on learning and knowledge creation, especially in the natural sciences. Above all, the ascendancy of the laboratory is reshaping the basic missions of other institutions (like universities), pushing some towards obsolescence whilst giving others a new lease of life.

For us, now taking on from where they leave off, we see each particular learning community (oral), developmental pilgrimium (scriptural), research academy (print) and socioeconomic laboratory (digital) as having its prospectively inter-institutional place, in transformative guise, which we shall illustrate specifically in the chapters that follow. For each particular individual, organisation and society, the process starts with their centering moral core, with a view to recognising and releasing individual and collective genius. Primacy lies, as such, not with a 'credit rating agency', economically so to speak, but with an agency that acknowledges and accredits the particular moral core(s) and path of individuation—of self to community and of acculturation—from core to topsoil, of a particular society. Thereafter, the recognition and release of GEN*E*-ius via community, pilgrimium, academy and laboratory in combination needs to ensue, duly encompassing nature, culture, science and enterprise.

3.7.2. Institutional Dynamics and the Historical Evolution of Knowledge

McNeely and Wolverton have in fact argued, overall, that *knowledge has been fundamentally reinvented a number of times throughout human history*. In each case they describe how one new institution—the library (for us the particular community), the monastery (for us a pilgrimium), the academy and the laboratory, if not also the largely invisible 'Republic of Letters'—has replaced the knowledge-based institution that preceded it. For example, new academic disciplines served to renovate and completely redesign the old-style universities, recognising their continuities with the ancient *universitas* in name only.

Indeed some, like the German philosopher Fichte in the late 19th century, advocated abandoning the term university, so thoroughly did the new 'research university' depart from the past. Sadly, from our transformative perspective, this did not happen and we are now carrying on from where he left off. We will now finally, to set the stage in this chapter, illustrate how this unfinished business has been picked up and furthered, albeit in faltering steps along the way, in the home country of one us, Ronnie 'Samanyanga' Lessem—that is, in Zimbabwe.

3.7.3. The Communiversity Vision

Towards a Communiversity: Substance and Form

For our so-called communiversity then, as a whole, while the integral *substance* is constituted of Integral *Development* and *Research* as means and Integral *Economics* and *Enterprise* as ends respectively, the communiversity *form* constitutes of a Learning Community (south), Re-GENE-rative Pilgrimium (east), Research Academy (north) and Socioeconomic Laboratory (west). Why so?

For each 'southern' (Community), 'eastern' (Pilgrimium), 'northern' (Academy) and 'western' (Laboratory) communiversity function, we incorporate the corresponding, underlying worldly substance. We start as such with Integral Development (11), because the very idea of an *integral* university (now communiversity) emerged out of such, as a means of societal development. From development, we turn to Integral Research (12), because social research-and-development constitutes our combined means. From means we then turn to ends in each communiversity case—that is, to Integral Economy (13) and Integral Enterprise (14). For while we invariably start with nature and culture, followed by science and technology, our integral end point is economic and enterprising.

TABLE 3: FORM AND SUBSTANCE OF THE COMMUNIVERSITY				
FORM/ SUBSTANCE	Learning Community (S)	Regenerative Pilgrimium (E)	Research Academy (N)	Socioeconomic Laboratory (W)
Integral Development	Community Activation	Awakening Consciousness	Innovation Driven Research	Embodying Development
Integral Research	Participatory Action Research	Cooperative Inquiry	Socio-Technical Design	Action Research and Learning
Integral Economics	Self Sufficiency	Developmental Economy	Social Economy	Living Economy
Integral Enterprise	Community Building	Conscious Evolution	Knowledge Creation	Sustainable Development

We now bring the two together, starting developmentally with community activation, as illustrated in the Zimbabwean case, with Zimbabwe being the home ground of co-author Ronnie Samanyanga Lessem.

Rapoko Grain and Muchineripi Rock: Learning Community – Grounds for Transformation via Nature and Community

- Community Activation
- Participatory Action Research
- Marketing to Community Building
- Community Based Economic Self-Sufficiency

For the Karanga people of Chinyika, on the one hand and for Chidara Muchineripi (15) on the other hand, from a natural, indigenous perspective as people of the soil, their life depends on the soil for they till it. They grow their crops on it and draw water from the ground. They bury their dead in the soil. Soil is their power. As such, for one elder poet:

"Why have the people forgotten what used to happen on Muchineripi rock?
Where your forefathers gathered rapoko and millet in abundance?
Where children played around while fathers and mothers pounded
rapoko ears with sticks and winnowed the grain from the chaff?
Where granaries were filled with golden brown rapoko grains?
Arise the children of Chinyika
Arise and be who you should be!"

When people arose from the ground as in Chinyika, as they did when they saved themselves from starvation midway through the first decade of the new millennium, it was the traditional *rapoko* crop to which they returned. Drawing as such on nature and on community, the village elders on the one hand and the village's leading women on the other, assembled on the symbolically all important Muchineripi Rock, near where their former chief was buried. The initial conversations which they held in a small hut on the top of the rock was what initiated the whole process of renewal. It was this communal process, accompanied by ancient rituals, that was to become, if you like, Chinyika's 'Socratic Method'.

Such face-to-face, more-than-human conversations in the round, engaging with one another and with nature, formed the primal backdrop then and constitute the natural and communal grounding now, for a learning community.

Ngoma Lungundu: Locally/Globally Emerging through Culture/ Spirituality – Re-GENE-rative Pilgrimium

- Awakening Integral Consciousness
- Cultivating Imagination via Cooperative Inquiry
- Human Resources to Conscious Evolution
- Culture Based Developmental Economy

Thereby, orally to begin with rather than drawing on their learned literacy, the people of Chinyika challenged the exogenous status quo whereby maize had become the externally imposed staple crop and introduced their newly indigenous *rapoko*. Through, in effect, a process of informative and transformative *co-operative inquiry* (16) of iterative action and learning, drawing on experience and imagination, conceptualisation and application, they proceeded to renew themselves. The overall symbolism of the journey, embodied in the Baremba and the story of 'the lost ark of the covenant'—*Ngoma Lungundu*—in that emergent respect, overtook that of the soil, embodied in the Karanga and in *rapoko*. In relation to Chinyika, as we shall see, the *Ngoma Lungundu* besides being an artefact has a spiritual power of renewal for the Lemba and Chinyika community in Gutu. This is an opportunity for the local community to look outside and connect with a global platform.

While the *Ngoma Lungundu* 'drum' (ark of the covenant) lies in peace and serenity in the museum in Harare, it is calling out loudly for the Lemba and the world, via Kada (17), to be reawakened to the values of personhood and to the integration of indigenous and exogenous knowledge. It is providing Southern African knowledge, creating communities with a challenge to revisit their history, religion and intellectual values for purposes of creating an integrated local and global community. Institutionally, as such, this becomes the sanctuary before and after which the community and university lodge themselves, locally and globally. From a Christian perspective, the ark of the convent with its inscribed commandments is lodged in the hearts of mankind, including here in

Zimbabwe. The first inscription is summarised by Christ, "... Hear, O Israel, Jehovah our God is one Jehovah and you must love Jehovah your God with your whole heart and with your whole soul and with your whole mind and with your whole strength." The second is, "You must love your neighbour as yourself. There is no other commandment greater than this."

This is, for Kada, what all individuals, organisations and nations should be concerned with: acknowledging the universal sovereignty of the Creator and the practical humaneness and value-sharing of southern African *ubuntu* ("I am because you are"). Africa, from its heart then, was privileged with the quality of brotherhood and human passion which it must share with the rest of the world—Steve Kada's mother's plea: "*Uri munhu here?*" (Are you human?). This is our overall communiversity's sanctimonious cause. To that extent, the Harare museum, with its Zimbabwean arts and artefacts, symbols and ceremonies, should be integrally as well as dynamically interlinked with the rural soil-nature-community, such as that at Chinyika. Such a museum, as a house of culture, should house not only the past and the present, but also imaginatively the projected future—as was the case for Shona sculpture—naturally and communally, culturally and spiritually, if not also scientifically and technologically, integrally *becoming Zimbabwe.*

Nhakanomics Research Academy: Newly Navigating via Science/ Technology Great University of Zimbabwe and the Future of Social Anthropology

- Innovation-Driven Institutionalised Research
- Socio-Technical Design
- Operations to Knowledge Creation
- Knowledge Based Social Economy

From nature reserve and community, to museum-as-pilgrimium so to speak, we turn now to a *nhakanomics* research academy that builds on what has come before, now extending beyond the specificity of a Chinyika to Zimbabwe, if not Africa as a whole. As such, for African American historian, the late Chancellor Williams (18):

"Today's world crisis then demands a new look at the civilisation we have. But it is right now in the crucial period that a whole continent of people who had been either asleep or quiescent for centuries, are suddenly rousing themselves. The world has never before witnessed a whole people rising up at once and demanding freedom. Africans in fact, education-wise, are spreading out all over the world to prepare themselves for the tremendous tasks ahead. One of the greatest discoveries of this age, meanwhile, was made in the field of anthropology, not physics. *It was the discovery that in the rush from primitive life man actually left behind some of the more fundamental elements needed for a truly civilised life. Chief among these was—and of course is—the sense of community, direction and purpose. This is why Africa is very important now. It can profit if it sees the precipice towards which we are drifting and takes the opposite course in an effort to build a different kind of society on a spiritual foundation."*

While Williams was writing in the 1980s, this was followed up some three decades later by the South African social anthropologists Jean and John Comaroff—now both Professors of African Studies at Harvard, while continuing to be associated with the University of Cape Town—who, in their *Theory of the South: Or, How Euro-America is Evolving Toward Africa* (19), maintained:

"The 'south' is treated less as a source of knowledge than as a reservoir of raw fact: of the historical, natural and ethnographic minutiae from which Euro/modernity might fashion its testable theories and transcendent truths, its axioms and certitudes, its premises, postulates and principles, just as it has capitalised on non-Western raw materials—human and physical, moral and medical, cultural and agricultural—by ostensibly adding value and refinement to them.

But what if we invert that order of things? What if we subvert the epistemological scaffolding on which it is erected? What if we posit that, in the present moment, it is the global south that affords privileged insight into the workings of the world at large?"

Following in their footsteps and based in the Centre for Culture and Heritage at the Great University of Zimbabwe, for Munyarazi Mawere (and his research colleague Artwell Nhemachena), social anthropology is the most integrative of disciplines (20). It brings together scholarly work in the humanities and natural sciences and social sciences; hence its interdisciplinary nature. It deals with the lives of people all over the world including one's own society, in terms of folklore, legal systems, political systems, economic systems, arts and medical practices as well as interrelationships between these in relation to social change and environmental adaptation. As such:

"... post-independent Africa needs 'bricoleurs' to put together the pieces that were broken by colonial establishments together for Africa to resurface 'alternative' social security, health provision, family set-up and alternative stories on climate and environmental change... The discipline is best placed to resurface 'alternative' industrialisation; dwellings, systems, foodstuff, 'alternative' understandings of weather and climate, mining and smelting systems. It is suited to resurface 'alternative' economies for which scholars at a global level are searching."

Global-Local Effecting via Economics/Enterprise: Providence Human Capital as an Integral Laboratory

- Embodying Integral Development
- Action Research
- Finance to Sustainable Development
- Life Based Living Economy: Economic Well-being

The laboratory, for McNeely and Wolverton, is the most evolved form of knowledge-based or knowledge-creating institution, whereas in our terms it is the Learning Community, Re-GEN*E*-rative Pilgrimium, Research Academy and Socioeconomic Laboratory, altogether integrally constituted in a particular society that wins through in terms of the communiversity. The point of departure for the laboratory, within or alongside a community, pilgrimium or academy, is the conventionally scientific—natural science based—one either agriculturally or industrially (now including information and communications technology) based. In Chinyika, via so-called agricultural extension officers, agriculture took pride of place over the indigenous knowledge of the people. As we evolve from agricultural and industrial towards social laboratories, such entities become much more rarified. For example, the kinds of 'social' laboratories that Dewey, Addams, Donham (see Khurana above) and Lewin established in America in the first half of the last century are very few and far between.

Yet it is that very social form of laboratory, which enables a 'learning centre' on Muchineripi Rock to evolve into a newly dynamic form of communiversity, from which a contemporary Harvard Business School, for example, would do well to learn. More generally then and in our Zimbabwean context for example, the attempt that Providence Human Capital is making to develop into a Socio-Economic Laboratory and its overall *chitubu* ('fountainhead' or 'wellspring' in the local Shona language) as its overall Re-GEN*E*-rative Pilgrimium, is set within a life based—as per *ntu* (meaning 'life' in Bantu)—living economy, what Canadian colleague Mark Anielski (21) calls a "well-being economy".

3.8. CONCLUSION: TOWARDS AN APPROPRIATE TECHNOLOGY

In light of the above, Ronnie Samanyanga Lessem received mail from Noah Gwariro, the Managing Director of Zimbabwe Power, who was a participant on our doctoral program, in response to comments Ronnie made on an early thesis submission, whereby he commented on the fact that Gwariro, though a mechanical engineer, was passionate in his youth about biology generally and herbal medicines specifically:

"In fact I am so very interested in renewable-solar and bio-digesters. Bio-digesters conserve forests by using cattle manure for example to generate clean burning gas in the huts. The technology for solar and bio-digesters are developing in Philippines after modifying basic designs from China and India. I am sure once we localise these versions a Chinyika version would evolve. I am elated about appropriate technology.

The solar projects would allow people to consistently have light for the studying of school children in their homes. The parents would charge their cell phones at home and be able to watch television and listen to the radio. We can arrange with Econet for example to make sure there is data transmission capability around Chinyika so that the whole ICT cycle benefits these pioneers of self-sufficiency by giving them internet access. On the biology and herbal side we could have botanical gardens to preserve and propagate herbs for local use."

We now turn specifically to the Learning Community, in theory and practice.

3.9. REFERENCES

1 Prado C.G (2000) *Starting with Foucault:* An Introduction to Genealogy. Boulder, Colorado. Westview Press. Second Edition

2 Lessem R et al (2013) *Integral Dynamics: Cultural Dynamics, Political Economy and the Future of the University.* Abingdon. Routledge

3 McNeely I and Wolverton L (2008) *Reinventing Knowledge: Alexandria to the Internet.* New York. Norton

4 Some M (1999) *The Healing Wisdom of Africa.* New York. Jeremy Tarcher

5 Adodo A (2012) *Nature Power: A Christian Approach to Herbal Medicine.* New Edition. Edo State. Benedictine Publications

6 Amjad S and Malik A (2018) *Integral Finance – Akhuwat: A Case Study of the Solidarity Economy.* Abingdon, Routledge

7 Sardar Z (1987) *The Future of Muslim Civilization.* London. Continuum International Publishing.

8 Hoppers C and Richards H (2011) *Rethinking Thinking: Modernity's Other and the Transformaiton of the University.* Pretoria. UNISA Press

9 Khurana R (2016) *From Higher Minds to Hired Hands: The Social Transformation of the American Business Schools.* Cambridge. HBS Press

10 McDonald D (2017) *The Golden Passport: Harvard Business School, Limits of capitalism and the Moral Failure of the MBA Elite.* Harper Business

11 Schieffer A and Lessem R (2014) *Integral Development: Transforming the Potential of Individual, Organization and Society.* Abingdon. Routledge

12 Lessem R and Schieffer A (2010) *Integral Research: Transforming Enterprise and Society.* Abingdon. Routledge

13 Lessem R and Schieffer A (2010) *Integral Economics: Releasing the Genius of your Economy.* Abingdon. Routledge

14 Lessem R and Schieffer A (2009) *Transformation Management: Toward the Integral Enterprise.* Abingdon. Routledge

15 Lessem R, Muchineripi P and Kada S (2014) *Integral Community: Political Economy to Social Commons.* Abingdon. Routledge.

16 Heron J (1994) *Cooperative Inquiry.* London. Sage

17 Parfitt T (2009) *The Lost Ark of the Covenant: The Remarkable Quest for the Legendary Arc.* New York. Harper Element

18 Williams C (1993) *The Rebirth of African Civilization.* Chicago. Third World Press

19 Comaroff Jean and Comaroff John (2012) *Theory from the South: Or, How Euro-America is Evolving Toward Africa.* London. Routledge

20 Mawere M and Nhemachena A (2017) *Death of a Discipline: Reflections on the History, State and Future of Social Anthropology in Zimbabwe.* Mankon. Bamenda. Langaa Research and Publishing CIG

21 Anielski M (2018) *An Economy of Well-being.* Gabriola Island. British Columbia. New Society Publishers.

SOUTH

PART 1: LEARNING COMMUNITY

Chapter 4:

Communal Learning in Theory

GROUNDING: COMMUNITY ACTIVATION

Building community is difficult, if not impossible, if people have lost contact with the ground as their point of strength. For it is only from a point of grounding and centredness that people can give back to their world, to their community. Without grounding, people will tend to take as much from the world as possible, since they are missing the nourishment that Earth offers.

Malidoma Some, *The Healing Wisdom of Africa*

Integral Development: Communal learning and activation is *primarily about relationships;* firstly between you and your immediate learning community, secondarily involving your external community, organisation and society.

Integral Research: In undertaking collective research, including the recovery of history, you *recognise and co-evolve folk culture,* thereby producing and diffusing new knowledge.

Integral Enterprise: Through reconciliation, without surrendering your individuality, but opening yourself up to the 'other', you enter into the space between, whereby you *exchange places with the other* in social/economic conversation that takes you beyond yourself.

Integral Economy: Boundaries between human community and nature are not rigid and hard, but permeable; *economics is not separate from nature and community.*

4.1. INTRODUCTION: DEVELOPMENT STUDIES TO *INTEGRAL DEVELOPMENT*

4.1.1. Communal Rounds

In covering the theory underlying communal learning, in duly 'southern' integral communiversity guise, we span the entirety of Trans4m's 'integral worlds'; that is, integral *research* and *development* as means and integral *enterprise* and *economy* as ends. In other words, each aspect of such integral worlds, both as means (integral research and development) and as ends (integral enterprise and economy) are incorporated into the fabric of our *integral communi-versity*. We start then with integral development.

From our integral developmental perspective (1), our starting point for working with a particular society, in our communiversity case is neither the individual, the organisation, nor society at large; it is an immediate community, either within or adjacent to a particular enterprise. For while an individual learner can all too easily detach him or herself from their immediate context, especially given the pervasive 'western' approach to education, this is altogether different from the engagement with a local community. As such, for Geoff Mulgan, founder of the British thinktank Demos:

> *"Community is deliberately a different word from society. It may refer to neighbourhoods or workplaces, but to be meaningful it must imply membership in a human-scale collective: a scale at which it is possible to encounter people face to face... and to nurture human-scale structures within which people can feel at home. Social science is ill at ease with such ideas."*

It is in this guise that we are faced now with the following developmental questions:

- How do we learn and develop as a community based on our own communal learning needs, aspirations and capacities?
- What do we know about the life of our communities and their ways to renew themselves?
- How do you best inter-relate local, indigenous and global, exogenous knowledge in the way your community can best learn?
- What are the true developmental issues faced by the specific community, within and/or around your enterprise, within which you work and learn?
- How does such learning relate to the major issues your society is facing and to the development capacities and issues of yourself, your group and your organisation?

4.1.2. Learning and Development as a Whole Life Project

For anthropologist Arturo Escobar (3), a renowned Colombian American 'southern' voice in the development arena, conventional 'development' thinking fostered a way of conceiving of social life as a technical problem, as a matter of rational decision and management to be entrusted to development professionals whose specialised, usually 'economic' knowledge allegedly qualified them for the task. Escobar argues that instead of seeing development, or indeed communal learning, as an emergent process rooted in the grounds of each community's history, cultural tradition, human psyche and existing indigenous institutions, these development professionals, or academics, sought to devise mechanisms and procedures to make society fit a pre-existing imported model that embodied the structures and functions of modernity. Thus, what needs to be studied is the mechanisms by which local cultural knowledge and economic resources, including land and natural resources, are appropriated by larger forces, such as unequal exchange between centre and periphery, rural and urban areas, upper and lower classes and dominant and dominated ethnic groups. As such, we now turn to economic anthropologist Stephen Gudeman.

4.1.3. On the Immersion in Local Value Domains

One True Model of Community

Stephen Gudeman (4), a graduate of both Cambridge University's School of Anthropology in the UK and also Harvard Business School in the US, is today a professor emeritus in the department of anthropology at the University of Minnesota. For Gudeman, there is no one 'true' model of economy, or indeed community, but only multiple meaningful formulations within particular cultures, each with their own value domains, in which we need to reflectively immerse ourselves as researchers. Thereby we uncover the origins of a particular community. As a representative of modern economic anthropology, a school of thought that uses anthropology in trying to understand economy in human terms, he calls on us to understand 'local models'.

Community and Market

For Gudeman, such a communal economy consists of two realms, which he calls *community* and *market*. Both facets make up the economy, for humans are motivated by social fulfilment, curiosity and the pleasure of mastery, as well as by instrumental purpose, competition and the accumulation of gains. In one guise (community), economy is local and specific, constituted through social relationships and contextually defined values. In the other guise (market), it is impersonal, even global and abstracted from social context.

Local Value Domains

In addition to community and market as the two constituting realms for economic practices and relationships, Gudeman distinguishes four value domains: *base, relationships, trade* and *accumulation*.

The first value domain is the base or foundation. It consists of a community of shared interests, which include lasting resources such as land and water, produced things and ideational constructs such as knowledge, technology, laws, practices, skills and customs. The base comprises of cultural agreements and beliefs that provide a structure for all other domains. The second domain, relationships, consists of valued communal connections maintained as ends in themselves. Through these relationships the base is created, allotted and apportioned to people in community. The third and fourth domains consist of trade and accumulation.

Accumulated value includes resources, relationships, goods, money and capital, all of which may become components of other domains. Amassed value is held, invested, consumed and displayed. Such an overall perspective of a social and economic base and its accompanying value domains has, for us, distinct 'southern' connotations; unsurprisingly, given Gudeman's anthropological background, which he shares with Zimbabwe's Munyaradze Mawere and South Africa's Comaroffs (see chapter 3).

For example, in areas of Panama, Columbia and Guatemala, where Gudeman has conducted extensive fieldwork, the base consists of material things, human character, work and divinity. The concept of 'force' or 'strength' (la fuerza) unites the several parts of the base, provides the mooring for a household and offers a rationale for caring for it. According to Gudeman, strength has divine and mundane referents; overall, it is life energy. For him, people must continually secure such vital energy from their surroundings. The often-heard expression "meeting the needs of the house" refers to the necessity of gathering and preserving the needs of the base.

In a market, people exchange goods, buying and selling at the best price available until they cannot better their personal holdings any further. Exchanges in community are different. Gudeman critiques that much of development work emphasises only the latter two of the four value domains—trade and material accumulation—while it is crucial to engage initially with the first two value domains: base and relationships.

Unleashing Community Potential

For Gudeman then, *development is not primarily about capital accumulation, but rather about innovation in you relationships*—your immediate learning community, your external community, organisations and society. Community in this wider sense offers a reservoir of possibilities and the key to development is to unleash the innovative potential that lies in it. For ways and means of recognising and releasing such potential, we now turn from communal learning and development to social research and innovation, specifically to so-called *participatory action research*. Together, these constitute social research (here participatory action research) and development (here community activation), leading to social innovation.

4.2. INTEGRAL *RESEARCH*: PARTICIPATORY ACTION RESEARCH (PAR)

4.2.1. Action Research as a Whole

The founding fathers of 'action research' (5) on which PAR is based are the American pragmatic philosopher and educator, John Dewey and the Jewish refugee from Nazi Germany, the social psychologist Kurt Lewin. Action research—for one of its contemporary co-creators Peter Reason (6) in England, together with Hilary Bradbury based in California—is:

> "... a participatory, democratic process concerned with developing practical knowing in the pursuit of worthwhile human purposes, grounded in a participatory worldview which is believed to be emerging at this historical moment. It seeks to bring together action and reflection, theory and practice, in participation with others, in the pursuit of practical solutions to issues of pressing concern to

people and more generally the flourishing of individual persons and their communities."

4.2.2. Action Research to Participatory Action Research

Participatory action research (PAR) then is the communal research orientation and indeed approach to action research, most closely aligned with community activation. The Colombian sociologist Orlando Fals Borda, who became a leading light in the PAR movement, had been working on the same alternative approach to social research whilst unaware of the international initiatives that had taken place in previous years. Fals Borda and his colleagues, now based at the University of British Columbia in Vancouver, were still using the generic term 'action research'.

Fals Borda argued that research that produced nothing but books was not sufficient and that a new type of research for social practice was needed. Thus, he called for a type of action research on the conditions and effects of various forms of social action and research leading to social action. At an action research conference held in 1977 in Tanzania, under the auspices of President's Ujaama project (7), oriented towards developing village cooperatives in his country, the concept of 'action research' used by Fals Borda met the previously coined concept of 'participatory research' and 'participatory action research' was later born.

The term was used for the first time by Orlando Fals Borda to name a new paradigm in social research; in fact, it was the only such research methodology thereby rooted in the developing world. Several decades later, the concept became popularised and known by its initials PAR. We now turn to PAR's key tenets as a participatory research methodology that indeed fosters community activation, albeit one that goes all the way, collectively speaking, from origination to transformation.

4.2.3. Combining Action and Knowledge

As a Scientific Methodology, Facilitates an Analysis of Social Reality

For Fals Borda (8), action and knowledge go hand-in-hand. Historical experience calls for rethinking the meaning of people's liberation. The dominant view of such liberation has been preoccupied with the need for changing the oppressive structures of relations in material production, which is certainly a necessary task. However (and this is the distinctive view of PAR), domination of elites is also rooted in control over social power to determine what is useful knowledge. In fact, existence of the gap in knowledge relations can offset the advantages of reducing the gap in relations of physical production.

People cannot be liberated by a consciousness and knowledge other than their own. It is therefore essential that people develop their own indigenous consciousness-raising and knowledge generation and this requires social power to assert this. The scientific character or objectivity of knowledge rests on its social verifiability and this depends on consensus as to the method of verification. All scientific knowledge is relative to the paradigm to which it belongs and the verification system to which it is submitted. An immediate objective of PAR is to give poor and deprived people control over their own verification systems.

PAR is Aimed at the Exploited, the Poor, the Oppressed and the Marginal

Stimulating the poor and deprived to undertake self-reliant initiatives requires two essential steps. The first is developing an awareness about the reality in which they live. In particular, they need to understand that poverty and deprivation are the result of specific social forces rather than an outcome of some inherent deficiency on their part or even 'fate'. Second, based on such critical awareness, they need to gain confidence in their collective abilities to bring about positive changes in their life situations and organise themselves for that purpose.

PAR Creates Awareness of the People's Own Resources

A typical PAR programme therefore stimulates direct social analysis by the landless. In many places this led to intense and sustained pressure-group action to confront social injustice and oppression by rural elites. In other areas, confrontational activity to resist social oppression by rural elites has been particularly intense for several years and led to many forms of harassment, both for the landless leaders and NGO workers.

So, in a PAR research process the community would ask itself the following questions:

- What was their experience?
- What did they learn about themselves from this?
- What would they, with their past experience, advise the landless in other villages who might want to get organised?
- What was the relation of their present activities with past ones?
- Would they like to document their story and draw its lessons more systematically after thorough discussion in the base of the organisation?
- Would they like to disseminate these so that fellow landless in other villages would not need to start from zero and could benefit from their experience?

PAR involves the full and active Participation of the Community

Overall, in PAR there is a break-up of the classical dichotomy between 'subject' and 'object' (manipulation and dominance) and its replacement by a humanistic mode of equal relation between two subjects (animation and facilitation). The essential difference between the latter approach and that typically undertaken by a political party or conventional development practitioner, in moving from analysis to transformation, is:

- *Starting from where people are:* their perceptions, knowledge, experiences and rhythm of work and thoughts, as opposed to preconceived agendas.

• *Stimulating people (animation) to undertake self-analysis* of their life situations and helping them to derive from such self-inquiry into the political-economic-cultural environment an intellectual base for initiating changes.

• *Assisting people to organise themselves* into People's Organisations (PO's) which are non-hierarchical in structure and democratic in operations.

• *Facilitating the actions for change,* with the external catalyst paving the way for internal self-reliance.

• Stimulating the People's Organisations to carry out *regular self-reviews,* to assess and learn from success and failure.

Table 4 : Ingredients and Techniques of a People's Science	
Collective Research	Dialogue, discussion, argument and consensus in the investigation of social realities
Critical Recovery of History	To discover selectively through collective memory, popular stories and oral traditions 'fleshed out' serving to recover history
Recognising and Co-evolving Folk Culture	Account is taken of art, music, drama, sports, story-telling and other expressions related to human sentiment and imagination
Production and Diffusion of New Knowledge	Different levels of communication are developed for people ranging from pre-literate to intellectual, using image, sound, painting, theatre, music and puppetry. The groups involved include cooperatives, trade unions, cultural centers.

4.2.4. People's Self Development and Transformation

Integrating Education with Life Processes

We now turn from Fals Borda to Bangladeshi educationalist M.D. Rahman.

Like many of his compatriots, M.D. Rahman (9) was inspired by popular mobilisations for social reconstruction and development in Bangladesh after its independence in 1971. As a teacher, Rahman had been stimulated by demands from sections of Bangladesh's student community for radical reform to integrate educational processes with processes of life. Yet most of the popular initiatives in the country faded, died or were repressed as reactionary forces gradually consolidated their hold on society's commanding structures.

Joining the ILO (International Labour Organisation) in 1977, Rahman was able to pursue the same interest, linking up with significant trends in the grassroots movements in several countries and initiating methodological experiments in field 'animation' work and in the sensitisation of animators, linking with intellectual trends, working with popular movements and synthesising and conceptualising from the ongoing experiences.

Organising the Rural Poor

According to Rahman, organising the rural poor can have several different objectives for an NGO:

- **Economic Uplift**: This means raising the incomes of the poor, giving them greater stability of income and some social security or insurance against unforeseen situations, old age and so on. If this is the sole or principal objective, external delivery of such can be in the form of *credit, technology* and *expertise*. However, emphasis on external delivery contradicts with the other objectives.

- **Human Development:** Creativity is the distinctive human quality for Rahman and the human development objective aims

125

to develop creative people. Creation is the product of thinking and action that is *communal participation*.

• **Achieving Social and Economic Rights:** The means of elimination of economic and social oppression and achieving equity in the use of public resources, implies the *exercise of collective power of the poor and often implies struggle*. The role of outsiders is to help develop a consciousness amongst the poor of short-run failures as a learning process upon which subsequent strategy is to be built.

• **Macro-social Transformation:** The above three objectives can be considered to be 'locally progressive' if they are pursued together; that is, progressive at a micro level. Their contribution to macro social transformation can be positive, if such micro work spreads on a broad enough scale. Since the great bulk of the flow of external resources is controlled by external forces, interested (according to Rahman) in dominating and exploiting the country rather than in its self-determination and development, *a self-reliant development effort is an absolutely necessary element for the country to shape its own destiny and stand up with pride*.

In fact, what we have recently discovered is that another such approach to participatory action research was extensively undertaken in Pakistan by development practitioner extraordinaire, Shoaib Sultan Khan, in the guise of *social mobilisation*.

4.2.5. Social Mobilisation

Reasons for Failure: No Cooperation, Incompetence and No Organisational Support

From the 1960s onwards, a small group of eccentric lateral thinkers in the Indian sub-continent, including Akter Hameed Khan Sahib (10) in India who became a mentor of Shoaib Sultan Khan (11), tentatively began to work out a whole new approach; that *development must come from within and that while organisations for the poor are useful, even*

126

essential, *their function is a simple one—provide the spark that starts the conflagration of organisations of the poor.* There was, however, a catch. In order to achieve the state of confident development from within, the rural poor had to be empowered, learn to believe in themselves and have confidence in their own abilities.

In fact, if ever a community project then failed it would be for one of three reasons. If people are unwilling to cooperate and work, nothing will happen; if an active, competent and honest activist cannot be found nothing will start or if it dies will soon fizzle out; and if a support organisation that is willing to listen to and respond to the wishes of the people is not there, local development initiatives will falter.

Three Development Principles: Self-Organisation, Group Skills, Capital is Power

In that guise they spoke dismissively of 'self-help'; for how could people help themselves if they had no resources and no idea how to self-organise? Self-organisation was a fundamental part of social mobilisation, in this case in the mountainous terrain of Northern Pakistan. Nothing would happen without it. *Self-organisation was the first principle. The second principle* was equally radical. Shoaib argued that *unless and until the managerial and productive skills of villagers were upgraded they would not be able to move forward* and would be easy prey to outsiders. He was not talking of technical skills here but of the skills that allow a group to work effectively together in unity and achieve a common goal.

The final principle was that capital is power, so ways had to be found whereby even the poorest villagers started generating their own capital through savings. As such, project identification amounted to the formation of village organisations, project preparation involved the villagers identifying their preferred group development option and project appraisal equated quite well to the partnership agreement between the village and the sponsoring organisation.

What is it, then, that makes social mobilisation unique?

What Makes Social Mobilisation: Economic Improvement/Community Spirit

It is this. *At the same time as economic improvement is promoted, so is community spirit.* Social mobilisation brings out the best in people, expects people to behave well and funnily enough, they usually do so. What is known as the 'rat race' in the West where everybody's top priority is to fill their own pockets is the very antithesis of social mobilisation where every pocket is filled, where people will work together for group gain that ultimately benefits individuals too, where life proceeds with decency.

We now turn from village-based communal mobilisation in South-Central Asia to such communal learning and development in Southern Africa (12), now set within an enterprise, rather than outside of it, as per marketing to community building, via 'southern' *ubuntu*.

4.3. INTEGRAL *ENTERPRISE*: MARKETING TO COMMUNITY BUILDING

4.3.1 Communal Building Rhythm of the Integral Enterprise

The South African Peace Nobel Laureate Bishop Desmond Tutu provides us with an intimate perspective into *ubuntu* in his acclaimed book *No Future without Forgiveness* (13):

> *"When we want to give high praise to someone ... we say* 'Yu, u nobuntu: *a person is a person through other persons'. I am human because I belong. I participate, I share. A person with* ubuntu *is open and available to other, affirming of others, does not feel threatened that others are able and good, for he or she has a proper self assurance that comes from knowing that he or she belongs in a greater whole and is diminished when others are humiliated or diminished, when others are tortured or oppressed, or treated as if they are less than who they are."*

In the following, we will guide you through the transformational GEN*E* rhythm of Community Building, as a progressive evolution of such *ubuntu* in an enterprise context, from **G**rounding in reciprocity and exchange to **E**mergence via *justice and reconciliation*, up to the **N**avigation via *social business* (social combined with business) to most especially *E*ffect through *workplace democracy* (workplace combined with democracy).

4.3.2. Local Grounding of Community Building: Reciprocity and Exchange

West African Markets Are Meeting Places

Such principles of social and economic exchange as well as of reciprocity are alive and well in parts of Africa today. Susanne Guiterrez (14) pointed out in her research in the 1980s on the market women of Nigeria:

> *"There is a clear reflection of European commercial and philosophical influences—in the emerging impersonal, formal and specialised attitude—in today's African institutions. In the marketplace, however, women are able to transcend these influences and bring to their daily lives the historical African sense of family and community. Regardless of the sophistication of the surrounding community, no matter how urbanised and industrialised it may become, the marketplace prevails as a centre of trade and communication, whether the traders are dealing in cement, tomatoes, or television sets."*

In fact, the cultural anthropologists Ellis and Ter Haar (15) have more recently given us a new perspective on money and markets in an African context:

> *"Throughout West Africa, the morality of exchange has been associated with the markets. West African markets are real meeting places, not just virtual or technical places of exchange. Some are regulated by sophisticated conventions on the pricing and sale of goods. They*

129

are rather like the 'agora' of the ancient Greeks, places to meet friends and talk as well as to do business; they are places of fundamental social importance."

We turn now to local-global emergence through healing and reconciliation, with Nelson Mandela to lead the way, taking us from private and civic to public enterprise. As we can see, such a communal perspective further transforms individual marketing.

4.3.3. Local-Global Emergence of Community Building: Justice and Reconciliation

Exchange to Reconciliation

The grounding in economic and social exchange goes back a long time in history. The reformation that has taken place in recent years, most poignantly in South Africa, is the turning of exchange and reciprocity into healing and reconciliation. In fact, the South African academic theologian John De Gruchy (16), in the context of South Africa's 'Truth and Reconciliation Commission' in his book on *Reconciliation – Restoring Justice*, has pointed out that:

"The Greek words translated in the New Testament by 'reconciliation' or 'reconcile' are compounds of the Greek 'to exchange' and this in turn is derived from the Greek word meaning 'the other'. The words thus carry with them the sense of exchanging places with 'the other' and therefore being in solidarity with rather than against such 'another'."

This indeed serves to cast 'exchange', whether economic or social, in a new light. It also serves to reinforce the original context of the 'market-place' as a place of social as well as commercial interaction. If we therefore de-construct 'market-ing' in that light, something new emerges—an idea which resonates with justice and reconciliation. Reconciliation, in this context, begins to become a reality when, without surrendering our individuality but opening ourselves up to the 'other', we enter into the space between. It is here, in these 'transitional spaces' that we exchange places with the other in a conversation that takes us beyond ourselves. Furthermore, in the process, our self-understanding begins to change. The aim of each step in the process is to break through the barriers of the past, discern common interests and so break open new possibilities that can take the process of exchange, supply and demand as well as profit further than we currently understand.

Marketing and exchange, in this reciprocal vein, emerge as a force for the healing of nature and society. In the process, together, they become a force for good, as well as a means of exchange of goods and services.

Covenanting Together to Restore Justice

Nelson Mandela (17) declared in his inaugural speech to the South African public in May 1994:

> *"We enter a covenant that we shall build a society in which all South Africans, both black and white, will be able to walk, without any fear in their hearts, assured of their inalienable right to human dignity—a rainbow nation at peace with itself and the world."*

Such reconciliation is about building bridges, about allowing conflicting stories to interact in ways that evoke respect, about building relationships including economic ones and helping restructure power relations. This means that we have to go beyond a political, social or economic agreement to co-exist across those rivers that divide and find ways to engender common endeavour, including that between producer and consumer. A covenantal relationship, in other words, goes further than a social or business contract because it is concerned about animate-civic-public reconciliation rather than mere private or commercial reconciliation in financial and economic terms. It involves building up 'equity', not only in a financial and economic sense, but also in a social and communal one.

Restorative Economics – Restorative Justice

Bishop Desmond Tutu (18), as we saw above in his *No Future Without Forgiveness*, written in the latter part of the 1990s, builds upon the notion of 'restorative' justice. He contrasts it with market economics, also building upon notions of exchange and reciprocity for a South African process of reconstruction and development (RDP).

> *"In South Africa today, the resources of the state have to be deployed imaginatively, wisely, efficiently and equitably, to facilitate the reconstruction process in a manner which best brings relief and hope to the widest sections of the community, developing for the benefit of the entire nation the latent human potential and resources of every person who has directly or indirectly been burdened with the heritage of the shame and the pain of the country's racist past … to take into account the competing claims on resources, with regard to the 'untold suffering' of individuals."*

The whole process of reconciliation has been placed in jeopardy by the enormous disparities between rich and poor, between the mainly rich whites and the mainly poor blacks. The rich provided the class from which most of the beneficiaries and perpetrators came from and the poor produced the bulk of the victims. This is why Tutu has exhorted whites to support the transformation taking place in the lot of blacks. For unless houses replace the hovels and shacks in which most blacks live, unless blacks gain access to clean water, electricity, decent health care, decent education, good jobs and a decent environment—we can bid reconciliation farewell. As things have actually turned out in the country, spiralling crime, arising at least in part out of a lack of economic reconciliation, has been a massive deterrent in the overall development of markets and communities. We now turn from South Africa to South-East Asia.

4.3.4 Newly Global Navigation of Community Building: Social Business

Creating a World Without Poverty

Mohammad Yunus (19) has by now gained international renown, including the award of the Nobel Peace Prize, for his work on micro lending in Bangladesh through the Grameen Bank. We now turn to his latest work, following on from where De Gruchy, Mandela and Tutu in South Africa left off in *Creating a World Without Poverty*.

For Yunus, mainstream free-market theory, which South Africa, for example, was obliged to conform to in the 1990s, suffers from a 'conceptualisation failure'—a failure to capture the essence of what it is to be human:

> *"In the conventional theory of business, therefore, we have created a one-dimensional human being to play the role of business leader, the so-called entrepreneur. We've insulated him or her from the rest of life, the religious, emotional, political and social. He is dedicated to one mission only—the maximization of profit. And today's world is so mesmerised by the success of capitalism it does not dare doubt the systems underlying such economic theory. Yet the reality is very different. People are not one-dimensional. They are multi-dimensional. This is where the social business comes in. Entrepreneurs will set up a social business not to achieve limited personal gain but to pursue social goals."*

The PMB versus Social Business

By insisting that all businesses must be profit-maximising (PMB), we have ignored the multi-dimensionality of human beings and, as a result, business remains incapable of addressing many of our most pressing social problems. Yunus in turn offers, based on his experiences with Grameen, the model of a social business. In its organisational structure, for Yunus, it is basically the same as the PMB, but it differs in its objectives. It employs workers, creates goods and services and provides these to customers at an amenable price; however, its objective is to create social benefits for those whose lives it touches. It is cause-driven rather than profit-driven, with the potential to act as a change agent for the world. A social business, however, is not a charity. It concentrates on creating products and services that create a social benefit and recovers its costs in the process through, for example:

- Providing nutritious food to poor and underfed children.
- Designing and marketing health insurance policies to provide affordable medical care to the poor.
- Developing renewable energy systems and selling them to rural communities at a price they can afford.
- Recycling garbage, sewage and other waste products in poor and politically powerless neighbourhoods.

We now turn from social business in general, to a particular expression of such, again in South Africa, which has drawn on the southern African philosophy of *ubuntu*. Albert Koopman (20) and Cashbuild, our case in point, are individual and institutional catalysts for *ubuntu* like economic and social exchange, culminating the process of 'southern' transformation of marketing into community building.

4.3.5. Global-Local Effect: Community Building/Workplace Democracy

Uncovering the Divine Will of Africa

The Cashbuild case is unique in South Africa to this day. With Albert Koopman at the helm of this provider of building supplies in the rural areas of the country, the company was not only ultimately transformed into a workplace democracy, but became distinctively profitable, socially as well as economically. Moreover, this initially took place in apartheid South Africa, where the conditions for such social and economic reconciliation could not have been less conducive. How, then, did Koopman manage such an ultimately successful process of mutual development between business and society, including conflict resolution, duly incorporating the advance of human rights with such a profitable enterprise? Cashbuild began as a wholesaler in 1978 and became a very successful business in a short space of time. Situated predominantly in the rural areas of South Africa and focusing on the black housing market, their staff consisted of 84% black, 13% white and 3% Indian. However, by mid-1982, with 12 outlets, profits started sliding. Everything 'northern' was in place—systems, procedures, technology, combined with a booming market—but something was going wrong and he did not know enough about the south at that point to realise where to start looking.

Key questions went through Koopman's mind. Why do the workers actually work? What is their social or Divine Will? What went wrong in Cashbuild with respect to capital and labour? What are we actually trying to achieve as a business organism? How do we bring together the rights of people, their spiritually based humanity and the economic process as represented in the workplace? Subsequently, he conducted a succession of brainstorming sessions to uncover the purpose of Cashbuild's existence. It soon became clear to us that one purpose existed in the management's mind and another in the workers'. Management 'up north' was pulling one way and the people 'down south' another. There was no transcendent purpose linking one with the other.

The Advent of VENTURECOMM

Koopman was sure that their belief in raising spiritual consciousness was valid, but he could not see how his employees were expressing their 'southern' social selves apart from the 'western' economic process. While they perceived their labour power as intimately associated with themselves as human beings, they still saw the company as viewing their labour content as part of the production – distribution – consumption process. They were being treated as commodities. What they were crying out for was for participatory democracy, thereby integrating their economic and social selves, so as to relieve labour power of its commodity character. It dawned upon Koopman that:

- No one can demand productivity from anyone, but I can create a climate within which social man is willingly productive.
- I cannot manage people, only things, but I can create a climate within which people take responsibility and manage themselves.
- One cannot demand quality from people, but I can create conditions at work through which quality work is a product of pride in workmanship.

A convention of some 200 workers was held and the following ground rules were established:

- Respect human dignity and individual freedom of speech.
- Allow everyone to have access to company results and performance standards.
- Give everyone a role in developing company policy.
- Improve the quality of life of all employees outside the work sphere through active community involvement.

It was proposed that a governing body of five people be constituted to each outlet—the VENTURECOMM—with each person being democratically elected to hold a portfolio, save for the manager who was appointed to the operations portfolio, based on his or her expertise. This portfolio was concerned with the 'hard' variables whereas the safety, labour, merchandise and quality of work-life portfolios were the 'soft' ones.

Moreover, each of these managers was continually assessed by lower levels in the hierarchy. In fact, this Cashbuild VENTURECOMM system was socialistic in that it instated social justice and offered security against destitution. It was likewise capitalistic to the extent that individual expression was given its due reward and group development its due recognition. The system thus gave expression to the work ethic and also to the enterprising spirit of people.

Cashbuild in today's South Africa is still a thriving commercial business with a well-developed marketing model, but, with Koopman having long gone, it is no longer, in Yunus' terms, a 'social business'. The fate of Cashbuild is replicated across the world's stage. Because the 'western' model of free market capitalism, economically, and the model of the shareholder-controlled, market-oriented corporation, commercially, is so universally predominant, marketing can hardly evolve, as was the case for Cashbuild in Koopman's time, into community building on a sustainable basis. In fact, such sustainability is ultimately dependent on such an integral enterprise being lodged within an overall integral economy, in this case promoting self-sufficiency.

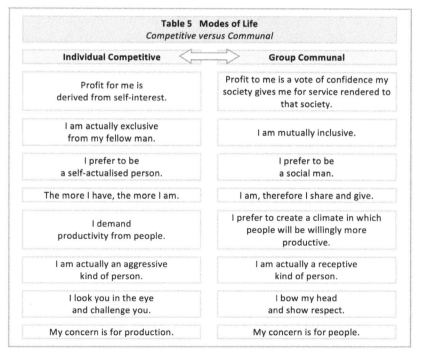

Table 5 Modes of Life Competitive versus Communal	
Individual Competitive	**Group Communal**
Profit for me is derived from self-interest.	Profit to me is a vote of confidence my society gives me for service rendered to that society.
I am actually exclusive from my fellow man.	I am mutually inclusive.
I prefer to be a self-actualised person.	I prefer to be a social man.
The more I have, the more I am.	I am, therefore I share and give.
I demand productivity from people.	I prefer to create a climate in which people will be willingly more productive.
I am actually an aggressive kind of person.	I am actually a receptive kind of person.
I look you in the eye and challenge you.	I bow my head and show respect.
My concern is for production.	My concern is for people.

4.4. INTEGRAL *ECONOMY*: COMMUNAL LEARNING TOWARDS SELF-SUFFICIENCY

4.4.1. Features of a New Subsistence Paradigm

The German economic sociologists Veronika Bennholdt-Thomsen and Maria Mies (21) have undertaken extensive research on economic subsistence, extending over several decades, particularly in Bangladesh. For them, as such:

1. How Would Work Change?

- Instead of wage work, *independent, self-determined, socially and materially useful work would be at the centre of the economy.*
- The fact that subsistence production subsidises the market (money) economy must be reversed; instead subsistence production needs to be liberated so that *wage labour and the market economy subsidise the larger social productivity.*

2. What are the Characteristics of Subsistence Technology?

- Technology must be *regained as a tool to enhance life, nurture, care, share;* not to dominate nature but cooperate with nature.
- Technology is to be designed in a way that *its effects can be healed and repaired.*

3. What are the Moral Features of a Subsistence Economy?

- The *economy is just one sub-system of society,* not the reverse.
- The *economy must serve the core life-system,* supporting the production and regeneration of life on the planet as a whole.

4. How Would Trade and Markets be Different?

- *Local markets would preserve the diversity of products* and resist cultural homogenisation.
- *Trade would not destroy biodiversity.*

5. Changes in the Concept of Need and Sufficiency

- A new concept of the satisfaction of needs must be based on *direct satisfaction of all human needs* and not on the permanent accumulation of capital and material surpluses by fewer and fewer people.
- The important concept and practice of the commons can be reclaimed to *resist the injustice linked to privatisation and the commercialisation of nature,* money becoming a means of circulation not accumulation.

4.4.2. Subsistence and the Commons

For Bennholdt-Thomsen and Mies, the boundaries between the human community and nature are not rigid and hard, but permeable. Economics is not separate from ethics, culture and spirituality. Production is not separate from and superimposed on reproduction. There is continuity between production and consumption. In reclaiming the commons via a subsistence economy they are linked to each other. Production processes will be oriented toward the satisfaction of needs of concrete local or regional communities and not toward the artificially created demand of an anonymous world market. Further, in such an economy the concept of 'waste' does not exist. Things cannot be consumed and things whose waste products cannot be absorbed within such a distinct eco-region cannot be produced. Such a local economy in a particular region requires, evidently, a community that feels responsible for sustaining the self-generative capacities of the region.

4.5. CONCLUSION: COMMUNALLY REINVENTING KNOWLEDGE

In the final analysis, in 'southern' guise, by way of communal 'grounding':

- Through INTEGRAL DEVELOPMENT you build **a Learning**

Community, thereby *cultivating ongoing learning relationships* between you and your immediate community, as well as with your external community, organisation and society.

• Via INTEGRAL RESEARCH you undertake **Participatory Action Research**, including the recovery of history, whereby you *recognise and co-evolve folk culture,* thereby producing and diffusing new knowledge.

• Through INTEGRAL ENTERPRISE, specifically turning marketing into **Community Building** you *promote reconciliation,* without surrendering your individuality, by opening yourself up to the 'other', *via social/economic exchange-and-conversation.*

• Via an INTEGRAL ECONOMY, specifically promoting **Self-Sufficiency,** boundaries between human community and physical nature are dissolved and made permeable; *economics is not separate from nature and community.*

We now turn from communal learning in theory to worldwide communal practice.

4.6. REFERENCES

1 Schieffer A and Lessem R (2014) *Integral Development: Realising the Transformative Potential of Individual, Organisation and Society.* Abingdon. Routledge

2 Mulgan G (2005) Resurgence. No. 172

3 Escobar A (2008) *Territories of Difference: Place. Movements and Life.* Durham. North Carolina. Duke University Press

4 Gudeman S (2001) *The Anthropology of Economy: Community, Market and Culture.* Oxford. Blackwell

5 Lessem R and Schieffer A (2010) *Integral Research and Innovation: Transforming Enterprise ad Society.* Abingdon. Routledge

6 Reason P and Bradbury H (2004) *Handbook of Action Research.* London, Sage

7 Nyerere J (1969) *Nyerere on Socialism.* Dar es Salaam. Oxford University Press

8 Fals Borda O (ed). (1991) *Action and Knowledge.* New York. Apex Publishing

9 Rahman M.D. (1993) *People's Self Development.* London. Zed Books

10 Yousaf N (2012) *Dr Akhtar Hameed Khan - Pioneer of Microcredit and Guru of Rural Development.* New York. AMZ Publications

11 Cossins N (2013) *The Man in the Hat: The Story of Shoaib Sultan Khan and the Rural Poor of Asia.* Lahore. Vanguard Books

12 Lessem R and Schieffer A (2009) *Transformation Management: Toward an Integral Enterprise.* Abingdon. Routledge

13 Tutu D (2002) *No Future Without Forgiveness.* New York. Doubleday

14 Gutierrez S (1986) *The Market Women of Nigeria.* London City University. Unpublished PhD Thesis

15 Ellis S. et al (2004) *Worlds of Power.* Johannesburg. Witwatersrand University

16 De Gruchy J (2000) *Reconciliation – Restoring Justice.* Canterbury. SCM Press

17 Mandela N (1994) *The Long Walk to Freedom.* Grand Rapids. Abacus.

18 Tutu D (2002) *op cit*

19 Yunus M (2008) *Creating a World Without Poverty.* New York. Public Affairs.

20 Koopman A (2001) *Transcultural Management.* Chichester. Wiley-Blackwell

21 Bennholdt-Thomsen, V. & Mies, M. (1999). *The Subsistence Perspective: Beyond the Globalized Economy.* London. Zed Books.

Chapter 5

Learning Community in Practice

NATURE POWER, SOULIDARITY CIRCLES, STUDY CIRCLES, COMMUNIPRENEURSHIP

What is commonly called credit by the banker is administered by him primarily for the purpose of private profit, whereas it is most definitely, communal property. In its essence it is the estimated value of the only real capital—the potential capacity under a given set of conditions, including plant and so on, of a society to do work.

Clifford Douglas, *Economic Democracy*

Exercise Nature Power: South, identified with Africa. Key features are: indigenous knowledge, community activation, agronomy, connection with the soil, respect and oneness with nature, a community of life.

Exhibit Soulidarity: By tasting the sufferings of others (community) outside your own self (individual), the collective alchemy of communal survival starts pulsating, setting it in a circumvolutory motion: the 'SOUL-idarity' impulse, the common thread between humans.

Study Circles: Non-hierarchical, action-oriented, involving the leadership of a locally rooted mentor and a sense of togetherness amongst the participants with a common shared goal set in the communicative process.

Communipreneuership: Comes into play when the productivity of a socio-economic ecosystem is brought about and owned by the community for the common good, thereby grounded in the co-creation of sustainable livelihoods.

5.1. INTRODUCTION: GROUNDED LEARNING IN A NATURAL/COMMUNAL SOUTH

5.1.1. Nature Power and Healing Radiance

Come Down to Earth so as to Regain our Health

We begin now, communiversity-wise and now in practice in the 'south', before turning 'east', 'north' and 'west' in turn, spanning what we term our integral realities or worldviews, so to speak, with communal learning in practice, thereby also including nature. Within our own Trans4m community, the first communiversity to emerge in the second decade of the new millennium was in rural Edo State, Nigeria. As such, naturally and communally, first let us remind ourselves of co-author Father Anselm Adodo's words of wisdom from his work, *Nature Power* (1):

> *"Nature Power is inviting the world to come down to earth so as to regain our health. The earth is the primary source of our creativity, intelligence and humanness. Before we set out to calculate, to create, to invent, to fabricate, the earth already was."*

The African universe, then, is a world of relationships, of interactions between the living and the dead, between the natural and the supernatural. A community is not just a place where human beings dwell. The African community comprises plants, animals, human beings, the spirit and the ancestors. Trees are more than trees; the sky is more than we see. There is more to plants and animals than we see with our eyes. *Everything in the universe is a language of Life and an expression of Life.* Therefore, they are sacred and holy.

144

Fusing Nature and Community

For Adodo (2) again, this time alluding to 'healing radiance' further to 'nature' power, holiness is a state of union with God, with oneself and with others. Others include your fellow human beings as well as plants, animals and indeed the whole of creation. For the traditional African as such, the drum, as text, is the carrier of the word, the primordial sacred sound by which the world came into being. The drum is to the traditional African as the Bible is to the Christian. The drum is the symbol of God's incarnation, of God present among us, of Logos. It is the sacrament of the divine in the human, of spirit in matter and the sacred in the profane. Sound for Africans is an emotive and creative force.

African traditional religions therefore generally believe in the presence of mysterious forces controlling activities in the world. These forces manifest in terms of spirits. They believe that it is through the manipulation of sound that they link up with this force and use it. Hence, great emphasis is placed on speech, incantations, singing and music and also dance.

Backdrop to Pax Herbals

Father (Dr) Anselm Adodo is a Benedictine monk in Edo State, the founder of Pax Herbals as an enterprise and also an academic in his own right. In his own words:

"In 1997, I was ordained a priest. That, however, did not change my normal course of work. A priest in the monastery can also work in the kitchen, farms and gardens as well as in the classrooms as a professor. I then became very busy with research in the fields of ethnobotany as I was fascinated by the world of plants. In my interactions with local healers, I observed how they applied local music and rhythms to treat depression and madness. I sat down with elderly local healers, traditional midwives, local bonesetters (orthopaedic specialists), local psychiatrists and psychotherapists in different parts of Nigeria to observe different methods of traditional medical

treatment. There were also professional counsellors and diviners who apply divination systems to proffer solutions to personal problems, success in business, protection against witchcraft.

The village of Ewu had a rich tradition of medical healing. There were traditional healers everywhere and traditional shrines can be sighted in many corners of the village. There was a mission hospital and a government hospital in the village, but majority of the people patronised traditional healers. Herbal medicine was identified with witchcraft, sorcery, ritualism and all sorts of fetish practices. Because herbal medicine was associated with paganism, African-Christians secretly patronised traditional healers, as the educated elite and religious figures did not want to be associated in any way with traditional African medicine. At that time, for a religious figure, especially a catholic priest, to be openly propagating traditional medicine, was seen as a taboo of the highest order.

I conceived the idea of Pax Herbals as a tool for changing the concept of traditional medicine from an esoteric practice by mysterious, fearsome old medicine men to that of a useful, profitable, rational and explicable venture in this context. The goal of Pax Herbals has since become to change the face of African traditional medicine. One of the burning issues for me is how to preserve this vast body of indigenous knowledge in writing, thereby making it explicit, so that it can be passed on to others."

From West Africa, specifically Nigeria, we turn to Southern Africa, specifically Zimbabwe, shifting our emphasis from natural to human learning community, altogether still in 'southern' grounding guise.

5.1.2. Chinyika: Political Economy to Social Commons

Chinyika Community Development Project

Out of the Chinyika community in Zimbabwe, in community developer and HR practitioner Steve Kada's words, a son was raised from the house of the Gutu chieftainship and was moved by the suffering of his own people. He woke up to the call of his ancestors to save his villagers from the scourge of hunger and poverty. Chidara Muchineripi then, who had become a successful business person and management educator, had a wakeup call from his slumber of individual success. He prompted in this direction while on our project-based Trans4m Masters in Social and Economic Transformation (MSET) in South Africa and thereby responded to his 'father's voice'.

As such he was reminded of his responsibility to his Chinyika people as the son of a chief. Emotively aroused, he initially decided to feed his brothers and sisters who were starving by buying bags of mealie meal (corn) and grain and distributing these to them. While in the process of responding to his 'father's voice', Chidara, having enrolled on the MSET programme, unknowingly together with his childhood friend and colleague Steve, in 2005, established the Chinyika Community Development Project. Chidara then reconnected with the voice that called his people to revisit the source of their food security in the past, the nutritious food and meals that came out of the sweat of their labour; a community that never starved.

The Grass that Turns to Gold

The voice echoed through poems and drama. One villager, at a field day function inspiringly recited the poem dedicated to *rapoko*:

> "*The grass that turns into gold*
> *The grass that gives people their livelihood*
> *The grass that is fed to people and their livestock*
> *The grass that connects the Chinyika people with the ancestral spirits*
> *The grass that has value beyond money*
> *The grass that makes and gives life to people.*"

This poem conveyed the value and the importance of finger millet, one of the 'key actors', as it were, for the Chinyika people. Through this re-visitation of the past, Chidara reconnected with the tradition and culture of growing indigenous small grains. For him, the voice of his father continued to echo throughout his lifetime.

Planting Himself in the Soil of his Ancestors

Thereafter, Chidara and Steve, after becoming co-researchers, spent endless hours together in Chidara's special gazebo thatched structure at his home in Harare. He was filled with great emotion as he narrated the story of his village people, promoted by the reminder through his education and research of his grounding. He would clench his fists, put his hands on each side of his body and stamp the ground as if in a dance. It was as if he was planting himself in the soil of his ancestors as he rooted himself in the centre and soul of Chinyika's traditional past. Chidara's father, as a chief, had passed on the oral tradition of a true African to his family and subjects. "A true African does not completely abandon his culture despite getting a Western education. Western education has its virtues but the African has to maintain his humane nature."

It is considered immoral, as such, to watch and let a poor person or family perish of hunger when another person has more than enough. Chief Chitsa of Chinyika, in addressing people on one of the field days said,

"Munhu ega ega, mwana ega ega anofanira kuziva kwaakabva"

which is translated as

"Each person, each child must look back and know where they came from and be responsible to himself and his community like what we have witnessed today."

This demonstrated that each one of us must be responsible to our people.

The Actor-Network: Public-Private-Civic Partnership

Chidara, responding to his Chinyika community in his capacity as designate chief and Steve representing the business sector as HR Director of Cairns Foods, played their respective catalytic roles. As such, they created a relationship between the private sector and the rural community, thereby institutionally extending—with the Zimbabwean Department of Agriculture ultimately also playing its governmental part—the *actor network*. On the one hand, Cairns Foods, through their agronomists, provided the Chinyika community with technical advice in growing traditional and horticultural crops. On the other hand, the Chinyika people provided Cairns Foods with a wealth of knowledge for purposes of product development. Cairns, in its own transformation process, began turning towards foods with a traditional base and flavour in addition to the current Western-oriented food products on the market.

Towards a Democratic Community

Through the re-awakening that has since been taking place among the Chinyika community, as well as in neighbouring communities today—extending from 5,000 people in 2006 to up to 300,000 in 2016—individual effort is being channelled and realised in the context of communal benefit. Such practical realisation is encouraged to the extent that it does not create selfish, egoistic individuals. The unifying force between the individual and the community is the focus on fighting the resurgence of food insecurity and the continued battle against poverty, to realise the capacity and strength that the people have in growing enough food and alleviating poverty.

In order to coordinate these developments, the leadership originally drew from the villages' horizontal structures. Through a democratic process in the traditional manner, the chief, headman, counsellors, village development committees and extension services personnel were all involved, consulted and contributed to the selection of the project leadership. The leadership, headed by Mai Tembo (Mrs Tembo), has clearly outlined its goals and strategy specifically to fight hunger through growing *rapoko* and in the long run eliminate poverty. They have clearly distanced themselves from the very sensitive partisan politics and they do not align the project farming activities with any political groupings.

The committees' main purpose has remained that of building a community consciousness that creates enlightened people's actions to fight both mind and material poverty; to thereby decolonise the mind.

The Role of Women Redefined: Musha Ndimai

In the process of putting together the project leadership, the role of a woman has been redefined. The challenge to take up responsibility has been greatly accepted by the women of the community. This has been evidenced by the number of women who attend the project meetings. In fact, the attendance at meetings, the field days involving demonstrations of ploughing, sowing and harvesting, have mostly been led by the Chinyika women. The influence of the 'mother' has been reflected through the number of active youth who are getting involved in the project activities. Mothers have also shown their cooking skills, which are exceptional when it comes to preparing traditional dishes of *rapoko*/millet 'sadza', thick porridge, meat and vegetables. When preparing for large gatherings, the mothers call upon their youth whom they have trained to help with cooking tasks, to assist with the heavy tasks of gathering firewood, drawing water and even food preparation itself.

Women's self-expression has moreover manifested itself through drama and singing. The large gatherings provide an opportunity for women to dramatise the social and economic challenges facing the community. Their drama illustrates the problems of irresponsible and lazy fathers and mothers who do not work hard in their fields; about fathers who spend most of their time drinking and neglecting families. They also highlight problems created by disease like HIV/AIDS. Although men participate in these dramas, it is usually the women's initiative. Mothers aim to educate both the young and old. More mothers have awoken to their traditional role—the home stands because of the mother—'*Musha ndimai*'.

The contribution then to a successful *rapoko* harvest cannot be underplayed. *The active participation of women has had a profound impact on the whole farming project.* The village harvest has so far recorded average yields of between 1 and 2 tonnes per household unit and most of the grain has been retained for consumption by the families. There was, however, surplus tonnage which community members agreed to sell and raise income for themselves. Today, then, that part of the country has food security.

We now turn from South to East and from Africa to Asia, specifically to Pakistan, where the tone and language changes.

5.2. EMERGING FROM THE SPIRITUAL/ CULTURAL EAST

5.2.1. Akhuwhat Means Brotherhood

Love is the Beginning of Our Journey and Beauty Our Quest

Amjad Saqib, as highlighted by our Trans4m PhD Fellow Aneeqa Malik (6) in their recent book, is the founder of Akhuwat in Pakistan, the largest non-interest micro-finance institution in the world as well as, as we shall see, much more. In his words:

> *"For us, the resonance of journeying through stages of self and communal metamorphosis is all too familiar with the journeying of the soul or pilgrimage (Hajj). The circumambulation resonates with the physical circumambulation around the Ka'bah, the ultimate spiritual journey for any Muslim. Circumambulating the Ka'bah represents the idea of oneness. In regards to social life, it means not to leave unity and to try to maintain this unity ... The Arabic verb 'tafa', from which the term for the circumambulation (tawaf) is derived, has the meaning to 'attain to the summit of a thing by spiralling around it'. Love is the beginning of this journey and beauty its quest."*

Mawakhat: Brotherhood and Solidarity

What, then, is Akhuwat's philosophy? Its model is quite unique in the way the world understands microfinance and poverty. This model is inspired by the *hijrah* (migration) of the Prophet of Islam from Mecca to Medina, two of the holiest cities for Muslims, located in Saudi Arabia. And the story starts more than 1400 years ago, in the time of the Prophet Muhammad (peace be upon him) of Islam. The story starts with self-sacrifice, migrating (taking a leave) from one's own self and caring for others, thereby sharing what you have with your brothers. This is a story of *mawakhat* (brotherhood) and solidarity amongst the Medina (virtuous city) community.

This pertinent story of migration in the history of humankind gave birth to the concept of spiritual brotherhood, *mawakhat*. The *mawakhat* model adopted by the *ansar* (helpers) of Medina under the guidance of Prophet Muhammad (peace be upon him) sets the precedent for how a model integral community and city should look. Although the physical migration in this case happened more than 1400 years ago in Mecca, in the Akhuwat case it is renewed.

A Cyclical Model of Gift Economy

According to Javaid Saeed, former tutor at Columbia College and the University of South Carolina, the failure of Muslims in understanding and applying Qur'anic doctrines in their totality is the cause of Muslim societies being generally static and not economically developed in the way they should have. According to Saeed, the Muslim condition compared to the more developed countries of the world is very weak and humiliating; they exist at the mercy of the countries of Europe and America, they receive most of the essential things of life from the more developed countries of the world and many Muslim countries receive economic aid from foreign countries.

From this viewpoint, Akhuwat has exemplified an immaculate financial model of communal and self-reliance, for in its entire history the institution has always banked on the benevolence of the affluent members of the society. At the same time, prototypically, they channel the obligatory *zakat* (charitable donations) money to the rightful deserving people of the society, i.e., the micro-entrepreneurs; hence they have successfully created a cyclical model of gift economy.

5.2.2. Solidarity and Mutual Support Can Become the Norm of a Just Society

The Soulidarity Impulse: Save Me From Poverty and From Wealth

In his Urdu book *Akhuwat ka Safar (A Journey of Hope)*, Amjad, as described by Aneeqa, recalls a prayer his father taught him which touched him deeply: "O Lord, save me from poverty." To that, he added, "Lord, save me from wealth." For him, Akhuwat is no longer a dream but has now become a social movement. It is no longer a passion limited to a few, but an institution for all. Society cannot be left at the mercy of a capitalistic and feudalistic financial system, a system mostly founded on the basis of exploitation. Banks lend to those who are already wealthy, while the poor and indigent are treated like untouchables. This divide in the 21st century is the worst form of financial apartheid.

A few people have appropriated the treasures of the world for their own use. If they had their way, they would even put a price on sunshine and the moonlight. Perhaps they have not understood the purpose of creation. 'Might is right' is not a rule that can be imposed upon humanity. Whatever belongs to the Lord, belongs to all.

The equitable distribution of resources must take place according to effort and skill. The poor are needy not of alms, but of cooperation. We give charity to the poor and make them dependent upon it. They are deprived of wealth and assets, but not of ego and pride and, through charity, we deprive them of those. Akhuwat has done nothing new, but by institutionalising Islam's basic system of interest-free loans, the rule of solidarity and mutual support can become the norm of a just and fair society.

Solidarity to Soulidarity: Constituting Virtuous Circles

More specifically then, for Saqib:

> "*By tasting the sufferings of Others (community) outside our own Self (individual), the collective alchemy of communal survival—the 'impulse of solidarity'—starts pulsating, setting it in a circumvolutory motion. And this is what we call the 'SOUL-idarity' impulse iteration, the common thread that runs between humans. It transmutates, in times of suffering originating in the* Ishq/*love realm, thereby horizontally taking effect as communal* ihsan *(perfection of beauty). For what is* ihsan *after all? It is a matter of taking one's inner faith* (iman) *and showing it in both good deeds and action* (amal) *and a sense of social responsibility* (Akhuwat) *borne from religious or spiritual convictions.*"

Through 17 years of existence, besides generating its own 'solidarity/circular economy', by rekindling the spirit of *ihsan*, Akhuwat has successively created its own 'community of Akhuwateers', that is, multiple virtuous circles. For Amjad, brotherhood (*Bhai-chara/Akhuwat*) is an unmatchable feeling of compassion that promises to empower people. By virtue of solidarity, the cyclic reverberation has spiralled through their many community initiatives that range from micro-finance and education to health and social services, to environmental reclamation and recycling, altogether termed virtuous circles. We now turn from 'south' and 'east' to 'north', from Africa (healing radiance) and Asia (virtuous circles) to Europe; that is, Slovenia (study circles).

5.3. NAVIGATING IN THE SCIENTIFIC/ TECHNOLOGICAL NORTH

5.3.1. A Nationwide Network of Slovenian Study Circles

From Democratisation to Local Development

The story of Slovenia's renewal, with which Trans4m have been intimately engaged for the past five years, consists of a multitude of stories, some of them taking place in small communities and others spreading across the entire country. Study circles (7), as such, have been offered in the frame of adult education by the Slovenian state since the independence of the country in 1992. As a non-formal form of adult learning they are based on civic freedom but are regularly monitored and supported by the state under certain conditions (licensed leaders, documentation, publicised results).

Their aim has changed from an initial emphasis on democratisation to their more recent focus on local development. The most frequently selected topic during the entire period of their functioning is identity and heritage—regardless of dichotomy of aims (e.g. personal/local learning), types of participants (retired/employed) and effects (most effective are those which use local history as means of community development).

Non-Hierarchical, Action-Oriented, Sense of Togetherness

The main components of Slovenian study circles are: *non-hierarchical, action-oriented, involving the leadership of a locally rooted mentor and a sense of togetherness amongst the participants with a common shared goal set in the communicative process.* This indeed is a form of community activation, north-south style. A study circle integrates individual and group initiatives by establishment of the 'common', including personal responsibility, overcoming the lack of intermediary bodies in post-modern society. This form of community activation moreover serves to build up social capital. Another role—building the ties of the community with the local natural environment—is more common in rural environments.

More specifically, four components then combine to make up the concept of the study circle in Slovenia, namely the *loose framework, the informal character of the study situation, the collective learning environment and the participants' genuine interest in knowledge*. Social capital is acquired at the very moment the participants are in a communicative relationship with each other and it is composed of knowledge, abilities and competences for a meaningful life, in public as well as in private life.

The main outcomes of Slovenian study circles (8) have been twofold:

• **Material Outputs:** Material outputs are booklets, local editions, exhibitions, etc. They are, however, not considered the only effect of such learning. Rather, a sense of belonging, community spirit and social cohesion are reported by participants and external evaluators as key effects.

• **Non-Material Outputs:** Study circles offer many non-material ones as this kind of learning fosters social responsibility, counterbalances consumption, raises self-consciousness and democratic decision-making, demolished in past periods of political nationalism or class-based pressures.

5.3.2. Building on its Nature and Tradition: The Emergence of Solčavsko

Dialogue-Based Learning Providing the Municipality with Project Ideas

Study circles are spread all over the country, but we now turn to a specific application of study circles in Slovenia by way of illustration. The Solčavsko region as such is located at the upper current of the Savinja River along the Slovenian-Austrian border. The area is surrounded by a mountain chain of the Kamnik-Savinja Alps and Karavanks. In the Solčavsko region, tourism remains closely connected with traditional activities: agriculture, forestry and handicraft. For centuries, the largest farms in the whole Alpine space have existed here and remained more or less self-sufficient. Study circles in Solčavsko starting in 2004 focused on learning for tourism development, aiming at the protection of natural and cultural heritage. Such study circles proved to be *not only an investment in internal cohesion through dialogue-based learning but also a stimulation of targeted activities, provided to the municipality as project ideas.*

All of these achievements did not come easily, partly because Solčavsko is an extremely heterogeneous region. Some people live on farms high up in the mountains. Others cope with conditions in alpine valleys. Also, the central settlement of Solčava is rather different than smaller settlements in the valleys and isolated farms. Hence, the municipality and region had to cope with a diversity of developmental models. However, looking to Solčavsko's past, present and future, the constant motive for all its development activities has been sustainability.

How, then, did Solčavsko manage to align its diverse and geographically dispersed population under a common goal? Again, study circles played a crucial role.

Connecting People and Identifying Development Opportunities

The first study circle in 2004 was provided in the upper area of the valley aimed at preservation, revival and development of the natural, cultural and ethnological heritage of the area. Following a positive experience and outcomes, several other study circles developed later with clear purpose and creative energy among people who up to then did not contribute their time and effort to the evolution of the common goal. The result was that an NGO, called 'Society for the Development and Conservation of Natural and Cultural Heritage Panorama' was established. Alojz Lipnik, later elected mayor of Solčavsko, continued to use the principles and the methodology of study circles for connecting people with common goals and seeking development opportunities for locals in the municipality of Solčava. He emphasised listening as the basis of co-operation and intergenerational flow. Lipnik stressed that:

"The experience of study circles is extremely valuable as well as knowing that it is necessary to listen to the people around you. Young people need help of their seniors to use their talents, knowledge and skills in order to find business opportunities in their hometown."

The main result of the municipality's multiple activities was the establishment of the public institution Center Rinka, which was aimed at managing visitors and introducing them to sustainable management of human and natural resources.

Center Rinka: A Multipurpose Centre for Sustainable Development

Institution Center Rinka encourages the development of local products in many different ways, but the main topics are always wood, wool and food production. All the events and activities at Center Rinka are held in close connection with local people, tourism providers and visitors of Solčavsko. Solčavsko remains a community of creative people with a clear development vision. It also involves young, educated locals with new projects, trying to help them find business opportunities and create green jobs: *local material, local people, local skills* and *knowledge.*

The Municipality of Solčava and Center Rinka prepare different projects to stimulate production and selling of local products and services. However, building and maintaining a truly creative community with a clear development vision is not an easy task. Center Rinka is continuously challenged to orient itself to the changing needs of the population as well as to the requirements of the environment.

Promoting the Good of the Community through Knowledge, Experience, Tradition

Solčavsko, then, in recent decades has co-evolved through study circles to serve 'the good of the community'. The motivation has been, mediated through the circles, *to take action for the common good instead of a displaying a shallow focus on individual good.* Development at Solčavsko is based on knowledge, experience and tradition. Incorporation of specific know-how and expert knowledge seems to be of particular importance but also involves drawing on the past. Education and cooperation with experts, scientists and institutions are truly important. The approach of taking small and moderate steps towards innovation is common in Slovenia's Alpine region. At the same time, there is a strong connection between nature and culture, including a commitment to a sustainable lifestyle. We now finally turn to the 'west' albeit mixed together with the 'south'.

5.4. ECONOMIC AND ENTERPRISE EFFECT FROM THE WEST

5.4.1. Communipreneurship: Co-creating Sustainable Livelihoods

For Nigerian Trans4m Fellows and Islamic bankers, Basheer Oshodi and Jubril Adejeo, what they term 'communipreneurship' (9) comes into play when the *productivity of a socio-economic ecosystem is brought about and owned by the community for the common good.* Although geographically based in the African 'south', the financial business that they are in also draws them 'west'.

Communipreneurship, as such a 'south-western' combination, is grounded in the co-creation of sustainable livelihoods, in order to effect prosperity in terms of job creation and wealth distribution in any given community. To make the advent of prosperity more prevalent across different communities in Nigeria for the exercise of the common good is what the organisation they have established, CISER (Centre for Integral Social and Economic Research) is all about, as a social enterprise that will serve to enrich prosperity across neglected rural communities in Nigeria.

5.4.2. Communal Cooperation

Towards Employing Self-and-Community: Nigeria's Experience

This then leads to communal cooperation. In his desire to promote and achieve the employment of self-and-community over the promotion of mere (self) employment, Adeojo critiqued the prevalent Porter's 5-market competitive (external) forces model (10). The critique was aimed at introducing the Integral 4 Community Co-operative Actions for employment of community.

The Integral 4 Community Co-operative Actions are:

- Contribution from the integrators
- Contribution from the people and community
- Contribution from the communiprises, i.e. complementary businesses, alternative businesses and technical support businesses
- Benefits for aspiring and new communipreneurs

Contribution from the Integrators

Unlike Porter's competitive forces, which are focused on the threats imposed by the bargaining power of the suppliers on businesses or enterprises, the integrators in this context are either suppliers or bigger businesses (commonly in the urban ecosystem) that aim to co-create sustainable business (or livelihood) opportunities for communipreneurs in the rural ecosystem (and even in their urban environment).

Contribution from the People and Community

In the case of Porter's forces, the bargaining power of the buyers and consumers also poses a threat to the growth and survival of the business, by driving down the prices of the products or services due to low market demand, as well as the changing taste of the consumers. In the case of the integral community co-operative actions, consumers and buyers are perceived as the people and the community that consume or use the product or service of the communipreneurs for the common good of the community.

The people and community see the communipreneurs as an integral part of socio-economic development for the community, purposefully in the areas of jobs creation as well as wealth distribution; as such, the people and community are committed to a continued relationship with the communipreneurs. They also provide resources needed by the communipreneurs such as labour, land and innovative ideas to improve the quality of the products and services.

Contribution from the Communiprises

In the case of Porter's competitive forces we have threats from alternative or substitute businesses. In the realm of communipreneurship, there is an emphasis on the need to have complementary businesses (or enterprises) to provide for necessary missing support services and contribute to the growth and sustainability of the communipreneurs and the enlarged community. The development of communiprises assists in financial co-creation, providing support through technological capacity, innovation, financial services, infrastructures and overall systemic thinking, towards well-being.

In the case of financial services, the communiprise can be the formal bank that provides basic financial services to the communipreneurs and the community. The financial institution will be close to the community and be part of the business, thereby providing supply-lending finance or partnership arrangements aimed at ensuring that communal ventures survive and grow. In this context, the communiprise supports the communipreneurs with proper business record-keeping, in terms of revenues and expenses in line with modern standards.

Benefits for Aspiring and New Communipreneurs

According to Porter's forces, there are barriers to entry for new entrants, but under the integral community co-operative there are some benefits to being new and aspiring communipreneurs, in order to serve and add value to the community at large. We have realised then, on the one hand, that in contemporary Africa, while entrepreneurs pursue profitability for their own prosperity, the communal good-life of the people can suffer. On the other hand, we also recognise that the self-same end result can apply to social entrepreneurs when they strive to achieve social impact, if they focus on making a profit for self and the enterprise. To further understand this conundrum, we dissected the impact of entrepreneurship into two forces: the *positive* and the *destructive*. We realised that the effects of the destructive force can be more long-lasting and completely outweigh that of the positive force.

We established that the effects of positive force of entrepreneurship on the community are as follows, but not limited to these:

- Livelihoods are created and wealth distributed as a result of the jobs offered by the entrepreneur.
- Via the above, those employed and their households are able to afford access to basic amenities including healthcare and education.
- Women are empowered when employed by the entrepreneur (who may also be a woman).
- Co-operative society is formed and funded by those who are employed to enable availability of credit supply for its members, for the common good of the community.

Yet moving on to the destructive force of entrepreneurship, for entrepreneurs to remain profitable in business, they may sacrifice many of their resources to achieve profitability. Some of these resources are human (those employed in the community), others are physical assets and financial. Such sacrifices result in some of the following consequences (but are not limited to these) for the community:

- Absences of the entrepreneur from the community, reducing its mobilisation.
- Disruption in the availability of basic amenities for the people.
- A survival mentality is generated in the community, inhibiting its

ability to progress and thrive.

• Rising poverty levels in the community, as those employed become unemployed, sacrificing employment of the community.

• The economy of the community becomes static or even deteriorates, as a result.

5.5. CONCLUSION

Interweaving finally, the theory of communal learning—from integral research and development to economy and enterprise, with the practice—spanning south and east, north and west, as per:

• INTEGRAL DEVELOPMENT: via communal learning you exercise **Nature Power**—South, identified with Africa. Key features are: indigenous knowledge, community activation, agronomy, connection with the soil, respect and oneness with nature, community of life.

• INTEGRAL RESEARCH: Study circles as **Socio-Technical Design**—non-hierarchical, action oriented, involving the leadership of a local mentor and a sense of togetherness amongst the participants with a common shared goal set in the communicative process.

• INTEGRAL ECONOMY: By tasting the sufferings of others (community) outside self (individual), setting it in a circumvolutory motion: the 'SOUL-idarity' economic impulse builds up **Self-Sufficiency**, weaving a common thread between humans and *oikonomia*.

• INTEGRAL ENTERPRISE: via **Community Building** you promote communipreneuership, whereby a socio-economic ecosystem is generated and owned by the community for the common good, thereby grounded in the co-creation of sustainable livelihoods.

We now turn from communal learning in practice, to re-GEN*E*-rative pilgrimium, firstly in theory.

5.6. BIBLIOGRAPHY

1 Adodo A (2012) *Nature Power: A Christian Approach to Herbal Medicine. New Edition.* Edo State. Benedictine Publications

2 Adodo A (2003) *Healing Radiance of the Soul: A Guide to Holistic Healing.* Edo State. Agelex Publications

3 Adodo A (2017) *Community Enterprise in Africa: Communitalism as an Alternative to Capitalism.* Abingdon. Routledge

4 Lessem R, Muchineripi P and Kada S (2012) *Integral Community: Political Economy to Social Commons.* Farnham. Gower

5 Saqib M A and Malik A (2018) *Integral Finance – Akhuwat: A Case Study of the Integral Economy.* Abingdon. Routledge

6 Saed J (1994) *Islam and Modernisation.* New York. Praeger

7 Oliver L (1987) *Study Circles: Coming Together for Personal Growth and Change.* Washington DC. Seven Locks Press

8 Piciga D, Schieffer A and Lessem R (2016) *Integral Green Slovenia: A Social, Knowledge and Value Based Economy at the Heart of Europe.* Abingdon. Routledge

9 Lessem R and Bradley T (2018) *Evolving Work: Employing Self and Community.* Abingdon. Routledge

10 Porter M (2004) *Competitive Strategy.* New York. Free Press

EAST

PART 2: RE-GENE-RATIVE
PILGRIMIUM

Chapter 6

Re-GENE-rative Pilgrimium in Theory

EMERGENCE: AWAKENING INTEGRAL CONSCIOUSNESS

... the mental space in which people dream and act is largely occupied today by Western imagery. Moreover, the spreading monoculture has crowded out viable alternatives in the industrial, growth-oriented society and crippled humankind's capacity to meet an increasingly different future with creative responses. The last forty years have considerably impoverished the potential for cultural evolution. It is only a slight exaggeration, he goes on to say, that whatever potential for cultural evolution remains is there in spite of development.

Wolfgang Sachs, *The Development Dictionary*

Integral Development: No living myth can be pinned down to one particular phase of its inherent development or to one consciously selected and favored aspect of itself. It too is a moving finger that writes and having written, moves on.

Integral Research: Experiential knowing lies at the base of a 'knowledge pyramid' as lived 'being-in-the-world'; supports imaginal knowledge as significant form and pattern; supporting conceptual knowledge, which supports practical knowing, the exercise of skill.

Integral Enterprise: The evolutionary knowledge spiral is a continuous, self-transcending process through which you transcend the boundary of the old self into a new self by acquiring a new context, a new view of the world, an evolved consciousness.

Integral Economy: Development programmes require a value-base that is meaningful to the people, relevant to their perceived needs and affirmative of their strengths. And where are such values to be found? They are present in indigenous religious traditions.

6.1. INTRODUCTION: AWAKENING INTEGRAL CONSCIOUSNESS

6.1.1. The Path of Co-evolution

Through our, so-called re-GEN*E*-rative pilgrimium we purposefully tap into the realm of a society's culture and spirituality (1), duly aligned, as we shall see, with the Biblical Quaternity Archetype (BQA) (2). Indeed, analogous to the individual level (or 'round', as we call it), it is here where we seek a community's or society's 'seat of creativity'. The regularly proclaimed, generalised 'self-help' approach to so-called 'development' often falls short in truly helping a particular society to connect with its own co-evolutionary potential, guided by its own cultural values and beliefs. 'Self-help' often means that the to-be-developed-people learn to help themselves become like the developed people.

To pick up a metaphor used in chapter 1, when we come to the pilgrimium we arrive, as it were, like a communal caterpillar entering into a collective chrysalis. It is a place of change. Thence, we add the dimension of journeying together. If the communi-butterfly is to emerge it will first need to have undertaken the communal hero's journey. As such, our 're-GEN*E*-rative pilgrimium' then takes its developmental place. So, in response to the need for consciousness-raising development, in this chapter we develop the pilgrimium story, starting with the story of our time from our ancient past and ending with the biblical quaternity archetype, ultimately spelling out our re-GEN*E*-rative pilgrimium.

To take us then out of a conventional, developmental cul-de-sac and re-enter the path of re-GEN*E*-ration, now in societal terms, we explore together the following questions:

- How does your community and culture regenerate itself co-creatively with others?
- How does your specific culture and spirituality inform such a regenerative path?
- How does the interaction between various cultures create fields for creative co-evolution?
- How can your own creative potential, rooted in our own cultural identity, ultimately also contribute to the regeneration of the world at large?

How can societal evolution build on the organisational co-evolution and the journey of the self that comes before it?

We begin with the African social philosopher Laurens Van der Post who takes us back to our shared origin, to the collective story of humankind. The German-born philosopher Jean Gebser takes on this original story, charting out the evolutionary stages of human consciousness. He emphasises the need to be in touch with our 'ever-present origin' in order to master the steps of human evolution that lie ahead of us. Then, we consider the conscious development of the ancient Celts, who exhibited a remarkable gift for making the ever-present origin an inclusive experience for all those they lived amongst.

6.1.2. Reconnecting with our Collective Story

The Story is Timeless

Van der Post complained that people always laughed at Bushmen stories and said they had no meaning. They had no meaning, he argued, because we onlookers had lost the key and the code. We had lost the meaning of the stories; thus, he started to decode them in 1952 (3). This was after he had returned to Africa, war-shattered, at a time when he was beginning his life again:

> *"My story was moving into a new phase and I had to begin it again. And it almost seems to me as if in this there's a parable for all of us, mankind. All of us who are discouraged, who sit back and say what's the point of trying, well this is heresy to me, because the story is timeless. Life is timeless. If we play our role in it we redeem it from time."*

The Story of Our Time

For Van der Post, in his book on *Jung and the Story of our Time* (4), everything in life is a story. The story of mankind then, is history and without history we have no meaning. Both are part of the same indivisible process. Stories provide us with our sense of wonder. They provide us with the sense of living mystery in life. They help us to heighten our sensitivities, our awareness. The story, moreover, presents the options and possibilities of life that might have been and still can be lived. C.G. Jung—Van der Post's great mentor about whom he even wrote a biography—said that in every disturbance of personality one could discern the elements of an interrupted personal story. And the person could only be cured or healed by the psychiatrist getting hold of the story. That story was the personality's, or indeed society's, most precious possession.

Africa is the cradle of humankind. From there our collective story unfolded. For Van der Post, modern man has cut himself off so dramatically from his origins that he can't do anything other than look down on them. Van der Post argues that it is modern man's excessive rationalism and fanatic adherence to outer physical reality—our 'north-western' reality viewpoint—together with his over-valuation of the demonstrable objective world around him, that has caused much of his own undoing. There are all manner of invisible and imponderable values which modern man has neglected in his or her own life and therefore ignored in the lives of those in his power, or those with whom he or she is thrown into contact; these factors sooner or later combine in rebellion against them.

Entering the Original Story – Facing the Shadow

For Van der Post, indigenous societies and particularly those in Africa, give the most dramatic example of life developing from an invisible point in time where history has as yet no size and magnitude, only position, ongoing into our own age. The bushman makes gods of all the animals that surround him; the Khoikhoi kneel to an insect, the praying mantis; the Bantu listens to the spirits of his ancestors in the roar of the lion and in the noise of his cattle stirring.

Then, suddenly, European man arrived on the scene. A long period of pure reason that began with the Reformation and had been stimulated by the French Revolution was deeply at work in the European spirit, setting him at variance with his instincts:

> "European man walked into Africa by and large totally incapable of understanding Africa, let alone of appreciating the raw material of mind and spirit with which this granary of fate, this ancient treasure house of the lost original way of life, was so richly filled. He had, it is true, an insatiable appetite for the riches in the rocks, diamonds and gold ... but not for the precious metal ringing true in the deep toned laughter of the indigenous people around him."

The Mythological Journey

Tell me then, Van der Post says, what the myth is within history that is seeking to express itself through the life of a nation and I'll tell you what that nation is and may become. To this day Africa is largely an Old Testament land which still needs temples and prophets and a David for Goliath (Mandela, for example) far more than it needs parliaments, politicians and trade unions. The particular myth of Van der Post's countrymen presupposed a great trek through a great unknown wilderness to a land of promise. It was a necessary and inevitable phase in the development of their myth.

> *"No living myth, however, can be pinned down to one particular phase of its inherent development or to one consciously selected and favoured aspect of itself. It too is a moving finger that writes and having written moves on. If we deny its onward movement it will go back and re-write the lesson on the rough blackboard of life with some extra lines on disaster thrown in after school hours. It works in this way because it contains the great rounded vision of life without bias, fear or favor for any of its parts."*

We now turn from Van der Post's *Dark Eye of Africa* to Gebser's *Ever-Present Origin*.

6.1.3. Ever-Present Origin

Evolutionary Stages in Society: Magical to Integral

Jean Gebser (5) was a Professor of the Study of Comparative Civilisations at the University of Salzburg in the middle of the last century. What was becoming increasingly evident for Gebser was that the individual was being driven into isolation while the collective was degenerating into mere aggregation. These two conditions, isolation and aggregation, were for him clear indications that individualism and collectivism were becoming deficient and a new form was required.

However, before we can describe the new, Gebser maintains that we must know the old, or, as per the title of Gebser's book, we must know our Ever-Present Origin. Looking back on human endeavour, Gebser distinguishes three structures of societal consciousness—magical, mythi-

cal and mental—and a fourth one to come—integral, altogether preceded by an original archaic structure. According to him, a true process of
development always occurs in quanta, which is in leaps, or in mutations.

Stage 0: Origin or Archaic Structure

Taken together, micro- and macro-cosmic harmony is nothing less
than the perfect identity of man and the universe in their original form.

Stage 1: Magical Structure

The man of magic has been released from his identity with the whole.
The more man became conscious of himself, the more he began to be
an individual. Man now stands up to nature. He tries to exercise her,
to guide her, striving to be independent of her, then he begins to be
conscious of his own will. Here is man the maker, fighter and indeed
entrepreneur.

Stage 2: Mythical Structure

While the magic structure leads to a liberating struggle against nature through a disengaged awareness of the external world, the mythical
structure, in turn, leads to the emergent awareness of the internal world
of the soul. To look into the mirror of the soul is to become conscious; to
apprehend the soul, through myth, is to become conscious of self. Everyone who is intent on surviving (with worth and dignity) must sooner or
later pass through the agonies of emergent consciousness. For Gebser,
as reflected by the German-Canadian Indologist Georg Feuerstein, the
mythic consciousness led humanity to an awareness of its internal environment... *imagination (imago = picture) or inner experiencing is distinctive of the mythic consciousness.* The mythic consciousness is 'introverted'.
It is this capacity, out of which myth and meaning are born, that became
lost when human consciousness evolved to the mental structure.

Stage 3: Mental Structure

Events of 500 BC in Greece had to be repeated, according to Gebser, around 1250 AD by European man. Then, however, his basis was considerably broadened because of three major achievements: the Greek theory of knowledge, the Hebrew doctrine of salvation and Roman legal and political theory. From the standpoint of the perspectival European world, this mental structure is 'rational', from the root *ratio* meaning to calculate, to think, to understand. Indeed, the names for the Indian lawgiver Manu, the Cretan King Minos and the Egyptian King Menes, are all most likely derived from the root *man*, the 'measurer'.

Stage 4: Integral Structure

By integration, Gebser means a fully completed and realised wholeness—the re-establishment of the inviolate and pristine state of origin by incorporating the wealth of all subsequent achievement. The concretion of everything that has unfolded in time and coalesced in a spatial array is the integral attempt to reconstitute the 'magnitude' of man from his constituent parts, so that he can consciously integrate himself with the whole. We now turn to the Celtic way, or pilgrimium, as we shall see lying in between Africa and Europe, starting thereby with integral development via community activation.

6.2. INTEGRAL DEVELOPMENT: COMMUNITY ACTIVATION THE CELTIC WAY

There was, then, a movement out of North Africa, which began in the 3rd millennium BCE and reached the shores of Britain in the 5th century CE. This was the Celtic way, that manifested something of the integrated society that Gebser points to and that Van der Post identified, in the 'great trek across the wilderness' for the African peoples. Recent analysis of the DNA of contemporary indigenous Irish and Scots communities (6) indicate that the familiar story of the Celts, having travelled across Europe in the Iron Age towards the Atlantic 5,000 years ago, has almost certainly got the map wrong. The Celtic peoples most likely originate from Berber and Tuareg tribes of North Africa, who travelled to the Western islands of Britain via the Iberian peninsula. However, it is the story of the influence of these peoples in Britain during the 5th–8th centuries CE that helps us tell the communiversity tale.

By the time of the Roman Empire's retrenchment from its North-Western borders, much of the southern half of Britain had come under the sway of Christianity. Despite the fact that neither Ireland nor most of Scotland had been Romanised, Christianity had quickly become established in those islands. But it was the 'insular Celtic' Christians who seem to have had the greatest impact in bringing the gospel to the indigenous peoples of northern and western Britain and Ireland. With waves of Anglo-Saxon invasions to the south and east, the various Celtic tribes moved north and west.

During the period of St Patrick and his successors (mid-5th CE) there is ample evidence for a widespread missionary movement and continuous journeying amongst the people of the 'Celtic fringe'. By the time of the establishment of Aidan's monastery (early 7th century) on Holy Island (Lindisfarne) there was an extension of the Celtic mission to encompass Anglo-Saxon communities down the east coast into the English Midlands and even as far south as modern Sussex.

There is a wide debate between scholars about the relative significance of differences between the Celtic and Anglo-Saxon Christian communities[4] (7, 8, 9). Bede (672/3–735 CE), the Saxon abbot of the double monastery of Wearmouth-Jarrow, who chronicled events of the previous century, saw Celtic ecclesiology and spirituality as flawed, because it opposed the authority of Rome. Even so, although his writings (10) show

---

4 See, for example, the alternative accounts of Ian Bradley, who reduces the distinctiveness of the Celtic church and those of Martin Robinson and Edward Sellner, who emphasise the differences between Celtic and Anglo-Saxon Christian communities, on the basis of precisely the same evidence (op cit). Whenever the Celtic church is discussed, strong ideological positions are swiftly adopted.

him to be strongly Roman-centred, as a Benedictine monk, he held great affection for the missionary zeal of the Celtic church. Nevertheless, whatever the differences between the two Christian traditions—and they do appear to be significantly deeper in terms of social and spiritual relations than even Bede contends—certain features of 6th–7th century Christian practice within Britain stand out.

In the first place, the monastic community was far more dominant than the ecclesiastical diocese. The connection between people—and their relationship to nature—was more important for the Celts than the commanding of territory and place, which was a distinctively Roman pre-occupation (sic). This may be seen as reflected in the communities of most indigenous—or Southern, in the integral world's understanding—peoples worldwide.

There was huge variety across the land concerning the nature of what a monastery was. Some were little more than groups of dwellings surrounding an anchorite cell, while others were the size of small cities. However, the important common feature was that Christian communities were established less on the basis of geographical territories than on the relationships between people, who shared a common identity because of their connection to a central monastic community.

In other words, pastoral practice revolved around presence rather than position, with the notion of community as superior to that of central authority. This was further reflected in the diversity of local liturgies that developed amongst Celtic Christian communities. Although, even in this, the range of diversity was usually very slim.

A second feature of the predominately Celtic church was that of the relative equality of women within the Christian community. The sheer number of women recorded as significant leaders within the church points to this. The pre-eminent position of such figures as Brigid, Hilde and Bride indicate the respect in which women were held as carriers of the gospel and charismatic leaders of their communities. This was, perhaps, a further reflection of the ancient Celtic conviction that the natural world, the human body and sexuality were all connected with a spiritual dimension.

The pagan Celts were notorious for their druidic rituals, a feature noted by Julius Caesar, who pointed to the power of the Druid priests in mediating healing and wholeness. Consequently, it is no surprise that the Celtic church of the 5th–8th centuries reflected a remarkably holistic gospel, especially when compared with the extreme dualism of the Church, as it had developed through much of the patristic period.

Sellner (op cit.) amongst others perceives this integration as further reflected in a passion for representing the beauty of nature in visual art, reflected in the aesthetic culture of these island Celtic Christians, with their high crosses,[5] knot-work, illuminated manuscripts, decorated vessels and intricately carved stonework. Veneration of the natural world—as a reflection of the Creator—was further developed in the significance they attached to sacred or 'thin' places, where they considered the boundary between heaven and earth to be attenuated. Consequently, holy sites such as Iona, Lindisfarne, Whithorn and Bradwell became places of pilgrimage. In this sense, liminality was an important theme of Celtic Christianity. Journeying was made along boundaries (cf. the earlier discussion of 'transitional spaces').

This in turn reflected a further distinctive feature of the Celtic way, which is characteristic as far back as the 3rd millennium BCE (11). It was their determination to journey without ceasing, especially across water, which characterised these communities. It may seem paradoxical to regard certain places as sacred and then to leave them behind. However, this was characteristic of the Celtic Christian movement, at least as recorded by Bede and other chroniclers. Part of this pilgrim mentality was reflected in enthusiasm for mission.

---

5 These, of course, reflect the ancient symbol of Jung's quaternity archetype, with their circle enclosing the cross, the image of barbaric Roman torture and execution, now redeemed as representative of the saving work of Christ.

At the same time, it demonstrated the Celtic desire for *peregrinatio* or the 'white martyrdom' of separation from all that would hinder their journey with Christ. Robinson (op cit.) identifies four facets of Celtic Christianity, in the Anglo-Saxon world, that conditioned their *peregrinatio*:

- Responding to the call of Christ, who called them to travel as part of the kingdom's discipline.
- The call to radical obedience, in taking up the cross and following.
- The breaking-in of the kingdom through the thin veil separating earth and heaven.
- Practical penitence.

This fourfold feature of the Celtic Church mirrored each of the four canonical Gospels, which, as we indicate below, align with the four worlds/pathways model of economic integration and the GEN*E*. They reflected the communal response of the Lukan travellers, seeking the kingdom way (Southern pathway); the cross-carrying, obedient following of Mark (Eastern pathway); the Johannine dissolution of the boundary between earth and heaven (Northern pathway); and the practical ethical penitence of Matthew (Western pathway).

As such, the Celtic Christian experience reflected a range of features that pertain to the communiversity. The learning community journeys together. It recognises the need for mutual sacrifice. It perceives and researches the thinness of the boundary between culture and spirituality, learning and life. Moreover, it seeks to practise its learning through innovations and enterprise that connect art and science, economy and community, enterprise and social solidarity. How, then, is such a developmental structure, or journey towards awakening consciousness reflected in the research world?

6.3. INTEGRAL RESEARCH: CO-OPERATIVE INQUIRY AND THE PATH OF RENEWAL

6.3.1. Research into Human Potential

Participatory and Developmental

John Heron was a pioneer in the creation of participatory research methodologies in the social sciences. As such, he was the founder and director of the Human Potential Research Project at the University of Surrey in England from 1970 to 1977, the first university-based centre for humanistic and so-called 'transpersonal' psychology and education in Europe. The emergent worldview that action research (see chapter 10 for an elaboration) espouses, for him, can be described as systemic, holistic, relational, feminine and experiential, but *its defining characteristic is that it is participatory and developmental* (12).

Within the context of co-operative inquiry that Heron established, human persons are linked in a generative web of communion with other humans and the rest of creation. *Human persons do not stand separate from the cosmos; we evolve with it and are an expression of its intelligent and creative force.*

Healing and Whole Making

A participative worldview invites us to inquire into what we mean by flourishing and the meaning and purpose of our endeavours. Given the condition of our times, a primary purpose of human inquiry is not so much to search for the truth but to heal. For Reason and Bradbury (13), in their *Handbook of Action Research:*

> "To heal means to make whole: we can only understand our world
> as a whole if we are part of it; as soon as we attempt to stand outside,
> we divide and separate. In contrast, making whole necessarily im-
> plies participation: the individual is restored to a circle or commu-
> nity and the human community to the context of the wider natural

world. To make whole also means to make holy: a participatory worldview restores meaning and mystery to human experience, so that the world is experienced as a sacred place."

6.3.2. Modes of Knowing: From Being to Doing

Grounding and Actualising

For Heron (14) and thereby integrally for ourselves, there are four modes of knowing which correspond with our four worlds and our GEN*E*. Moreover, his modes of knowing—from being to doing—open up the door to the 'four worlds'. As a result:

- *experiential knowing*, our 'south', lies at the base—Grounding—of a 'knowledge pyramid', comprising the direct, lived 'being-in-the-world'.

It supports

- *imaginal or presentational knowing*, our Emergent 'east', which supports
- *propositional or conceptual knowledge,* our Navigational 'north, which upholds
- *practical knowing,* the Effective exercise of skill, our 'west'.

What is above serves to actualise what lies below. In our terms, mankind's origins, in the African south, reflects the historical base of the knowledge pyramid, or indeed spiral. The Celtic way represented the emergence of a more imaginal way of life that connected faith, culture and society in a journey of discovery. Equally, the Celts explored the boundaries between artistic knowledge, reason and spirituality, as people who had travelled into the navigational North.

Ultimately, the 'western' frontier, mankind's final port of historical call, practical knowing in other words, or know-how, serves to actualise the knowledge quest. It is grounded on and empowered by all the prior forms of knowing—southern, eastern and western. Specifically, moreover, the practical is immediately supported by propositional or conceptual knowing, which it celebrates and affirms at a higher level. It affirms what is intrinsically worthwhile by manifesting it in action.

This dynamic up-hierarchy, grounded in the 'south' and effectively bearing fruit in the 'west', is different from the classical top-down one, whereby the west controls everything below, without being empowered by any of it—that is the 'rest' of the world. Such a pyramid, in effect, can be seen as a spiral, which expands our knowing and is free and unfettered, or contracts if we are socially damaged. So, to re-iterate what has been said before, albeit in a newly becoming guise:

- *Experiential reality* is the lived experience of the mutual co-determination of person and world.
- *Imaginal reality* is significant form and pattern, in perceptual and other imaging, that interconnects analogically and metaphorically the whole network of other significant forms and patterns.
- *Conceptual reality* is the combined sense and reference of concepts.
- *Practical reality* is excellent practice and its effects.

There are two important features of this fourfold, integral epistemology. Firstly, there is a pyramid of support or grounding. Experience of 'being-in-the-world' is the ground of exercising imagination with its significant patterns of imagery. Both of these together are the ground of propositions, concepts or theories about it. Experiential knowing constitutes the ground of fourfold knowledge; intentional action is the effective culmination of it and imaginal as well as conceptual knowing mediate between the two. For Heron, because of their relatively autonomous form, each of these—southern, eastern and northern—can function in a limited way without the other three, *except* for 'western' practical knowing. As such, in our terms, 'the west needs the rest'.

Participative Spirituality

In his more recent work in the new millennium, Heron has explicitly grappled with what he terms *participative spirituality*, defining the 'sacred' as:

- The all-inclusive illimitable presence of *what there is*.
- That which calls human beings to *comprehensive flourishing*.

'Science', for him then, is an activity which exercises critical rigour in articulating human experience. Sacred science thus involves four ways of knowing which are mutually supportive and correlative with each other. Practice firstly, as the outcome of an inquiry, *fulfils* all other modes. It fulfils them because it involves them all, integrates them, gives them human purpose, imbuing them with intentionality and completes them by manifesting them. Secondly, it *celebrates* them by showing that the reality which they articulate manifests excellence. This celebration is not a proof of them. It brings them forth, in and through the values of human flourishing. It is a declaration by concerted doing. What is important here is the word 'concerted'*:* people acting together and interacting through consensus. The grounding is epistemological or knowledge-based, the actualisation is axiological or morally-founded.

The Co-operative Research and Development Cycle

Translated into a research and development cycle, this entails:

- Firstly, a strong emotional base—in the individual case, confidence; in the societal case a well-developed, positively functional, open and formative local identity.
- Secondly, imaginative development through metaphor, analogy and story; in the societal case, an open-ness to different worlds and a culture that can fuse such diverse elements together into newly imaginative configurations.
- Thirdly, individual discrimination of the salient intellectual features of the material within a global view; in the societal case, a

philosophical and scientific elite, combined with social and political institutions that can accommodate complexity.

• Fourthly, the opportunity to practice with others; in the societal case, an open society which is able to accommodate diverse perspectives and has ways and means of resolving the conflicts arising and making, consensually, the decisions required.

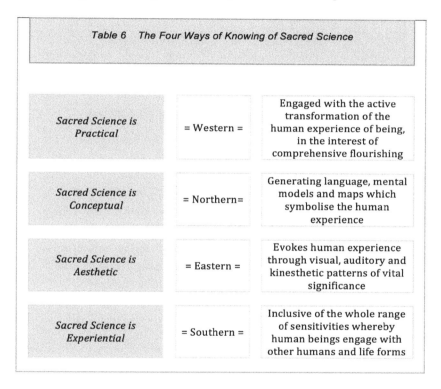

Table 6   The Four Ways of Knowing of Sacred Science

Sacred Science is Practical	= Western =	Engaged with the active transformation of the human experience of being, in the interest of comprehensive flourishing
Sacred Science is Conceptual	= Northern=	Generating language, mental models and maps which symbolise the human experience
Sacred Science is Aesthetic	= Eastern =	Evokes human experience through visual, auditory and kinesthetic patterns of vital significance
Sacred Science is Experiential	= Southern =	Inclusive of the whole range of sensitivities whereby human beings engage with other humans and life forms

We now turn from integral research to integral enterprise and from cooperative inquiry, along the research path of renewal, to *imaginally* based conscious evolution.

6.4. INTEGRAL ENTERPRISE: HUMAN RESOURCES TO CONSCIOUS EVOLUTION

6.4.1. Self-Conscious Human Beings

Removing Labour from its Commodity Status

For eastern European polymath and social philosopher Rudolf Steiner, 'labour' needs to be removed from the economic process of production, distribution and consumption. As such, people in organisations should not be viewed as a human resource or as a factor of production, but rather as self-conscious human beings. What Steiner (15) had to say in *Towards Social Renewal* at the turn of the last century was:

> *"The modern worker abhorred instinctively the fact that he or she had to sell labour power to an employer in the same way that commodities are sold in the marketplace. It is not possible therefore to divest human labour power of its commodity character without first finding a means of extracting it from the economic process. Efforts should therefore not be devoted to transforming the economic process so that human labour is justly treated within it, but towards extracting labour power from the economic process and integrating it with social forces which will relieve it of its commodity character."*

The Liberation of Capital

Furthermore, for his German follower, Folkert Wilken, in *The Liberation of Capital* (16):

> *"The continual inventiveness of human beings is ultimately the source and actually the only source, of capital. In such a context capital is an intellectual, cultural, even 'spiritual' force originating in continuing innovation. As such it creates both the possibility of and the desire for, a liberation of the person from physical labour, to find his or her 'true' place in a world of mental and cultural activity."*

In fact, it was the renowned American Buddhist philosopher, Robert Pirsig, in his classic work on *Zen and the Art of Motorcycle Maintenance* (17), who said:

"You can find the Godhead just as easily in the gears of a motorcycle transmission as in the heavens above."

Basho: Place of Nothingness and Everythingness

The philosophical and spiritual backdrop to the conscious evolution of Japanese large-scale manufacturing in the second half of last century, in fact, was provided by the work of Kitaro Nishida (18), Japan's leading 20th century philosopher. His logic appears in various forms, but most directly in the Japanese term basho, literally 'place' and by extension 'field', 'matrix', 'medium' and even 'world'. In this sense, there is for Nishida distinct *basho*, each having their place in the final enveloping *basho*, or 'place of no-thingness', or indeed 'every-thingness'. Each of these 'worlds' presupposes and exhibits the contradictory identity of objectivity (explicitly known) and subjectivity (tacit knowing). Nishida, by his own admission, follows in the footsteps of Germany's notable philosopher and phenomenologist of 'being' Martin Heidegger and France's renowned existentialist philosopher Jean-Paul Sartre. Moreover, his philosophy has much in common with ancient Vedic wisdom.

For all such philosophical systems, firstly, the physical or biological world is at one end, while the psychological human-historical world is at the other. *Each such human-historical world has its own 'basho' or locus of self-transformation.* Each one is dynamically formative, organic and teleological; these properties being absent from the physical world. Its self-organising, self-transforming character becomes an analogue of the 'creative act' in the existential mode of human awareness.

Nishida relates such to the 'I–Thou' relationship of Jewish philosopher Martin Buber. The abstractions of science can never escape from their own basis in individual experience of the historical world. In human-historical life, secondly, there is always a dialectic of the affirmative and the negative: the former, for Nishida, is the world of matter and the latter is the world of consciousness. The former is the world of objects; the latter is the world of intentional acts. What the Japanese organisational sociologists Nonaka and Takeuchi have done with their approach to conscious organisational evolution, in terms of 'knowledge creation', is to transform Nishida's 'worlds', *basho*, (not human resources) into fields of knowledge: *Ba*.

6.4.2. The Evolutionary Spiral

Transcend the Boundary of the Old Self into a New Self by Acquiring a New Context

Nonaka and Takeuchi draw substantively on Nishida, as well as upon the central European philosopher of *Personal Knowledge,* Michael Polanyi (19). Their 'eastern' evolutionary knowledge spiral is a *continuous, self-transcending process through which you transcend the boundary of the old self into a new self by acquiring a new context, a new view of the world, an evolved consciousness and knowledge*; indeed, a new social construction. In short, it is a journey 'from being to becoming'. You also, in the process, transcend the boundary between self and other, through interactions amongst individuals or between them and their environment.

It is important to note that the movement through such modes of development forms a spiral, not a circle or a straight line. In such a developmental spiral, the knowing interaction between tacit (subjective knower) and explicit (objective known) is amplified through these four levels of meaning, which correspond with our Four Worlds.

Socialisation (S), Externalisation (E), Combination (C) and Internalisation (I)

These four modes of development or knowledge are socialisation (S), externalisation (E), combination (C) and internalisation (I). As the so-called SECI spiral, they visualise the knowledge creation process, which lies at the heart of a knowledge-creating organisation. The spiral becomes larger in scale as it moves up and through these levels, expanding horizontally and vertically across organisations.

It is a dynamic process, starting at the individual level and expanding as it moves through communities of interaction that transcend sectional, departmental, divisional and even organisational boundaries. Development as such, or indeed conscious evolution, is a never-ending process that upgrades itself continuously. This interactive spiral process takes place both intra- and inter-organisationally, transferred beyond organisational boundaries. Through dynamic interaction, one organisation's development can trigger that of outside constituents such as consumers, affiliated companies, universities or distributors. For example, an innovative new manufacturing process may bring about changes in the suppliers' manufacturing process, which in turn triggers a new round of product and process innovation within the organisation. As such it is a *self-transcending process* in which you reach out beyond the boundaries of your own existence, *transcending the boundary between self and other, inside and outside, past and present, building altogether upon one or other Ba.*

6.4.3. Ba: Shared Context in Motion

Ba in General

Based on the philosophy developed by Nishida, as further evolved by Nonaka and Takeuchi (20), *Ba* is here defined as a shared context in which being and becoming and thereafter knowing and doing, are communicated, created and utilised. Generation and regeneration of *Ba*, or indeed consciousness, is the key, providing the energy, quality and place to move along the evolutionary spiral. *Ba*, then, *means not just a physical space, but a specific time and space.* The key concept in understanding Ba is 'interaction'. Development, or transformation, alludes to a dynamic and indeed dialectical human process, as opposed to 'labour force', human resources, or even human capacity.

Four Types of Ba

There are then four types of *Ba*. In our Four World terms, these are originating *Ba* (southern—socialisation), dialoguing *Ba* (eastern—externalisation), systemising *Ba* (northern—combination) and exercising *Ba* (western—internalisation). These, altogether, are defined by two dimensions of interaction. One dimension is the 'type' of interaction; whether the interaction takes place individually or collectively. The other dimension is the 'media used' in such interactions; whether the interaction is through face-to-face contact or virtual media such as books, manuals, memos, e-mails or teleconferences:

- *Originating Ba is defined by individual and face-to-face interactions.* It is a place where individuals share experiences, feelings, emotions and mental models. From such originating *Ba* emerges care, love, trust and commitment—for us, 'southern'—the ground for evolution within and among individuals and organisations.
- *Dialoguing Ba is defined by 'eastern' collective and face-to-face interactions.* It is the place where individuals' mental models and skills are shared, converted into common terms and articulated as concepts. Dialoguing *Ba* is more consciously constructed than originating *Ba*, involving the conscious use of metaphor and analogy, as well as negation and affirmation, to make the tacit explicit.
- *Systemising Ba is defined by 'northern' style depersonalised and virtual interactions.* Information technology, through on-line networks, groupware, documentation and databanks, offers a virtual collaborative environment for systemising *Ba*.
- *Exercising Ba is defined by personalised, individual as well as virtual*

188

'western' style interactions. Here, individuals embody explicit facts and concepts communicated through virtual media, such as written manuals or simulation programmes, making the explicit tacit.

We now turn from conscious evolution to a culture-based, developmental economy and thereby from micro-enterprise to macro-economy. In the process, moreover, we turn from the Japanese Far East to the Middle Eastern origins of The Bible (Jewish and Christian Scriptures) and the People of the Book (*Ahl al-kitab*), with faith traditions remaining a common denominator for each.

6.5. INTEGRAL ECONOMY: REGENERATIVE PILGRIMIUM – TOWARDS MEANINGFUL ECONOMICS

When we enter the economic realm of the pilgrimium, we recognise that there are a vast number of different systems which act to re-GENE-rate our understanding and consciousness of economics. We have been taught that there is no alternative (TINA) to neo-liberal capitalism, but this is a shibboleth. As we journey from the developmental way of Africa and the Celts, through the co-operative research of Heron's sacred science and the conscious evolution of the Japanese *Ba*, we ultimately reach a journeying place in which the entire economy and society are regenerated and can be consciously conceived as spiritually constituted.

6.5.1. Semiotic Economics – A New Eastern Journey

Discovering the meaning-making that undergirds different economic systems is a journey in itself. It can come as a considerable surprise to recognise that the models of supply and demand, price, profit and the market are not the entirety or even the dominant understanding of what economic means, when viewed across the landscape of human history and culture. In his classic work on the way in which capitalism had become dis-embedded from social relations, Jewish-Christian economist Karl Polanyi (21) pointed to the historic nature of reciprocity or gift-exchange as the basis of a former economic world. Equally, he saw the mid-20ᵗʰ century as an era when the state's role in redistribution had become magnified to compensate for market failures and dislocations.

In the GEN*E*alogical journey outlined here, we can associate reciprocity with the southern way of community. Nor is it consigned to history, as Polanyi thought. It is a way that remains alive and well even in the most 'advanced' economies. The economic acts that we do for one another in families, communities and voluntary organisations, represent about one-third of the extent of GDP, in a country such as the UK, if we calculate our care gifts in pounds sterling. The UK Office of National Statistics calculates this to be equivalent to £1.1TN per annum. However, we seldom think of it like that. Reciprocity is simply give-and-take because we love one another, which sounds so un-economic.

Equally, we can see that a journey to the north brings us into the field of redistribution. The systems and processes we generate, largely through fiscal policy, to garner taxes and government borrowing—through gilts, bonds and on international money markets—in order to fund welfare, health, education, employment support, environmental sustainability and the like, are characterised by a northern ability to use technology and sophisticated methods for seeking greater income equity. Then, of course, the markets, politics and capitalist economics bring us foursquare into the Western world.

Yet Polanyi's schema—as in so much economic analysis, even when it is able to look, through the lens of political economy, beyond the marketplace—misses the journey East. That is because we frequently neglect to consider the core values, cultural norms and spirituality that emerge through economics that comes from a pilgrimium journeying place, over the horizon. What are the names of the places to which we might travel, economically, on an alternative pilgrimage?

Table 7 Four Ways of Semiotic Economics		
Economics that effects alternative markets	= Western =	Purposeful investing for a meaningful **impact**
		Prayerfully instituting the principles of **Kingdom** of God economics
Economics that systemically navigates towards a common good	= Northern =	Reversing the hierarchy of money and gift, where home becomes the economic **core**
		Measuring economic **well-being**, to create an economy of welfare and care
Economics on an emergent journey into co-operative solidarity	= Eastern =	Evolving **mutual support** between rich, middle income and poor people
		Asserting stakeholder **rights** to economic co-operation
Economics that is grounded in natural capital and the commons	= Southern =	Rooting sustainable production/consumption in natural **cycles**
		Holding land and property in common for **posterity**

In Table 7 we refer to 'semiotic economics'. By this we mean the journey into the meaning-making that takes place under the conditions of different economic systems. Each of these are alternatives to neo-liberal market-based capitalism. Equally, each is either a continuation of historic, indigenous and often ancestral systems, or frequently represents contemporary models of the economy, which may be unrecognisable or invisible to dominant economic understanding.

Semiotics is the science of uncovering the relations between objects, signs and their interpretive outcomes. However, as we argue elsewhere (22), this also represents a missing Eastern journey. Objects ground meaning. Signs help us to navigate them. Interpretations are the effects that meanings have on us and the world, as they shift, multiply and generate new meanings; bouncing off each other, like electrons in a nuclear field. In other words, semiotics has a south, a north and a west, but it misses the undergirding pre-signifier elements which emerge meanings from objects. We term these 'archetypes of signification', following the language of Jung's understanding of the psychological structures of the collective unconscious.

When we apply this logic to economics we begin to comprehend—on our journey—that there are prior questions that we need to ask in relation to human and real world objects, in order to make meaningful economic decisions about them and our choices. For example, picking up the indications in Table 7, alternative markets require us to ask: what is value and what is grace? When we journey into the economics of well-being, we need to ask: what is love and what is wealth? When we journey into the economics of co-operation, we need to ask: what is solidarity and what are rights? When we journey into the economics of the commons, we need to ask: what is nature and what is culture?

6.5.2. A Semiotic Economics Pilgrimium

In our opening chapter, reflecting back to Newman's original *The Idea of a University*, we commented that the pilgrimium is a place in which to journey, rather than one in which to be still and contemplate the eternal. Just as Newman had to discover his call in the journey towards creating the Catholic University of Ireland, as well as in his Sicilian illness—instead of within the security of Oriel College, Oxford—the pilgrimium of semiotic economics requires us to step out of our familiar spaces into uncharted (at least to us) territory.

Such a progression is depicted in the opening words of Dante's *Divine Comedy:* (in English translation) "In the middle of the journey of our life I found myself in a dark wood, where the straight way ahead was lost". The image of being lost in a wood and needing to find our way out is a familiar one of nightmares and fairy stories. But Dante's phrasing is surprising, when we take a second look. He does not say: "In the middle of the journey of life"; strikingly, he writes about "the journey of *our* life" (my emphasis). The journey of the soul, even through the seven circles of hell/heaven is a shared, collective one and a pilgrimage. We do not undertake the mythic, mystical and horrific journey as solitary, isolated and lone individuals, but in solidarity, collaboration and co-operatively, as a caravanserai, to use a different Eastern metaphor.

That said, the space of the pilgrimium through which the journey passes may not be physical. It will often be psychic and cognitive. Even so, the point that we are making, in referring to the Eastern pathway of semiotic economics, is that the cognitive is, primordially, dependent on the sub-structures of the psyche. Consequently, we can depict the framework of the semiotic economics journey. It has four basic steps, as part of its methodology, which can be generalised and specified, for example, in relation to Kingdom economics. These are:

- Identify the economics object e.g. for Kingdom (of God) economics: the spiritual gift-graces, or 'charisms' (GEN*E* grounding/Southern Realm).
- Uncover the cultural/ spiritual/ integral/archetypes of signification e.g. the (initial pre-conscious) emergent desire to enter into grace; and to discover the joy of sacrificial giving-away, as practical needs become clear (GEN*E* emergence/Eastern realm).
- Specify the sign/symbolic question (signifier) to be addressed e.g. how do we develop systems of economic sacrificing (GEN*E* navigation/Northern realm)?
- Effect the co-creation of local material interpretations e.g. take part in practices for cancelling debts, at global as well as personal scales (think local, act global, in the GEN*E* effects/Western Realm).

6.5.3. Journeying through the Biblical Quaternity Archetype

Previously, one of us, Bradley (ibid.) introduced the pattern of the Biblical Quaternity Archetype (BQA). Throughout this volume we have connected the idea of the communiversity to the models of the four worlds and the fourfold GEN*E*. Equally, when we examine the depth structure of the Judaeo-Christian scriptures we discover precisely the same fourfold pattern.

This is most immediately evident in the fact that the Second (New) Testament Gospels are (only) four in number: Luke, Mark, John and Matthew. These were selected for the canonical authorised text of the Bible—from the many accounts and collections of sayings of Jesus of Nazareth circulating in the 1st century CE—which was broadly settled by the end of the 2nd century. Furthermore, close examination of these texts reveals that they present four interlocking perspectives that specifically parallel the Jungian model of personality types, which is the basis for the four worlds/GEN*E*. Of course, this happened 1700 years before Jung and, in fact, develops a more ancient fourfold pattern of understanding humanity's place in the world, the origins of which are lost in the mists of time.

Looked at in this way the Gospels have a rather different order from that contained in the conventional Bible. Luke-Acts presents an intuitive-feeling (NF/Southern) mode that is grounded in an understanding of community. Equally, with a clear resonance for the pilgrimium, St Luke's two volumes tell the story of a journey in—to Jerusalem and the events surrounding Jesus of Nazareth's crucifixion and resurrection—and a journey out—to the ends of the known world—by the new community of the post-resurrection disciples of Jesus Christ. Then Mark's Gospel, which in reality is the Gospel of Peter, dictated to John Mark, presents a sensing-perceiving (SP/Eastern) mode that emerges from the immediacy of Jesus' encounters with the supernatural world. It, too, is organised around the pattern of journey, which St Luke borrowed from Mark's Petrine text, so that both South and East focus on what we here call the pilgrimium experience of communiversity.

In navigational terms, St John's Gospel presents an intuitive-thinking perspective (NT/Northern), which directs the reader on their faith journey through a series of signs, culminating, to close the first half of his narrative, in the raising of Lazarus and at the end of the 'book of suffering', the post-resurrection appearances of Christ. Finally, the Gospel of Matthew, with its emphasis on ethical behavior, much of which is drawn from the worlds of money and finance—unsurprisingly since, from tradition, Matthew was a tax-gatherer—offers a sensing-judging (SJ/Western) perspective.

As such, reading the Gospels in this light, the Northern and Western texts complete a pilgrimium journey around the GENEalogical cycle, where the final piece of the jigsaw is the Gospel which, in the dominant Western tradition, opens the New Testament. Perhaps we should not be surprised that a Western worldview had placed the Gospel of Matthew—with its practical focus on taking responsibility for changing behaviour, significantly in respect of money and possessions, paralleling the First (Old) Testament Pentateuch (Law of Moses), with the Beatitudes standing in for the Ten Commandments—at the forefront of the Christian scriptures.

But, correspondingly, if we read the Gospels in the order of the GENE—from Luke, through Mark, John and onto Matthew—we receive a quite different picture of the spiritual journey, from a literal journey to practical advice on the conduct of human behaviour and relationships. That is the model of the BQA, which parallels the Jungian pattern of personal temperaments, the four worlds and, crucially, the GENEalogical progression of the pilgrimium.

6.5.4. The recursive GENEalogy

There is, however, a further twist in the perspective that the BQA provides. In the largest representation of its cycle, from one Gospel to another, there is a recursive turning from Luke to Mark. From the sunny uplands of a joyful communitarian pilgrimium we are taken into a much darker world, where the journey is characterised by sacrifice and, even, a question-mark (sic) hanging over the resurrection of Jesus (if we allow the Gospel to finish with its original ending). Of course, the theme of servant leadership and sacrificial service is a vital aspect of the Lukan narrative too, but it is not the brooding context that it is for St Mark (i.e. St Peter).

That said, taking the order of the BQA, we can turn back to the way of a present hope through the navigational signs contained in John. This leads us onward in our pilgrimium to the ethical teaching of Matthew and a world in which we are able to reinterpret the role of money and possessions in an upside-down way, where it is far more blessed to give than to receive. So, the journey concludes or rather, the map for our life-journey indicates an ethic of the Kingdom of Heaven.

However, we need to take the recursion between Luke and John via Mark seriously. If we look to the even greater cycle of salvation history as understood in the Christian tradition, we discover a continually repeating pattern. The same is true when we cast our gaze in a microscopic way into the individual narratives of each Gospel or, indeed, countless passages throughout the Jewish as well as the Second Testament scriptures. The well-understood pattern of biblical salvation history is also a fourfold sequence: from Creation, through Fall, to Redemption and Salvation.

This pattern can equally be applied to the four worlds, so that Creation and the worlds of community and nature are tied together. Similarly, we can see the connections between Fall, culture and spirituality; then, we may link Redemption, science, systems and technology. Finally, there are parallels between our understandings of Salvation and the worlds of effecting politics and enterprise.

Nevertheless, what the pattern of biblical salvation history points to is a break in the flow of the journey. We can depict this in a variety of ways. There is a natural tendency for humankind to attempt to circumvent the GENEalogical cycle. This involves turning from community to politics and markets before it has experienced the releasing of spiritual consciousness and discovered the complexity of navigational systems, through which to co-create new enterprises. Equally, we can talk of the South trying to turn West before it turns East and thence North.

In terms of salvation history, this is the repeating biblical pattern of a Fall taking place. It involves all people; from the mythic everyman, Adam, to the very real and human St Peter, trying to take the easy way out of avoiding pain in order to reap the fruits of success. This is, again, another way of looking at the pilgrimium, as a reGENErative experience.

The collective journey of pilgrimage within the communiversity is one that will inevitably exhibit an initial effort to take the line of least resistance. Communiversity developers will be prone to mount a path to a fix enterprise or, as is sometimes commented, in respect of entrepreneurs, to 'storm the castle'. However, the BQA and recursive GENEalogy indicate that such an attempt will be futile. There is no escaping the pattern of salvation history if we are to genuinely seek the Eastern path of the pilgrimium, entering into a consciousness of the painful aspects of spirituality, by which to connect our communities to their navigational compasses. We must first explore our needs before we develop systems that can utilise our strengths.

Throughout this depiction of pilgrimium—from the developmental path of the Celts out of Africa, through the co-operative research of John Heron and the conscious evolution of Rudolf Steiner, Nishida, Nonaka and Takeuchi—we have seen a spiral at work. But the significance of the pilgrimium lies in the way in which the journeying community can hold its members to account, to seek the Eastern way. It is a way that is so often missing in social science, in development, research and enterprise, yet it is vital if we are to develop an economics that is true to the meanings of humankind. To do so is to visit not only a 'road less travelled' but one where we expect our needs and weaknesses to be laid bare, before we can journey further, guided by the compass points of our navigational systems.

6.6. CONCLUSION: RE-GENE-RATIVE PILGRIMIUM

We have now traced a path from integral development to a re-GENE-rative pilgrimium, spanning integral research and development, enterprise and economy. Specifically:

- Through INTEGRAL DEVELOPMENT you build on the **Story of our Time**, as a journey from the mythic to the developmental, whereby no living societal myth can be pinned down to one particular phase of its inherent development. It is a moving finger that writes and having written, moves on.
- Via INTEGRAL RESEARCH you undertake **Cooperative Inquiry,** whereby conceptual knowledge arises out of lived 'being-in-the-world', restoring meaning and mystery to human experience, so the world is experienced as a sacred place.
- Through INTEGRAL ENTERPRISE, specifically turning human resources into **Conscious Evolution** you transcend the boundary of the old self into a new self by acquiring a new context, a new view of the world, an evolved consciousness.
- Via an INTEGRAL ECONOMY, specifically promoting a culture based and spirituality via **Semiotic Economics**, whereby principles for the improvement of present lives can be culled from cultural and spiritual traditions and re-articulated in ways that mobilise the people to take responsibility for social change.

We now turn to the re-GENE-rative pilgrimium in practice.

6.7. REFERENCES

1 Schieffer A and Lessem R (2014) *Integral Development: Transforming the Potential of Individuals, Organisations and Societies.* Abingdon. Routledge.

2 Bradley, T (2019) *Innovating Arts, within the Cultural-Economy nexus of the Liverpool City-Region: Towards a Communiversity, using the Biblical Quaternity Archetype model.* Unpublished PhD thesis. Johannesburg. Da Vinci Institute.

3 Van der Post, L (1955) *The Dark Eye of Africa.* Cape Town. Lowery Press.

4 Van der Post, L (1976) *Jung and the Story of our Time.* London. Vintage.

5 Gebser, J (1985) *The Ever-Present Origin.* Ohio. Ohio University Press.

6 Cunliffe, B (2018) *The Ancient Celts.* Oxford. Oxford University Press.

7 Bradley, I (2018) *Following the Celtic Way – a new assessment of Celtic Christianity.* London. Darton, Longman and Todd.

8 Robinson, M (2015) *Rediscovering the Celts: true witness from Western shores.* Birmingham. ForMission Publishing.

9 Sellner, E.C (2006) *Wisdom of the Celtic Saints.* United States. Bog Walk Press.

10 Bede, St (2008) *The Ecclesiastical History of the English People. Oxford World Classics.* Oxford. Oxford University Press.

11 Kruta, V. (2005) The Celts: History and Civilisation. London. Hanchette Illustrated.

12 Heron J (1997) *Cooperative Inquiry.* London. Sage

13 Reason P and Bradbury H (2006) *Handbook of Action Research.* London. Sage

14 Heron J (1994) *Feeling and Personhood.* London. Sage.

15 Steiner R (1977) *Towards Social Renewal.* Springfield. Rudolf Steiner Press

16 Wilken F (1982) *The Liberation of Capital.* London. Heineman

17 Pirsig R (1974) *Zen and the Art of Motorcycle Maintenance.* New York. William Morrow

18 Nishida K (1992) *Inquiry into the Good. Connecticut.* Yale University Press

19 Polanyi M (1998) *Personal Knowledge.* Abingdon. Routledge

20 Nonaka I and Takeuchi H (1995) *The Knowledge Creating Company.* Oxford. Oxford University Press

21 Polanyi, K (1944). *The Great Transformation – origins of our time.* New York. Farrar & Reinhart.

22 Bradley, T (2019) Introducing the Fourth Way of Semiotic Economics. Chapter 2, in Lessem, R, Bradley, T, Malik, A & Oshodi, B. *Islamic to Integral Finance.* Manchester. Beacon Books.

Chapter 7

Re-GENE-rative Pilgrimium in Practice

Pax Africana - Akhuwat - Geoculture - Liver Birdsong

The sacred circle, the cosmogenic round, the wheel of the arising and passing away of the created world and all its manifest forms is like a symphonic composition arranged in three movements: prelude, crescendo and finale: emergence, fulfilment and dissolution. Mythologies of the cosmogenic round trumpet the coming into being of humanity and the world as we know it from a from a transcendent ground of being; then they score the complex relationship between humanity, this ordinary world of space and time and the great mystery of being; and finally the herald the dissolution of this phenomenal world back into the transcendent mystery from which it emerged.

Clyde Ford, *The Hero with an African Face*

Self Discovery in Nature: Monastic life originated in the human heart. It started the moment God said, "I am one, let me be many". God desired to express God's self in creation; *the search for truth means self-discovery in nature and through nature.*

Seeking Soulidarity: There is a spiritual semblance to every travel you take, *leaving your comfort zone behind.* Making your *halal* (rightful) living is an *ibadah* (worship) and travelling to another land (*hijrah*) to find a livelihood is also considered worship.

Manifesto on Geoculture: The goal of geomancy is to provide our modern culture with methods of understanding the flow of life forces and with *methods of perceiving the hitherto less known dimensions of existence.*

7.1. INTRODUCTION/SOUTH-BENEDICTINE MONASTERY/CHINYIKA COMMUNITY

7.1.1. Searching for Answers to the Questions of Life

A Place Where Spiritual and Intellectual Virtues Might Bloom

We now turn from theory to practice, beginning this practical chapter on the Re-GENE-rative pilgrimium with the journey of co-author Father Anselm Adodo (1), also a Trans4m Communiversity Associate, from Benedictine Monastery to a Pax Africana Communiversity with a view to communitalism (further elaborated on in chapter 11):

> *"I did not join the monastery because of a sentimental fear of hell, or due to any puritan's tendency or childish piety. It was based on my belief that the monastery might just be a place where my spiritual and intellectual virtues might bloom. On my first explorative visit to the Benedictine Monastery in Edo State, I knew I had come to the right place."*

Perched on a hill one thousand feet above sea level, St Benedict monastery was founded by a group of Irish missionary monks, with the aim of spreading the monastic tradition to West Africa. They chose Edo State, geographically located right in the middle of Nigeria, linking the north, east, west and south. Today, the St Benedict Monastery is one of the most culturally diverse monastic communities in Africa, representing 15 different ethnic groups in Nigeria.

The Monastic Context : Vital to the Evolution of a Transformed Worldview

When Anselm joined the Catholic Benedictine Monastery as an 18-year-old boy, it was like an adventure, a fairy tale, an 'Alice-in-Wonderland' journey into the unknown. He was searching for answers to questions about life. A monastery is a cultural unit with age-long traditions, practices and way of life. It is a place where a group of people live together in a community to devote time to prayer and meditation. The Catholic Church has a long history of monasticism dating back to the pre-Christian era.

For him, the monastic context was vital to the evolution of his spirituality and transformed worldview and was the foundation of his work as a social innovator. As a young monk, he studied church history, spirituality, scripture and read many of the spiritual classics. Such a daily immersion in the spiritual classics and the spiritual thoughts of others had a transformational effect on his thinking about God, others and the world. Anselm was also assigned to various offices at different times: as a gardener, farm manager, assistant liturgy director and assistant bursar. The bursar is the general coordinator of the monastery's economy. In 1992, he took his final vows (a life-long commitment to live in the monastery as a monk) at the age of 21. For the next seven years, he was involved in further intensive studies.

The Story of Ewu Monastery and the Search for the Truth

In 2004, after 17 years of living in the monastery as a monk, he was privileged to be assigned the task of editing a book that tells the story of the St Benedict Monastery, as part of the celebration to mark the silver jubilee of the existence of the monastic community of Ewu. In the book titled, *The Story of Ewu Monastery: Silver Jubilee Reflections,* Anselm wrote:

"Monastic life did not start in the desert lands of Egypt, or in the fertile green farms of Canaan, or in the Garden of Eden. Monastic life did not originate in the high mountains of the Himalayas, or on the holy mount of Horeb. Monastic life originated in the human heart. It started the moment God, the almighty and all-powerful said, 'I am one, let me be many'. God desired to express God's self in creation."

In his study of philosophy, he was fascinated by the unending search of human beings from different traditions, cultures, races and religions for truth. The history of humanity is simply the history of human search for knowledge of the truth. What, then, is the truth? How is truth to be found? Is truth absolute or relative? What is reality? Aside from philosophy and theology, he also made a foray into the social sciences and studied anthropology, sociology and history of development.

Meeting the 'Angel' in the Bush: This Plant Will Eradicate Viral Infections

What, then, was Anselm searching for on the morning of November 2nd 1995, on a lonely pathway in the monastery's farmland? Was he was searching for the truth? What was the 'truth' doing in a bush at 7:30 in the morning? He was strolling quietly on the lonely farmland, fully alert and listening to the rhythm of the swaying trees, the chirping of the colourful birds and the beatings of his heart. There, on an open plot of farmland was a little girl, dressed gorgeously in a bright golden gown, truly angelic, playing all alone in the open farming plot of land. It was usual for mothers to bring their children to the farm. However, it was very unusual and forbidden, to leave one's child out of eyesight and very unusual to dress a child so gorgeously when going to the farm.

Anselm moved closer and asked the child, who looked like a four-year-old, "Where is your mother?" Silence. He walked around and raised his voice saying "hello" many times. No answer. Then the little girl smiled and held out a hand—a beautiful, innocent hand—in which she was holding a freshly uprooted weed. Of course, he was not going to accept a piece of familiar fresh weed from a beautiful four-year-old in a strange location. Then she spoke: *"This plant will eradicate viral infections in a sufferer who uses it".*

The Gospel of St John: You Will Know the Truth and the Truth Will Set You Free

For Anselm, his search for truth meant self-discovery in nature and through nature. This is the key to happiness, health and wholeness. Every day he watched as people died from common diseases that could have been remedied by herbs growing around them. People—*my people*—perish, he thought, for want of knowledge. His people then needed to embrace knowledge, so they could experience freedom. This was how he interpreted the quotation from the Gospel of St John: "You will know the truth and the truth will set you free." His inner calling was to explore knowledge, not just for the sake of exploration, but also as a tool for innovation, inner freedom, healing, transformation and self-discovery. Truth heals.

The village of Ewu had a rich tradition of medical healing. There were traditional healers everywhere and traditional shrines could be sighted in many corners of the village. There was a mission hospital and a government hospital in the village, but the majority of the people patronised traditional healers.

Pax Herbals as an Antidote to Witchcraft, Sorcery, Ritualism

Herbal medicine was associated with witchcraft, sorcery, ritualism and all sorts of fetish practices. Because herbal medicine was associated with paganism, African-Christians secretly patronised traditional healers and the educated elite and religious figures did not want to be associated in any way with traditional African medicine. At that time (1996), for a religious figure, especially a Catholic priest, to be openly propagating traditional medicine was a taboo of the highest order.

He then conceived the idea of Pax Herbals as a tool for changing the concept of traditional medicine from an esoteric practice by mysterious, old men to that of a useful, profitable, rational and explicable venture in this context. The goal of Pax Herbals was to change the face of African traditional medicine. Although Pax Herbals was established in 1996, it was not registered as a private liability company until 2002. The company is officially described as *a Catholic research centre for scientific identification, conservation, utilisation and development of African medicinal plants.*

Some of its stated objectives, as stated on its website (Paxherbals.net) are:

- To serve as a centre for genuine African holistic healing that blends the physical and the spiritual aspects of the human person.
- To become a model comprehensive health care centre where the western (North, West) and traditional (South, East) systems of healing are creatively blended.
- To be an example of how proper utilisation of Traditional Medicine can promote grassroots primary culturally acceptable, affordable, relevant health care systems.
- To disseminate knowledge of the health benefits of African medicinal plants through documentation, publications, seminars and workshops.
- To carry out researches into ancient African healing systems with a view to modernising them and making them available to the wider world through education.
- To demystify African Traditional Medicine and purge it of elements of occultism, fetishism and superstition and promote its globally acceptable rational use.
- To be a truly indigenous herbal phyto-medicine centre that combines respect for nature and community with wealth creation.

Communitalism: Communis, Spiritus, Scientia, Economia

In contrast, the foreign gods—that all too often go along with conventional medicine—include materialism, consumerism, neo-liberalism and preference for a Western way of life over a traditional way of life. For Adodo, Africa's romance with this has been disastrous, despite the obvious benefits, such as globalisation, education and modernisation.

Some seventeen years after he established Pax Herbals, while on our Trans4m PhD doctoral program, Father Adodo has taken a systematic approach to looking at the imbalances in his society, focusing on a particular community in Edo state and proposing solutions. This led to the theory of *communitalism*, a theory built on the four dimensions of Pax: *communis, spiritus, scientia* and *economia*. The four Pax's taken together make Pax Africana, which expresses the integral nature of life. Each is associated with a female *Orisa*, a mythic goddess. The four are brought together as a commune, a community of knowledge, bridging the gap between community, spirit, nature and reason.

We now turn from Nigeria to Zimbabwe.

7.1.2. The Chinyika Story

A Microcosm of a Macrocosm

The colonisation of Zimbabwe, for the primary instigators of this Chinyika story, Dr Paul (Chidara) Muchineripi (2)—son of the local chief and his longstanding friend and Human Resource Director Dr Steve Kada (both Trans4m PhD graduates)—by the British had the profoundly debilitating effect of an imposed and dominant 'western' conventional economic system. From 1980, the country was subjected to restructuring according to exogenous 'western' or indeed 'northern' thinking and the exogenous economic philosophies that prevailed. The indigenous communities under the dominant colonial system were shaken from their cultural roots. The country evolved into a newly colonial political and economic system, thereby falling under exogenous, crudely capitalist sway.

The state of poverty in the Chinyika locality is historically rooted, therefore, in the inflexible economic structure; a dual formal-informal economic system, the coexistence of what was perceived as a 'superior' white (formal) and 'inferior' black (informal) economic systems. In pre-independence Zimbabwe more generally, the rich white elite, who resided on the railway line cities, like Salisbury and Bulawayo, enjoyed superior sets of conditions to those in the hinterland of the rural areas like Chinyika. Chinyika, locally and the country as a whole nationally, being a microcosm of the international and continental social and economic structures, found themselves embodying the global reality of dependency.

Towards Social and Economic Transformation in Southern Africa

Chidara and Steve had been spending hours and hours together during their masters programme (Masters in Social and Economic Transformation), which was run by Trans4m in South Africa. In the first decade of the new millennium as such, travelling from Zimbabwe together to South Africa and lodging in a small hotel room, it was as if they were back to their 1980 college days when they had been studying together. History was repeating itself; from two young men to two old men replaying their lives.

Furthermore, it was revealed to Steve that Chidara's wife's totem was *hwesa/mbeva* or mouse, which was also his African totem. They began to review their relational status. Chidara became Steve's *mukuwasha* brother-in-law because his wife was Steve's sister in terms of their culture. It made him happy that his 'sister' was married into the Karanga royal family since Chidara is Gutu Chief designate. What became of even greater significance was that the totem *mbeva*—the mouse—is that of the Lemba (or Baremba) people. Chidara's wife Nakirai is Lemba and her whole tribe currently live in Gutu, where Chinyika is based.

It dawned on Steve through providence that he had been walking on the road to his ancestral linkages. Steve's home is in Mutasa on the eastern side of Zimbabwe where his original birthplace is in Katerere, the land of the Hwesa Mbeva, who are a group of Lemba descendants. In December 2009, Ronnie-becoming-Samanyanga visited Zimbabwe, together with Trans4m's co-founder Alexander Schieffer, to come and meet the Chinyika community. While they were interacting with the Chinyika people, the MP for the Gutu area visited the gathering, to introduce himself and address the people. He however later said that his main mission was to meet his brother, the white Jew who was present. After this, further investigations by Steve led to more findings regarding the assertion by the Wa-Remba MP that his people were black Jews. They realised that Professor Tudor Parfitt from the School of African and Oriental Studies in London had carried out extensive research and written a book—*The Lost Ark of the Covenant* (3)—about the Wa-Remba in Zimbabwe, especially those in Gutu, Shurugwi and Limpopo.

The Lost Ark of the Covenant: Ngoma Lungundu

Professor Parfitt's research (which has taken him many years) was based on the search for the lost ark of the covenant of the Jews. As such he researched into the history of the Wa-Remba or Baremba and their ark—the *Ngoma Lungundu*—which is said to have been brought into Zimbabwe and hidden in a mountain cave in the southern part of the country. Parfitt ultimately stumbled upon the *Ngoma Lungundu* stored in the archives of the Harare museum and announced his findings. What followed was a political, theological and academic commotion over the alleged authenticity of the discovery. The significance for Steve is that he now finds himself having the right to assert who he is locally in the Zimbabwean nation and also in a global context.

In relation to Chinyika, the *Ngoma Lungundu*, besides being an artefact, has a spiritual power of renewal for the Lemba and Chinyika community in Gutu. This is an opportunity for the local community to look outside and connect with a global platform. While the *Ngoma Lungundu* 'drum' (ark of the covenant) lies in peace and serenity in the museum, in Harare, it is calling out loudly for the Lemba and the world via Kada, to be reawakened to the values of personhood and to the integration of indigenous and exogenous knowledge. It is providing Southern African knowledge-creating communities with a challenge to revisit their history, religion and intellectual values for purposes of creating an integrated local and global community.

Moved by the Suffering of his Own People: Revisiting the Source of Food Security

This is, for Kada, what all individuals, organisations and nations should be concerned with: acknowledging the universal sovereignty of the Creator and the practical humaneness and value sharing of southern African *ubuntu*. Africa, from its heart, was privileged with the quality of brotherhood and human passion which it must share with the rest of the world. Out of the Chinyika community, moreover, in Kada's words, a son was raised from the house of the Gutu chieftainship and was moved by the suffering of his own people. He woke up to the call of his ancestors to save his people from the scourge of hunger and poverty.

Chidara, then, who had hitherto become a successful business person and management educator, had a wakeup call from his slumber of individual success, prompted by his participation in the masters programme in social and economic transformation and then responded to his 'father's voice'. More importantly, awareness gripped him and reminded him of his responsibility to his people as the son of a chief. Emotively aroused, he initially decided to feed the people who were starving in Chinyika by buying bags of mealie meal (corn) and grain and distributing these to them.

While in the process of facing this challenge and responding to his 'father's voice' to take care of his people, Chidara enrolled on the Trans4m Masters (MSET), as indicated above, unknowingly together with Steve in 2005. That was the beginning of the establishment of the Chinyika Community Development Project. Chidara then reconnected with the voice that called his people to revisit the source of their food security in the past, the nutritious food and meals that came out of the sweat of their labour; a community that never starved. Today, 300,000 villagers in and around Chinyika, some of whom had been starving a decade ago, are fully food secure.

We now turn from 'south' to 'east' on the pilgrim's way, for a distinct change in tone as the two worlds mark out their different pilgrims' intentions.

7.2. AKHUWAT: AN EASTERN CASE OF PAKISTANI SOULIDARITY

7.2.1. My Source Being Clay Moulded out of a Soil Rich with Ancient Wisdom

For Aneeqa Malik (3), co-author of *Akhuwat - Islamic Finance: A Case of a Solidarity Economy*, a participant on our PHD (Process of Holistic Development) programme, a question arose after emigrating from Pakistan to a new land (the UK) and facing the challenges that came with it.

"Although I spent most of my life outside my country of birth and origin, my soul remained attached to my source-identity, the source being my clay moulded out of a soil rich with ancient wisdom and heavily impregnated with mystical lyricism. The lyrics continue to reverberate in the inner silence of my soul—the echoes of the silent wisdom of my Eastern truth. For I grew up absorbing the soul-wisdom of my soil, which to this date reverberates with the wisdom of the mystical giants who formed the Islamic view of my region, Pakistan, through poetry and Sufi preaching which came from a deep inner place."

From an Islamic viewpoint and in the South Asian context, the Sufi saints of the region were the people who contemplated ontological Islamic philosophy, thereafter consciously embedding and embodying cultural values and the wisdom locked in that particular soil. Hence, Aneeqa terms it the 'soul-wisdom of the soil', which she believes she is carrying within her.

7.2.2. The Regime of Selfish Wealth Had To Be Razed

Dr Muhammad Amjad Saqib, founder of the world's largest 'economic brother-hood', Akhuwat, or more conventionally termed interest-free micro-finance bank, joined the elite Civil Service of Pakistan in 1985. Having stood out as a public servant, just as his career was to move towards higher echelons, he resigned in 2003 with the intent of facilitating societal change through Akhuwat—which had already been founded by him in 2001 and had meanwhile started taking strides towards the force it was to become.

The salient feature of his public service career—one that perhaps changed the course of his life—was his last assignment as general manager of Punjab Rural Support Programme (PRSP). It was here that he had the opportunity to closely examine the various initiatives of poverty alleviation, education management, participatory development and conventional microfinance. This made him realise that 'something different had to be done'. This desire to do 'something different', something more effective as panacea for the poor, spurred him on to conceive and introduce an interest-free microfinance model based on the idea of *mawakhat* or brotherhood.

7.2.3. Create Brotherhood Between Emigrants (*Muhajireen*) & Helpers (*Ansar*)

Akhuwat eventually launched in March 2001. Modestly and discreetly, they started conferring small loans without interest to the poor while working from within a mosque. They had decided not to run it as a business. Akhuwat has a virtue-based approach to poverty alleviation and had designed its various social and economic development activities as an expression of solidarity with the marginalised and disadvantaged groups of people. Akhuwat's vision of development is known as *mawakhat*, meaning 'solidarity'—a paradigm of justice and compassion.

Mawakhat refers to the creation of brotherhood between emigrants *muhajireen* and the helpers (*ansar*). Prophet Muhammad established brotherhood between the *muhajireen* and *ansar*. He paired off each *muhajir* with one *ansar* and declared them brothers. The generous *ansar* gave over one half of their wealth to their new brothers so that they could live comfortably in Medina. As such, Amjad's call was to fight the biggest challenges facing Pakistan: poverty elimination and reviving the spirit of *mawakhat*/solidarity endowment. In doing so, he successfully devised a localised financial solution which veritably came out of the pages of Islamic history and the Prophetic tradition of *mawakhat*. This model of finance has been helping Pakistan in two ways: on the one hand, it is providing access to finance for the poorest of the poor of the society and on the other hand, the resources provided to the poor have been conducive in helping the growth of local micro-enterprises at a grassroots level, thereby generating a self-sufficient economy for Akhuwat's community through a process of metamorphosis, a latter-day *hajj*.

Muslims of Medina embraced the Muslim migrants who settled in Medina, leaving everything they had behind for the sake of God, with love and sincerity. They (the *ansar*) did not and would not, begrudge any kind of help they could offer to them. However, the migrants were not familiar with Medina's climate, customs and working conditions. They did not bring anything with them when leaving Mecca. For this reason, they needed to be familiarised with Medina's working conditions and with the Muslims of Medina, who came to be called the *ansar* (the helpers) because they offered all kinds of help to them. Therefore, the Prophet Muhammad gathered the *ansar* and the migrants together five months after migrating to Medina. He appointed 90 Muslims, 45 of whom were from the ansar and the other 45 from the migrants, as brothers. This is the spirit and philosophy of *mawakhat*.

7.2.4. Journeying of the Soul or Pilgrimage as a Communal Metamorphosis

In Amjad's words, as such:

"For us, the resonance of journeying through stages of self and communal metamorphosis is all too familiar with the journeying of the soul or pilgrimage (hajj). The circumambulation of the soul resonates with the physical circumambulation around the Ka'bah, the ultimate spiritual journey for any Muslim."

Circulating around the Ka'bah represents the idea of oneness. In regards to social life, it means not to leave unity and to try to maintain it. Its meaning regarding individual life contains deep truths. Specifically, just as the sky has seven layers; man has seven souls. Each revolution around the Ka'bah represents a phase, a stage; man covers a phase and is elevated up to the seventh sky, above the material realm. It also means to rise from the lowest realm of the soul, which has seven realms, to the highest one—that is, from *nafs al-ammarah* (soul commanding to evil) to *nafs al-mutma'innah* (tranquil self), from the animal life to the spiritual life. It is a kind of worship taken from the order of the universe. The planets rotate around the sun, the electrons around the nucleus, the moth around the candle; rotating around such a centre means allegiance to love. This cyclical procession is called *tawaf* (circumambulation), the ritual of taking seven rounds around the holy Ka'bah.

7.2.5. Acts of Kindness to Our Fellows Sets Solidarity Impulse in Motion

Tafa: Attain to the Summit of a Thing by Spiralling Around It

The Arabic verb *tafa* in fact, from which the term for the circumambulation *(tawaf)* is derived, has the meaning to 'attain to the summit of a thing by spiralling around it'. Hence, it is thought that through the *tawaf*, the pilgrim participates with the angels in their circumambulation of the Divine Throne. This is so because cosmologically, the Ka'bah is regarded as the reflection of the archetypal Divine House in the seventh (or fourth) Heaven above and beyond which stands the Throne of Allah, around which the angels are constantly rotating.

The two complementary ideas of circularity and centrality are involved in the establishment of a *haram*, a sanctuary, where the physical (man) meets the spiritual (Divine). For Saqib and Malik, this represents the solidarity impulse which pulsates in the centre (Ka'bah/sanctuary) and the cyclical procession around it spirals down as the Divine bounty *(barakah)* transcends in circularity.

Barakah Rounds: Acts of Kindness Set the Solidarity Impulse in Motion

The Arabic word *barakah* (Hebrew/Jewish: *berekah*) is the establishment of divine goodness in something; what it exudes cannot be sensed by people, nor can it be outwardly quantified, nor is it limited by anything, but rather, something with *barakah* in it has an unexplainable increase and benefit in it from Allah. An example is when one gives charity, *barakah* enters one's remaining wealth such that it increases in benefit without increasing in the actual amount. For Akhuwat, any journey (*hijrah*/migration) one takes to achieve God-proximity and recompense through one's acts of kindness towards fellow beings sets this solidarity impulse in motion.

In fact, the loan disbursement ceremonies are held inside sanctuaries (mosques, churches and temples), raising awareness with a renewed purpose, as the whole purpose of creating religious spaces in most Abrahamic religions was to congregate communally in them for various reasons; from prayer gatherings to discussing matters of communal concern and benefit. In doing so, Akhuwat has demonstrated the belief that without action (*amal*), knowledge (*ilm*) is of little use on its own. Through this distinctive model of *mawakhat* (solidarity), Akhuwat has successfully

215

generated a solidarity bond by raising awareness of self-and-community through the practical example of the historic Prophetic tradition of *Hijrat-un-Nabwi* (the Prophet's symbolic emigration from Mecca to Medina).

7.2.6. *Hijrah*: My Spiritual Quest Continues

As Akhuwat's philosophy of *mawakhat* was born of *hijrah* (migration) to another land, this, for Aneeqa, was the main theme of her transformational journey too. In his Urdu book *Kamyab Loug (Successful People of Chiniot)*, Amjad Saqib writes about migration as an imperative to finding one's livelihood after travelling to another land. For Amjad, there is a spiritual semblance to every travel one takes, leaving one's comfort zone behind. As per Islamic religious tradition, moreover, making one's *halal* (rightful) living is considered as an *ibadah* (worship) too, as well as travelling to another land (*hijrah*) to find one's livelihood.

For us, the wayfarers on the wisdom of the soul path, we believe what lies at the core of a community's well-being (SOUL-idarity) is the well-being of the soul. It is the awakening to the true identity of the self. The true Self has been patiently awaiting our attention, but we have been so occupied with the drama of the little self that we have not even noticed that there is something far greater which is our true nature. The superficial aspect of each of us, which is the cause of divisive ideas such as I, me, mine, yours, is the source of all of our pain and confusion. When we venture beyond our little self, we discover something far greater, something that has been given names such as Self, God, Allah, Brahma, Atman, Tao, or Buddha-nature. But no matter what we choose to call it, this is our true home, the source of the greatest bliss, the greatest peace and the greatest understanding.

Akhuwat is a Message of Equal Partnership

For Amjad, this transformation in (any) society, but Pakistan in his context, comes by extending *mawakhat* to one's community. Akhuwat is a message of equal partnership—a vision of an ideal society, where there exists no divide between the wealthy (haves) and the poor (have-nots). Ever since Amjad's engagement with inter- and intra-communal work, what he found most interesting and often fascinating is the microbial nature of human communities, similar to the concept of community ecology in plant and animal ecology. Although our thicker communal concentration in urban spaces has now detached us from the ecology of nature, this trans-migration has made us human beings more brazen than mineral; hence, the chemical imbalance has rendered us barren from the inside.

Now deeply immersed in the spirit of *mawakhat*—a spiritual paradigm of solidarity—this solidarity impulse is the transcendental spirituality amongst communities. This impulse, moreover, is transformational, doing its rounds from one community to another, generating virtuous circles. This is apparent in Saqib's depiction of *mawakhat*, whereby this solidarity impulse originating from the holy city of Medina is now doing rounds in Akhuwat's Pakistani community of 'Akhuwateers' (its family of borrowers, donors, volunteers and institutional ecosystem).

In fact, for biologists, analogously as such, microbial communities are defined as multi-species assemblages, in which organisms live together in a contiguous environment and interact with each other. Microbes strongly interacting with each other in a microenvironment comprise a local community. As such, the complex nature of microbes affects the biogeochemical transformation of communities and how energy flows through them. Now, because microbes possess mechanisms for the horizontal transfer of genetic information, the metagenome may also be considered as a community property. In Akhuwat, then, the emergent quality of its solidarity impulse creates virtuous circles of benevolence, as per the '*barakah* rounds'.

What, for Saqib and for Akhuwat, does this more generally involve?

7.2.7. *Ishq – Ilm – Amal – Akhuwat*

We conclude this 'eastern' perspective on the developmental pilgrimium with Amjad's words that reflect his deep love and compassion for his country and his people, with a deep longing to find a cure for its many societal ailments. For the path of compassion which leads to soul transformation starts from the invocation of *ishq* (divine love), as repeatedly expressed by him.

Ishq is an Arabic word—also used in Urdu, as well as many other languages—that means 'love'. The word is related to *ashiqah*; a vine. The common belief is that when love takes root in the heart of a lover, everything other than God is effaced. As love is the source of creation (transcendence) and the real sustenance of all beings, if man knows how to give it—to the world around him as sympathy, as kindness, as service—he supplies to all the food for which every soul hungers. *Ishq*/love then is the driving force transmutating in the heart of a believer, igniting the flame which translates into a form of supreme knowledge *(ilm)*.

In Islam, *ilm is not confined to the acquisition of knowledge only, but it also embraces socio-political and moral aspects.* Knowledge is not mere information; it requires the believers to act upon their beliefs and commit themselves to the goals which Islam aims to attain. The next stage after *ilm* is *amal*—putting into action the knowledge acquired through good deeds, for originality of thought combined with action *(amal)*, for Amjad, can transform the destinies of nations. Finally, through Akhuwat, thousands of people have been granted loans and no interest is taken on these loans. This is a splendid beginning indeed towards interest-free banking. The compassionate seek the compassionate and they are able to find each other. At this point, at its final stage, it arrives home by grounding itself in the community.

In Akhuwat's case, this is its community of Akhuwateers who have been travelling the path of *mawakhat* from *ishq* to *ilm* to performing *amal* and finally, grounding all the knowledge accumulated on the path to practise communal solidarity with renewed SOUL-idarity. We now turn from 'east' to 'north' and from our fellow travellers in Pakistan, Nigeria and Zimbabwe to Slovenia, in the heart of Europe.

7.3. SLOVENIA: REDISCOVERING THE CONSCIOUSNESS OF NATURE

7.3.1. Healing the Earth

In the beginning of the 1980s, Slovenian artist Marko Pogačnik (4), with whom we recently became associated through our citizens' initiative on Integral Green Slovenia, started to search for a more sensitive, heart-oriented approach to ecology as an alternative to the head-oriented approach of modern science. He realised that ancient cultures knew a holistic approach to the landscape—what is known in China as Feng Shui, Vastu in India and Geomancy in Europe. Since then, he set out to develop an updated approach to geomancy as a form of holistic ecology. Translated into modern language, Geomancy means 'interpreting the Earth and environment as a multidimensional organism'.

To be practical, he initiated the Healing the Earth Project, dealing with blockades and traumas that the modern, anthropocentric civilisation has inflicted upon the Earth and its beings. For this purpose he invented 'lithopuncture', a kind of earth acupuncture consisting of systems of stone pillars with engraved signs called 'cosmograms'. Their purpose is to establish a non-verbal communication with the consciousness of a given place and its beings. His best-known project is the lithopuncture system located on both sides of the border between the Republic of Ireland and Northern Ireland, created in 1993 as a peace project preceding the actual peace process which started a year later.

7.3.2. Back to Earth, Our Home Planet

The present-day high tide of global awareness, according to Pogačnik, is an outcome of the efforts of many people worldwide to comprehend the earthly cosmos as a complex unity, searching for creative ways to embody this new approach in their lives. However, we can go no further towards making the Earth our global home if we do not set out, once and for all, to abandon our egocentric attitudes towards our evolution and to act as a civilisation in tune with *Gaia*, as Earth consciousness.

But instead of functioning as a global network of mutual support between nations and religious communities, globalisation, as currently practised by our civilisation, exploits the cultural and social differences between the peoples of the earth to promote the profitability of global corporations. The unimaginable masses of money, for example, which have travelled around the planet in the last few decades, represent a serious threat to the stability of the Earth. For the most part, this is not money grounded in real goods or creative actions, or, at least, in gold bars lying in the cellars of national banks, but instead it represents, metaphorically and psychologically, a gigantic amount of mental energy that goes by the name of finance. Finance has by and large lost its relation to the reality of life and yet is the cause of many destructive actions on Earth, among others the dangerous developments in weapon production and the unlimited enrichment of individuals and elite groups.

When seen in the context of changes on the Earth, the apparently catastrophic events, whether in the realm of finance, economics, or social systems, also have a positive face. The key lies in the concept of transformation. Transformation is not a simple linear change. It demands that something which is out of the cosmic order to break down to give place to the new. In effect, according to Pogačnik, we are today facing a recycling process on the level of civilisation.

7.3.3. Towards Geoculture: The Slovenian School of Geomancy

In his *Manifesto on Geoculture* (5), Marko Pogačnik states:

"Over the last decades we have been witnessing the following steps being made on a global level towards a new culture tuned to the essence of the Earth:

A new ecological consciousness and movement represents the first basic step, signalling the will of humanity to change its attitude towards the Earth planet.

The next step involves diverse efforts to create an awareness of the multidimensional nature of the Earth and her creation, including human beings as part of earthly cosmos. Out of these efforts the art and experimental science of geomancy is developing as a form of holistic ecology. The goal of geomancy is to provide our modern culture with methods of understanding the flow of life forces and with methods of perceiving the hitherto less known dimensions of existence.

The present ecological and economic crisis confronting our civilisation demands a third step, to move further ahead on this path and create a kind of partner culture upon the planet. We need to rediscover and cultivate the love-based dimensions connecting human beings and Gaia—and to manifest them in everyday life. We need to create a new kind of culture upon the Earth that will enable the further development of the human race as well as that of the Earth, including all its beings and dimensions. Let us call this already evolving future culture: Geoculture."

In order to develop this Geoculture, we first need to transform our dogmatic and rationally based concepts about what the Earth is and who we are as human beings and to change our cultural norms and practices accordingly. We now finally turn from south, east and north to the west—that is, to Liverpool and to one of us, Tony and my Biblical Quaternity Archetype (BQA), duly associated with our re-GENE-rative pilgrimium, now in practice as illustrated in his production of *Liver Birdsong.*

7.4. FROM THE BQA TO ARTISTIC PRODUCTION: *LIVER BIRDSONG – THE LIVERPOOL BLITZ MUSICAL*

7.4.1. Methodology from artistic creativity

One of the core issues RAiSEd (see Research Academy in Practice) by our work towards Communiversity Liverpool was the extent to which arts-based social innovation can, transformationally, assist in re-balancing some of the problems of social formation in that contemporary city. In addition, on the basis of developing a semiotic economics approach, connected to research tenets drawn from an analysis of the integral GEN*E* represented in the Second (New) Testament scriptures (see Pilgrimium Theory, BQA), we framed these questions:

- How could any biblical critical tenets be utilised in the analysis of the specific social innovation to be developed to address the imbalance problems identified in respect of marginalisation within the Liverpool City Region (LCR)?
- Can we generate a contribution—as an original piece of artistic culture—that addresses some, or all, of the imbalances in the LCR?
- What process of bringing together a co-creative community will be required to achieve this cultural contribution?
- What lessons can be learned for future social innovation development, from the impact of any cultural origination within the LCR, addressing the local imbalances and problems identified above?

These questions become more numerous, complex and practical as we move into the Western world. That is because they connect to a very specific piece of artistic creativity, collaborative community development and preliminary articulation of an eco-system that it is expected will flow from it, which builds on the 'south', 'east' and 'north'. We discovered in the early stages of work towards the communiversity that artistic creation—involving the forming of a new musical theatre production company and work towards the initial professional staging of a show—was a significant method that addresses, directly or tangentially, many of the imbalances in the city. Such connection was not by way of providing solutions, but instead utilised the semiotic economics method of revealing the signification of those local cultural challenges, in order to raise consciousness within the community, which lies at the core of the pilgrimium *peregrinatio*, already identified in the chapter on Pilgrimium Theory.

Liver Birdsong – the Liverpool Blitz Musical, written by Tony Bradley and Rebecca Myers, had the specific intention of indicating challenges to the position of women in Liverpool, connecting the generations to the city's wartime history. It offered opportunities to young professionals, especially women, to break into the theatre world; for Liverpool talent to tell Liverpool stories to Liverpool people. It had its world premiere to mark the 75th anniversary of the Liverpool Blitz of 1940 and will be revised on tour for the 80th anniversary, as *Songbirds – the Blitz Musical*, in Autumn 2020–Spring 2021.

Equally, in doing so, it sought to *show* (sic) that artistic creativity offers a particular methodology for connecting integration to individuation. By integration we mean an attempt to offer a work of creative origination that supports the city's GENE*a*logical development. By individuation, we mean to draw a connection—through the characterisation, plot and dramatic production to the theory of personality maturing that derives from Jungian psychology (see Pilgrimium Theory). Artistic co-creation involves a different type of pilgrimium *peregrinatio*, but offers a vital contribution to communiversity practice, in releasing the community to awaken consciousness trans-rationally.

7.4.2. The Methodology of Artistic Integration – The Artist as Integrator

Within the integral model, the emergence of renewed institutional development occurs through an awakening of consciousness, in shifting the interpretation of institutional evolution of organisations, from 'leadership' to 'integrators'. However, there is a significance in considering *The Integrators,* as Ronnie does elsewhere (6), which is precisely to show that the focus of leadership is changing into the 21st century, from a cult of entrepreneurial personality to the ability of drawing together the human potential and capital of a diverse community. This is required by the complexity of organisations that are needed to tackle the local-to-global challenges that are emergent in societies, political institutions and, most notably, the planetary eco-systems that are revealed as becoming increasingly unstable. As such, we attempted to act as integrators of the teams behind a new musical, *Liver Birdsong,* directly addressing the city's history and contemporary life.

Characteristically, in respect of artistic creative collaboration, the focus was on the embodiment of emergent spirituality in the work itself. This is an important point. Whereas it is reasonable to emphasise integrative personalities—who emerge the values that lead to systems and technology for research-to-innovation co-laboratory-based innovation—artistic creation operates in a different way, counter-intuitively.

Following Ernest Gombrich's (7) famous quote, in *The Story of Art*— that there is "no such thing as Art, only artists"—we might conclude that there is no methodology of artistic creativity. The argument runs that every work of an artist is *sui generis*. Of course, this is a profoundly and ironically, acultural understanding. Art emerges from culture and, recursively, helps to articulate it and create it anew. But, it is not only the product of geniuses, any more than is science or any other field of human endeavour. It arises from its history, environment and creative zeitgeist—the 'spirit of the age' in which it is produced. In this respect, we attempted to develop an artistic methodology that *acted* to integrate the city and its people using its culture but, also, addressed its imbalances. It sought to signpost an artistic method of cultural and personal individuation.

7.4.3. The Method of Cultural Individuation – Transformation Through Characters and Story

Accordingly, our emphasis as writers and composers, was not on ourselves as integrators or social animateurists, but on the specific cultural products that we used to convey an awakening consciousness. Indeed, we saw that this process was emergent. We did not set out with any clear plan, beyond the most flimsy story-board, or even a dramatis personae of characters. Rather, those emerged with their own voices, to sing their own songs and to introduce us—and the city's audience—to their own spirituality and the values of Liverpool women during the Second World War.

Of course, such statements by creative writers always sound peculiar and, possibly, pretentious. They speak as if their creations have an independent life of their own and visit them from some ethereal region beyond the world which we inhabit. Well, of course, herein we are back to Jung and the archetypes of the collective unconscious. Oddly, I realised that we had created a story about four women who worked at Royal Ordnance Factory (ROF) Kirkby. But, furthermore, these *four*—Maggs, Daisy-Mae, Carla and 'Cockney' Lil—appeared to conform, in broad ways, to the temperaments of the Jungian model of personality. At the same time, the unfolding of the story-line, plot and narrative arc showed a process of individuation for each of the four characters, so that it was only in the diverse destinies that they exemplified their realised temperamental characteristics, both personally and as a community.

Daisy-Mae Beech was grounded in her Liverpool homeland but found empathy difficult until she lived through the trauma of her own sexual assault and the murder of her assailant. By the end of the show we imagined that she would become an Intuitive-Feeling (NF/Southern G) person. Carla Evans emerged as sweetly spiritual from the outset; however, this sweetness would turn into bitterness, as she becomes engulfed in the conflagration, in the ruins of the air raid shelter on Durning Road which was the actual setting of the real-life event that the show depicted in fictionalised form. By the end of the show Carla revealed something of the truth about being a Sensing-Perceiving (SP/Eastern E) person.

Initially, we saw 'Cockney' Lil Ford as objective and best able to navigate her way through what it meant to be a woman in 1940s Liverpool, having been transferred from the Woolwich Arsenal, as so many workers historically were. However, whilst she retained her objectivity throughout, it was in the way she navigated towards a fuller life in her adopted city that she revealed her underlying identity. By the end of the show we could see the capacity of this young woman as an Intuitive-Thinking (NT/Northern) personality.

And finally, the lead heroine of the musical, Maggs Williams, at first appeared to us in a rather unappealing light. We didn't understand why she behaved the way she did. At an early point in the writing process we questioned whether her life could turn around, as enemies become friends, to effect new innovation. But, by the end, her Sensing-Judging (SJ/Western *E*) character had become individuated, as she displayed the truth of her SJ nature, in revolving in the direction of making amends to Daisy Mae and understanding the character of an Intuitive-Feeling persona.

In briefly introducing what we saw as the fourfold nature of the central female characters, we recognised the archetypal nature of this creative method. At the same time, it suggested that this was not, in any surface cognitive sense, intended or utilised as a scaffolding for some type of stylised morality play. Rather, it pointed to the fact that the archetypes will out. The fourfold nature of reality and its processes, in the recursive GEN*E*alogy, was revealed in all sorts of ways, not least in art reflecting life and vice versa.

Our initial intention as writers was to tell a story of real heroism in wartime Liverpool, to address some of the city's negative consciousness and lack of historical understanding. But, what emerged was something far more primal. We were taken on a pilgrimium journey, as was the audience, so we were told, as the characters each go through an integral

GENEalogical cycle. They had their recursions, especially for Daisy Mae and Maggs, from South to West (see Pilgrimium Theory chapter). But, so did the writers, the production and the show itself. In other words, there was a spiral dynamism to the process of the art-work, which opened up new social innovation possibilities in a renewed integral cycle.

7.4.4. Using a BQA Tenet – An Example from St Luke's Creation Grounding

BQA Tenet: *It Began with Adam – All Communities are Grounded in God's favour, through Christ: Seek Your Distinctive Community Favour*

The power to work and write creatively is something of a mysterious process. The very start of activating our small community to address some of the imbalances of the city began in this enigmatic fashion. One email that I sent to Rebecca Myers on 3rd March, 2015 indicates this:

Hi Bex

On the drive back from teaching at Blackburn last night, the following arrived in my head.

This is the turning-point for Maggs, with Hal. I hope that it isn't cheesy but hits the right note between the horror of the situation, the romance and a turn of faith and hope.

The incident of finding the new-born baby with the mother dead beside it is recorded in the historical documents for that night—so this needs to be historically accurate, although the child has never been traced—reveals something else about the re-birth of the city. That baby would be 75 this year!

It includes the song: 'There's a lot to do'.

During the early weeks of my writing the script of *Liver Birdsong* we had been wrestling with the way in which the central character (Maggs Williams)—a tough, feisty, working-class Scouse young woman—would turn towards falling in love. How would she move from meeting to a depth of connection with Hal, one of the male leads, a US Marine Chaplain, as they were embroiled in the events of the Durning Road bombing on the night the show is set?

As I comment in the email, the entire scene, song sequence (*There's a Lot to Do*) and dialogue 'arrived in my head' as I was driving back from teaching at one of my University's Network colleges. This happened repeatedly over a period of six weeks. On my lengthy commute from my home in the English Lake District to Liverpool and back each day, I would find songs, fragments of conversations between characters or scenes simply appearing in my mind. There is something about particular moments when 'nature power' is released, when there is a genuine community activation taking place, where the serendipitous activity of the unconscious leaks through into consciousness and an artistic work begins to unfold. This spiritual process could, equally, be analysed using tenets drawn from the Biblical Quaternity Archetype.

Adopting this analytical approach delivered four tenet commentaries for each of the four stages of the salvation history model (see Pilgrimium Theory) for each of the four canonical Gospels. This would develop sixty-four analytical sections, through which the biblical tenets could be utilised to commentate on the development of social innovations in the city, which represent part of the co-creation and contribution journey of Communiversity Liverpool.

Whilst this artistic production-spiritual interrogation methodology diverges considerably from the type of 'data analysis' utilised in a standard piece of Mode 1 type empirical research, it entirely conforms to the approach of Integral Research. Although this was methodologically constructed, using a model of biblically-derived analysis, it could be replicated, we believe, through deriving analytical tenets from any source of profoundly inspiring values and spirituality, for motivating consciousness-raising. Once again, this reveals the unique approach of the communiversity for enabling cultural and social transformation in a manner that is closed off to conventional Mode 1 universities.

In this respect, the creation of *Liver Birdsong – the Liverpool Blitz Musical* revealed—along the way towards the GEN*E*ration of Communiversity Liverpool—that through art and artistic innovation, we tap into a trans-rational aspect of personal, community, cultural and social life. Equally, this could be understood by using analytical lenses that draw from spiritual and depth psychological traditions, rather than the standard instruments of empirical social science. The pilgrimium journey that it took us on—including writers, performers, stage and production staff, audience members and representatives of the city—awakened possibilities for transformation of the future city by better understanding the significance of the city's history, in the light of our spiritual tradition. As we entered into the stories we were, the city was better able to embrace the stories it could become.

7.5. CONCLUSION

- INTEGRAL RESEARCH: First things go wrong; then, in God, things can go right. *Whether they do go right or not depends on whether the articulation is made to the inner moral core* of the Godhead, which can then impact social innovation.
- INTEGRAL DEVELOPMENT: *The search for truth means self-discovery in nature and through nature.* Pax Herbals is a means of changing traditional medicine from an esoteric practice by fearsome old medicine men to that of a useful, profitable, rational venture.
- INTEGRAL ENTERPRISE: In every travel you take, leaving your comfort zone behind; *making your* halal *(rightful) living is an* ibadah *(worship) and travelling to another land* (hijrah) *to find a livelihood is also termed* ibadah.
- INTEGRAL ECONOMY: We need to *create a new kind of culture upon the Earth that will enable the further development of the human race as well as that of the Earth,* including all its beings

and dimensions. Let us call this already evolving future culture: Geoculture.

We now turn from Re-GEN*E*-rative Pilgrimium in practice, to socio-oeconomic research academy in theory.

7.6. REFERENCES

1 Adodo A (2017) *Integral Community Enterprise in Africa: Communitalism as an Alternative to Capitalism.* Abingdon. Routledge

2 Lessem R, Muchineripi P, Kada S (2014) *Integral Community: Political Economy to Social Commons.* Abingdon. Routledge

3 Saqib A and Malik A (2018) *Integral Finance – Akhuwat: A Case of Solidarity Economics.* Abingdon. Routledge

4 Piciga D, Schieffer A and Lessem R (2016) *Integral Green Slovenia.* Abingdon. Routledge

5 Pogacnik, M. (2013). *Manifesto on Geoculture.* www.markopogacnik.com (Accessed: 11 August 2015).

6 Lessem R (2016) *The Integrators – the next evolution in leadership, knowledge and value creation.* Abingdon. Routledge.

7 Gombrich E H (1995, Revised). *The Story of Art.* London. Pearson.

NORTH

PART 3: RESEARCH ACADEMY

Chapter 8

Navigation: Research Academy in Theory

EMANCIPATION: INNOVATION DRIVEN
INSTITUTIONALISED RESEARCH

Economic models that focus centripetally on one economic form to the exclusion of others perform a premature selection on a necessary institutional variety that is never given the opportunity to emerge.

Max Boisot, *Framework for a Learning Society*

Innovation-Driven Institutionalised Research: Through individual and institutional *learning and development, research and knowledge creation* you aim—in conjunction with the other communiversity entities—for overall social innovation.

Socio-Technical Design: As a friendly outsider, individually and institutionally, you adopt a problem-solving approach to your social research-and-innovation, altogether aimed at socioeconomic benefit, *using a co-creative approach.*

Organisational Knowledge Creation: Involves *socialisation* defined by face-to-face interactions; *externalisation* via the use of metaphor and analogy; *knowledge combination* via IT/ documentation; *externalisation* through personalised action.

Knowledge-Based Social Economy: While maintenance learning involves the acquisition of fixed outlooks, methods and rules, long-term societal development requires *innovative learning—renewal, re-structuring and problem re-formulation.*

8.1. INTRODUCTION: INTEGRAL DEVELOPMENT & THE COMMUNIVERSITY

8.1.1. Learning and Development

We now turn, first in theory, from the developmental pilgrimium, as per the awakening of integral consciousness, to the research academy, as per innovation driven, institutionalised social research. From our *integral* developmental (1) perspective, as such, the co-creation of knowledge, following upon communal learning and a developmental pilgrimium, in our overall communiversity case, takes organisational place within such a research academy. Given the unfortunate fact that little of our education and research seems to address and resolve the major social issues we face today in a particular society, be it in the UK or Zimbabwe, we are called upon to look at learning and knowledge creation anew. The researcher or knowledge creator is thus invited—now from a 'northern' perspective—to explore at both an individual and an institutional level the following questions:

- How do we, individually, organisationally and societally, learn and know?
- What do we need to know based on deep reflection of our selves, our organisations, our communities and our society, about the development issues we face?
- How do we address, individually and collectively, these development needs with relevant new knowledge, generated by myself, together with others?
- What learning models, knowledge creation concepts, forms of

236

research and education and learning tools can inform me and my context?

• How do I envisage building up my learning and research from an individual to organisational and societal perspective, indigenously and exogenously, ultimately in the form of a research academy?

We now turn, first of all, to the individual learning cycle and thereafter work our way through research, knowledge creation and societal learning.

8.1.2. The Learning Cycle: Learning is Development

What Do You Know About How You Learn?

It may be strange to revisit here, from an integral developmental perspective, as per social research and development so to speak, what should have been clear to us: the way in which we learn and create new knowledge. Understanding how we learn, we consider a necessary, scientific precondition for individual as well as organisational and societal development. And yet, although we are schooled from an early age, we often have relatively little knowledge about learning in general and about our personal learning style in particular.

It is somehow bizarre that in our formal education, from pre-school to school to university, we not only discover little about how we learn individually, but also how this relates to collective learning. Of course, we may study such individual learning processes in a programme of pedagogy, but even this will be restricted to individual, as opposed to organisational or community-based learning.

While our objective in this book is not to fully fill that gap, we nevertheless feel it is important to have at least a reasonable sense of how we learn, individually and collectively, as such an understanding is amongst the most needed qualities for development. This is particularly true in our integral case, as we are seeking to continuously create new knowledge from the ground up, relevant to a particular context. Such a primarily inside-out approach is totally different from the typical outside-in approach to economic development, in which preconceived knowledge is merely applied to a context, usually with unsustainable results.

The Integral Learning Cycle of David Kolb

One of the most helpful introductions into learning in our specific context comes from the US-American educationist David Kolb (2), world-renowned for the development of his experiential learning theory. Like Swiss psychoanalyst Carl Jung (3) in the case of psychological types (see Table 8), Kolb maintains that it is our preferred learning style that determines how and what we learn, or indeed not learn or even avoid learning.

Kolb's model works on two levels, as he explains in *Experiential Learning*. The first level is represented by the learning cycle that includes four learning stages that, ideally, progressively build on each other. Kolb argued that his learning stages are to be seen in circular or even spiralling form. The learner is supposed to engage with the full circle of experiencing, reflecting, thinking and acting. Concrete experiences lead to observations and reflections. These reflections are then assimilated and translated into abstract concepts, which then inform a person's action, where the person actively tests and experiments. This fourth and final step, in turn, enables the creation of new experiences, which makes the cycle start all over and turns it into a spiral. These four stages of the learning cycle are also somewhat analogous to John Heron's four modes of knowing, as we saw in chapter 6: experiential, imaginal, conceptual and practical.

The following table introduces each of them and illustrates also the corresponding steps in Jung's typology and in our own transformational process—the GEN*E*-ius—that underlies the Integral Development.

238

Table 8 Kolb's Learning Stages Compared with Jung's Psychological Types and the GENE-ius Rhythm of Integral Development		
Kolb's *Learning Stages*	*The functional* *Types of Jung/* *Heron/s Modes*	*The GENE-ius* *of Integral* *Development*
① *Concrete Experience* (CE)	Feeling/ Experiential	Grounding
② *Reflective Observation* (RO): Reflection on that Experience	Intuiting/ Imaginal	Emerging
③ *Abstract Conceptualisation* (AC): Formation of abstract Concepts based on Experience	Thinking/ Conceptual	Navigating
④ *Active Experimentation* (AE): Testing of new Concepts	Sensing/ Practical	Effecting

As much as we have to gain greater clarity on stages, styles and development phases of learning, we also desperately need a broader understanding of the methods of knowledge creation that are used. For this exploration we now turn to what we have termed *Integral Research* (4), which was originally developed for individuals pursuing their research in the social sciences. We will see the conceptual resonance between Kolb's learning cycle on the one hand, and Integral Research's four research paths and trajectories on the other.

8.1.3. Integral Research: Transformative Approach to Research & Development

Where Conventional Research Falls Short

It has been our long-standing passion to conceive of learning and research in a transformational way. Learning, for Kolb as for ourselves, should not primarily be geared toward recipients gaining factual knowledge, but should rather be liberating and transformational for the individual and, by extension, for their communities, organisations and societies. In other words, social science research-and-innovation should generate relevant knowledge to address issues and draw on and serve to co-evolve innate capacities in particular social and economic contexts.

Towards Integral Research and Innovation

Such an approach, here leading towards innovation-driven, institutionalised research, allows us to choose between four research paths that jointly fulfil the following criteria:

- Reflect different modes of thinking and being (if not from all over the world, at least from all over Europe as well as America).
- Are culturally rooted and relevant to the specific context to which they are applied.
- Interconnect research method and methodology, critique and action, thereby stretching over what we term a full trajectory from research origination (method) to research foundation (methodology), emancipation (critique), transformation (action).

Table 9   The GENE
Grounding to Effect: Origination to Transformation
You, personally, communally, institutionally, societally, locally engage with the original *Grounding* of your individual and collective, locally based Life World.
Emergence allows you to understand a core social need that *emerges* locally and globally within this context, founded upon the natural and cultural gifts that a society brings to bear in your addressing such, in association with others.
The *Navigation* phase requires you to draw indigenously and exogenously on social sciences, newly globally, if not also the humanities, to prepare for a new conceptual synthesis, emancipating you from local and global constraints.
Through your *Effecting* transformation you ultimately and socially innovate, drawing on your burning desire, related to a burning issue, releasing genius globally-locally, thereby making a true contribution to your own context.

In Table 9 above we introduce the transformative rhythm of the GEN*E*. We start out with descriptive or narrative, grounded theory or experimental research method (Level 1), that is the grounding and origination of your individual and collective endeavours, as a social science researcher or innovative practitioner.

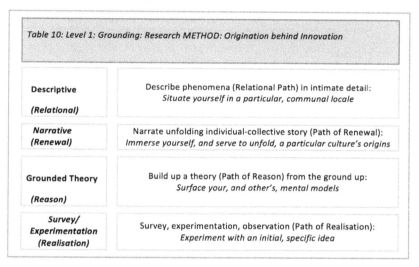

Table 10: Level 1: Grounding: Research METHOD: Origination behind Innovation

Descriptive *(Relational)*	Describe phenomena (Relational Path) in intimate detail: *Situate yourself in a particular, communal locale*
Narrative ***(Renewal)***	Narrate unfolding individual-collective story (Path of Renewal): *Immerse yourself, and serve to unfold, a particular culture's origins*
Grounded Theory *(Reason)*	Build up a theory (Path of Reason) from the ground up: *Surface your, and other's, mental models*
Survey/ ***Experimentation*** ***(Realisation)***	Survey, experimentation, observation (Path of Realisation): *Experiment with an initial, specific idea*

Through Level 2, you emerge, individually and collectively, from the local, to the local and global, in your overall orientation. This foundation level is comprised of the more sophisticated but still conventional research wisdom on the one hand and provides the emerging local-global foundation for your social innovation on the other. For the analytically based research trajectory, it serves to locate you in one or other of *four respectively phenomenological or interpretive, rational or empiricist* (positivist) methodologies. In parallel, for those of you pursuing the innovation trajectory it serves to establish the underlying paradigm—humanistic immersion, holistic fusion, rational social science or pragmatic problem solving—from which you are working.

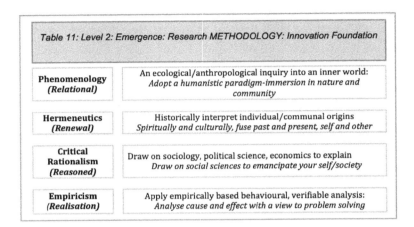

Table 11: Level 2: Emergence: Research METHODOLOGY: Innovation Foundation	
Phenomenology *(Relational)*	An ecological/anthropological inquiry into an inner world: *Adopt a humanistic paradigm-immersion in nature and community*
Hermeneutics *(Renewal)*	Historically interpret individual/communal origins *Spiritually and culturally, fuse past and present, self and other*
Critical Rationalism *(Reasoned)*	Draw on sociology, political science, economics to explain *Draw on social sciences to emancipate your self/society*
Empiricism *(Realisation)*	Apply empirically based behavioural, verifiable analysis: *Analyse cause and effect with a view to problem solving*

Through Level 3 you encompass the more contemporary, unconventional wisdom, spanning so-called 'critical' and 'emancipatory' methodologies', that is *feminism, critical theory, postmodernism* and *critical realism.*

Table 12: Level 3: Research CRITIQUE: Emancipation towards Innovation	
Feminism *(Relational)*	Feminism promoting knowledge as personal liberation: *Build upon the wisdom inherent in nature to uncover indigenous knowledge and worldviews*
Critical Theory *(Renewal)*	Critical theory as emancipatory dialectic *Transcend historic capitalism/materialistic consciousness to evolve new forms of spiritual and social awareness*
Postmodernism *(Reasoned)*	Postmodernism as alternative discourses: *Build a knowledge creating, post-industrial community, drawing on diverse knowledge sources*
Critical Realism *(Realisation)*	Critical realism as a generative underlay: *Uncover empirical facts, key events and underlying Generative mechanisms*

On the one hand, these serve to provide an overtly radical, socio-political outlook upon your research; on the other hand, they serve, from a socially innovative perspective, as a basis for social and economic emancipation, building upon a major social movement, locally and globally, of your time and place. Level 4, for the first time involves action research; it serves, transformatively moreover, to ultimately bring about fully integral innovation through *participatory action research, cooperative inquiry, socio-technical design* and *generic action research*. The origins of 'action research' in America, in fact, in the middle of the last century, lay not only in its desire to make the social sciences more relevant to the problems of the day, but also to emancipate psychology and sociology, most specifically, from the shackles of an analytical and empiricist bias that inhibited radical transformation.

Table 13: Level 4: ACTION Research: Transformation for Innovation	
PAR **(Relational)**	Communal problem solving to promote self reliance: *Alleviate communal and environmental decay;* *serve, locally, to heal the planet, globally*
Co-operative ***Inquiry*** ***(Renewal)***	A democratic process of inquiry, using diverse knowledge modes: experiential, imaginative, conceptual and practical *Serve to democratise education and research*
Socio-Technical ***Design (Reasoned)***	Co-generative democratic workplaces: *Build non-hierarchical, networked communities and societies*
Action ***Research*** ***(Realisation)***	Continual cycling between action and reflection: *Promote social change, challenging,* *and overturning existing power bases*

8.2. INTEGRAL RESEARCH TO SOCIO-TECHNICAL DESIGN

8.2.1. Transformative Orientation to the Path of Reason

Your Research is Geared Towards Social Betterment

So much for integral research as an underpinning for our research academy, we now turn specifically to socio-technical design as the 'northern' branch of action research. For the originator of action research, Kurt Lewin (5), "nothing is as practical as a good theory" and "the best way to understand something is to try to change it." The social sciences themselves began as a form of engaged political economy, aimed at social betterment, if not also transformation.

Only as the social sciences were split out into the various existing conventional disciplines and subjected to harassment and purges because their social activism offended the rich and powerful, did the social sciences become separate from such transformative action. Greenwood and Levin (6) view such analytically based social sciences as today an impoverished derivative, albeit a methodologically and theoretically sophisticated one, of the originally transformatively oriented social sciences to which they see action as the natural heir.

You Use a Co-creative Approach

Organisationally instigated action research, as such, can be thought of as a process consisting of at least two distinct phases. The first involves the clarification of an initial research question (analysis), for us a burning issue, whereas the second involves the initiation and continuation of a 'social change and meaning construction process', for us a transformation. Both culminate in the creation of opportunities for learning and reflection in action (see Figure 1), within a co-generative process between insiders and outsiders.

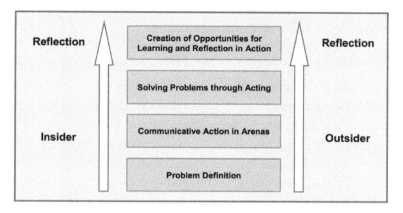

Figure 1: Co-generative Approach to Organisational Research & Development

You Act as a 'Friendly Outsider'

A professional action researcher, or indeed a research institution as such, must know how to be a 'friendly outsider'. This role is vital in action research because the external perspective is a key element in opening up local group processes for change. But this outsider, individually or collectively, is 'friendly' in a special sense. He, she, or it, must be able to reflect back to the local group's ideas and understandings about them, including criticism of their own perspectives, in a way that is experienced as supportive rather than negatively critical or domineering.

The friendly outsider must also be expert at opening up lines of discussion; a kind of good Socratic teacher. Often local organisations or groups are either stuck in positions that have hardened or have become pessimistic about the possibilities for change. Flexibility and opportunities for change are pointed out to local people, along with encouragement in the form of moral support and information from other cases, where similar problems existed but change turned out to be possible. Another key role of the friendly outsider is to make evident the tacit knowledge that guides local conduct. This can be in the form of critical reflections or supportive comments about local capabilities. We now turn to socio-technical design in more depth.

8.2.2. Socio-Technical Design in Depth

The crux of the action research-based knowledge generation process is the encounter between local insights and the understanding that the outsider, individually or institutionally, brings to the table and the fusion of these insights into a shared form of understanding that serves as the basis for solving practical problems. An affirmation or proposition from one of the parties (thesis) is brought forward and is met with demanding and challenging questions and counterpropositions (antithesis) and out of this friendly encounter of points of view an understanding (synthesis) will gradually evolve.

Such organisationally based action research is based on the affirmation that all human beings have detailed, complex and valuable knowledge about their lives, environments and goals. This knowledge is different from scholarly knowledge because everyday knowledge is embodied in people's actions, long histories in particular positions and the way they reflect on them. This kind of knowing is different from much conventional scientific knowledge because practical wisdom, practical reasoning and tacit knowledge are its central characteristics. *Action research, then, centres on a co-generatively structured encounter between the worlds of practical reasoning and those of scientifically constructed knowledge, integrating practitioners and professionals in the same knowledge generating process that it calls 'co-generative' learning.*

Furthermore, a local theory is context-bound and makes sense in the context of years of local processes matching interpretations with concrete experiences. In action research, *the central intent is to generate knowledge that bridges these knowledge worlds.* Conventional social researchers, who have severed the connection between research and action, rarely know whether they are right or not, as their findings are seldom acted upon and the practical results from their research rarely have direct consequences for them. Local knowledge belongs mainly to insiders, but outsiders can also develop varieties of local knowledge through research based on local engagement over the long term. For Greenwood and Morten, because *action research privileges local knowledge, it necessarily works with the role of narrative in the research process, as well as in writing up the results.* For most logical positivists (conventional social researchers), as well as those using formal qualitative techniques, the strong presence of narratives is taken to be hopelessly 'unscientific' and incapable of producing valid knowledge. In this respect, the rational-pragmatic bias of action research is combined with a holistic and humanistic orientation.

This brings us to the Knowledge Creating Company.

8.3. INTEGRAL ENTERPRISE: OPERATIONS TO KNOWLEDGE CREATION

8.3.1. Knowledge Creating Rhythm of the Integral Enterprise

Enabling Conditions for Knowledge Creation

Following in the footsteps of Kolb's Experiential Learning, our own Integral Research and Greenwood and Levin's Socio-Technical Design, we now turn to the Knowledge Creating Company/Academy, altogether in the context of our prospective Research Academy. For the leading Japanese organisational sociologists Nonaka and Takeuchi (7), as we also saw in chapter 6, the path taken by a knowledge creating enterprise (for us including a communiversity) is to turn knowledge creation into continuous innovation, so as to gain subsequent comparative advantage.

A first step as such is to define the 'field' or 'domain' that gives a mental map of the world in which an enterprise or academy exists and provides a general direction regarding what kind of knowledge they ought to seek to create. Most organisations only have products and services in mind when formulating strategy. Such products and services have clear boundaries. In contrast, boundaries for knowledge are more obscure, helping to expand the organisation's economic, technological and social scope. A case in point, for example, is Matsushita's knowledge based vision in 1990:

- We are in the 'human innovation business', a business that creates new lifestyles based on creativity, comfort and joy in addition to efficiency and convenience.
- We produce 'humanware technology', technology based on human studies such as artificial intelligence, fuzzy logic, neuro-computers and networking technology.

Nonaka and Takeuchi identify three key 'enabling conditions' for the knowledge creating enterprise:

- First, develop intentionally the organisational *capability to acquire, create, accumulate and exploit knowledge.*
- Second, *build up autonomous individuals and groups,* setting their task boundaries by themselves to pursue the ultimate intention of the organisation.
- Third, provide employees with *a sense of crisis*—as well as a lofty ideal—such so-called 'creative chaos' increases tension within the organisation.

How then does the so-called 'hypertext' organisation serve to promote such?

Structuring Knowledge Creation: The Hypertext Organisation

The Project Layer

Nonaka refers to a 'hypertext' organisation because of its layered nature and scope, which serves to develop, channel and distribute knowledge through the duly formed networks. The top stratum of this kind of enterprise, or indeed communiversity academy in our case, is comprised of the 'project team' layer. Multiple project teams engage in knowledge creating activities such as new product and systems development. In all such cases the team members are brought together from a number of different units across the business system and are assigned exclusively to a project team until the project is completed.

The Bureaucratic System

Alongside this project layer, but occupying a lower order of knowledge creating significance, is the conventional academic 'bureaucratic system' with its normal hierarchy of authority. The project layer, on the one hand, is engaged with developing new knowledge through self-organising groups. The hierarchical system, on the other, is primarily concerned with categorising, ordering, distributing and commercialising or operationalising such knowledge. In terms of the Nonaka and Takeuchi's knowledge spiral (SECI) as below: whereas the project layer is primarily focused upon 'southern' socialisation and 'eastern' externalisation, the hierarchical system is more engaged with 'northern' combination and 'western' internalisation. Underlying both project layer and business system, for Nonaka and Takeuchi, is a 'knowledge foundation'.

The Knowledge Foundations

This third layer does not exist as an actual organisational entity, but is embedded in a communiversity vision, organisational culture and technology.

The vision arises from these spiritual, aesthetic and scientific knowledge grounds. If made explicit, it provides the direction in which the communiversity should develop its social as well as technological innovations. Moreover, it clarifies the overall 'field' in which it wants to play. Furthermore, while vision and culture provide the experiential and imaginal base to tap tacit knowledge, technology taps the explicit knowledge generated in the other two layers.

A knowledge creating academy ultimately must have the organisational ability to acquire, accumulate, exploit and create knowledge continuously and dynamically. Moreover, it must be able to re-categorise and re-contextualise it strategically for use by others in the organisation or by future generations. As Nonaka and Takeuchi have indicated, a hierarchy is the most efficient structure for the acquisition, accumulation and exploitation of knowledge, while a task force is the most effective for the creation of new knowledge.

The Knowledge Creation Process: SECI

Organisational knowledge creation, therefore, should be understood in terms of a process that institutionally amplifies the knowledge created by its people and crystallises it as a part of the knowledge network of the communiversity. In this context it is possible to distinguish between several types of knowledge creating activity, which correspond with the four poles of our integral realities, as well as our GENE rhythm, through which the knowledge created by an individual is transformed and legitimised. These, as illustrated in chapter 6, are also aligned with expressions of Ba, that is, different manifestations of time and place, as per our 'four worlds'. Moreover, while the knowledge creating company or research academy has 'northern' connotations, its reach extends integrally, communiversally throughout.

Socialisation – Southern – Grounding: Learning Community

In the first instance an informal community of social interaction provides an immediate forum for nurturing the emergent property of knowledge at each organisational level. This is the 'southern' *grounding* rhythm, incorporating altruism, empathy and a sense of reciprocity. Since the informal community of which such behaviour forms a part might span organisational boundaries, it is important that a research academy is able to integrate aspects of emerging knowledge from different parts of the communiversity. Thus, the potential contribution of informal groups to organisational knowledge creation should be related to more formal notions of organisation structure, both within the organisation and without.

Such *tacit to tacit* socialisation, moreover, relies on shared experience that enables members to 'indwell' into others and to grasp their world from 'inside'. This shared experience also facilitates the co-creation of 'common perspectives', thereby contributing to the 'common good'. In other words, communication is like a wave that passes through people and culminates when everyone synchronises himself with the wave. To succeed in that respect, it will have to countermand the prevailing individualistic and formalistic culture.

Externalisation – Eastern – Emergence: Developmental Pilgrimium

Once mutual trust and a common implicit perspective have been formed through shared experience, the team needs to articulate the perspective through continuous dialogue.

This process activates so-called 'externalisation', from *tacit to explicit,* whereby participants, acting out of a 'gardening' mentality, engage in the mutual co-development of ideas. This constitutes a holistic 'eastern' *emergent* orientation. Such dialogue, moreover, should not be single-faceted and deterministic but multi-faceted. This dialectical thinking, in effect, is a spiral process whereby affirmation and negation are synthesised to form knowledge, based upon the use of metaphors, extending on to analogies and concepts. The emergent concepts, then, provide a basis of crystallisation, or knowledge combination.

Combination – Northern – Navigation: Research Academy

The third mode of knowledge conversion involves the use of social processes to combine different bodies of *explicit* knowledge held by individuals, through such academic mechanisms as formal meetings, academic workshops, seminars and conferences, as well as research publications. The reconfiguring of existing information through the sorting, adding, re-categorising and re-contextualising of such explicit knowledge in 'northern' *navigational guise* can, at the same time, lead to new combinations of knowledge. Our own integral worlds, constituted of integral realities (south to west), realms (anthropological to economic), rhythms (grounding to effect) and rounds (individual to societal) are an example of such.

Modern computer based data processing systems, in fact, provide a graphic example of such knowledge 'combination', as does, for example, the 'balanced scorecard', constituting such explicit forms of knowledge creation that are rational in orientation.

Internalisation – Western – Effect: Socioeconomic Laboratory

Finally, in the conversion of *explicit into tacit* knowledge—that is 'internalisation'—action is important. We are now in the realm of 'western' pragmatism and transformative *effect*. Individuals internalise knowledge tacitly, through direct, hands-on experience, thereby both reaching out for and holding onto what they have hunted for. Moreover, for explicit knowledge to become tacit, it helps if the knowledge is verbalised or diagrammed into manuals, documents or stories, as any good consultant knows. The quality of that knowledge is influenced by both the variety of the experience and also the degree to which they are related. It is effected, moreover, to the extent that knowledge is embodied through deep personal commitment, thereby transcending the subject-object divide. It is here, specifically, that academy and laboratory combine forces.

Overall, each of the four knowledge creating modes produces different outputs. Socialisation (learning community) yields what the Japanese term 'sympathised knowledge' such as shared values and technical skills. Externalisation or catalysation (developmental pilgrimium) produces 'conceptual knowledge', resulting in the new product or organisational designs. Combination (research academy) gives rise to so-called 'systematic knowledge' such as academic curricula and research publications. Internalisation, finally, yields 'operational knowledge' (socioeconomic laboratory), which encompasses project management and enterprise outcomes. We now turn from such a knowledge-creating, integral enterprise to integral economics and specifically from knowledge creation to a knowledge-based social economy, altogether serving to build up our all-encompassing research academy.

8.4. INTEGRAL ECONOMICS: WELFARE TO SOCIAL ECONOMY

8.4.1. No Limits to Learning

Overcoming the Human Gap

In the 1970s, a cross-cultural team of social scientists were brought together by the so-called *Club of Rome*: the late Jim Botkin (8), a management and technology consultant from America (and a fellow student of one of us, Ronnie Lessem, at Harvard Business School), Mahdi El-mandjra, a senior government adviser from Morocco and Mircea Malitza, a Minister of Education from Romania.

That something fundamental is wrong with our entire world system was quite evident to them from the outset; in the seventies, they recognised that humanity was unable to assure the minima of life to all its members, to be at peace with itself, or to be in harmony with nature. Once wars were waged in quest of salt; today in quest of energy, and tomorrow, food may become the salt of contemporary economy. *If current trends continue, we are destined to lose drastically in terms of habitat, health and quality of life, perhaps even the very capacity for survival.*

Evidence of this first became visible in the growing disenchantment that has come to surround the 'technological fix'. In food production, for example, the programme known as the Green Revolution has been criticised for creating additional social, economic and environmental problems in the course of solving food production concerns. Second, emphasis on 'the human element' became apparent, as global issues have expanded to include more social, political and cultural issues than purely material and physical ones. What was missing then and still is now, is the human element embodied in what Botkin and his co-authors term 'the human gap', affecting not just a single organisation or community, but a whole economy and society.

The Gap between Growing Complexity and our Capacity to Cope with It

The human gap is the *distance between growing complexity and our capacity to cope with it.* It is known as a 'human gap' because it is a dichotomy between a growing complexity of our own making and a lagging development of our own capacities. Due to the predicament of humanity increasingly being seen as deriving from the human gap, they examined how learning can help bridge this gap; not only individual learning but also groups of people, organisations and even societies. Human potential, overall then, is being artificially constrained and vastly underutilised, so much so that for all practical purposes there actually appears to be no limits to learning. What kind of learning, for an economy-and-society as a whole, does this involve?

8.4.2. Maintenance Learning versus Innovative Learning

Learning That Brings Renewal, Re-structuring and Problem Reformulation

Traditionally, for Botkin and his colleagues, societies and individuals adopted a pattern of continuous 'maintenance learning', interrupted by short periods of innovation which was stimulated largely by the shock of external events. Maintenance learning, then, is the acquisition of fixed outlooks, methods and rules for dealing with unknown and recurring situations. Typically, this is the case today, with such 'maintenance' outlooks being adopted by 'trade war' Trump in America, Brexit Tory Party Britain, or 'bond note' ZANU PF Zimbabwe.

But for long-term survival, particularly in times of turbulence, change or discontinuity, another type of learning is even more essential. It is the type of learning that can bring change, renewal, re-structuring and problem reformulation—and which Botkin calls 'innovative learning'. The shift to innovative learning, however, is an extremely challenging one. Indeed, what could be more challenging than for all people to join the renewed efforts aimed at narrowing the gaps that divide humanity as a whole, or indeed the United States of America, Great Britain or Zimbabwe, focusing our energies towards a peaceful, profoundly human, overall enterprise? Moreover, despite the fact that the methods for and commitment to innovative learning are still at present underdeveloped, such learning is a subject area that promises to provide a basis for mutual cooperation and dialogue among East and West, North and South.

Prophetically then, Botkin announced some thirty years ago that our diverse worlds either needed to learn to restructure the local/national/international order cooperatively, or commence a period inescapably more combative and crisis-prone. The question is not *whether*, for Botkin and his colleagues writing thirty years ago, we will usher in learning, but *what kind* of learning we are bringing about. Would humanity, whether in Zanzibar or Zimbabwe, be taught by shocks, the lessons of which entail prohibitive costs and deadly delays, or will people learn how to shape those events?

However relevant Botkin's claim still is, the context in which such innovative learning needs to take place has changed fundamentally. Now well into the new millennium, we are increasingly faced with imminent climate change, networks of terror and populist political responses to such, which require a revised approach to learning and continuous adaptation. At the same time, with globalisation comes increased social injustice. A new navigational perspective is thereby required, via a research academy which links concern for the social agenda with renewal of the knowledge basis of economy and society.

8.5. CONCLUSION: LEARN, PROBLEM SOLVE, CREATE KNOWLEDGE, SOCIALLY INNOVATE

We began with Kolb's individually based learning cycle and ended with Botkin's societally oriented innovative learning, with our integral research, Greenwood's socio-technical design and Nonaka's knowledge creating enterprise lodged in between. Altogether, moreover, we provided the conceptual base for the Integral Communiversity research academy, set alongside its learning community, developmental pilgrimium and socioeconomic laboratories, altogether underpinned by integral life; that is, integral research and development, economy and enterprise. Altogether, as such:

- Through INTEGRAL DEVELOPMENT, as a **Research Academy,** you engage in *learning and development, research and knowledge creation.*
- Through INTEGRAL RESEARCH, via a **Socio-Technical Design,** you adopt a *problem-solving approach* to your organisationally based research with a view to innovation, altogether aimed at social benefit.
- As an INTEGRAL ENTERPRISE, through **Knowledge Creation,** you involve firstly face to face *socialisation*; secondly, externalisation through the conscious use of metaphor and analogy; thirdly, *knowledge combination* via documentation; finally, *externalisation* through personalised action.
- In the context of an INTEGRAL ECONOMY, set specifically within a knowledge based **Social Economy** you use *innovative learning* to bring about *change, renewal, re-structuring* and *problem reformulation.*

We now turn from theory underlying a research academy to its practice in the south, east, north and west.

8.6. REFERENCES

1 Schieffer A and Lessem R (2014) *Integral Development: Transforming the Potential of Individuals, Organisations and Societies.* Abingdon. Routledge

2 Kolb D (1983) *Experiential Learning: Experience as the Source of Learning and Development.* New York. Prentice Hall

3 Jung C (2018) *Psychological Types: General Description of the Types.* Createspace Independent Publishing

4 Lessem R and Schieffer A (2010) *Integral Research and Innovation: Transforming Enterprise and Society.* Abingdon. Routledge

5 Lewin K and Gold M (1999) *The Complete Social Scientist: A Kurt Lewin Reader.* Washington DC. American Psychological Association

6 Greenwood D. and Levin M (2006) *Introduction to Action Research: Social Research for Social Change.* New York. Sage

7 Nonaka and Takeuchi H (1995) *The Knowledge Creating Company.* Oxford. Oxford University Press

8 Botkin, J., Elmandjra, M. & Malitza, M (1979) *No Limits to Learning: Bridging the Human Gap. A Report to the Club of Rome.* London: Pergamon.

Chapter 9

Research Academy in Practice

OFIRDI NIGERIA, *iSRA* PAKISTAN, *RAiSE* UK, *DA VINCI* SA

In the process of scientific investigation as understood in our times, the decisive stage is neither the collection of data that, in a way, starts the whole process, nor the application of theoretical findings to practical issues, which is the final stage. The decisive stage is what comes between them—the interpretation of raw information, the theoretical processing of the data collected and the production of those particular utterances which we call scientific statements ... the one essential shortcoming of scientific activity in the colonies was the lack of the intermediate stage. We missed the central operation of theory building. The medium stage then took place in the so called "mother country". Thus science in the colonies was characterised by a theoretical vacuum—the lack of those intellectual and experimental procedures that, being at the heart of the entire enterprise, depended on infrastructure that existed only in the ruling countries. This theoretical vacuum was substantially the same as the industrial vacuum that characterises economic activity.

Paulin Hountondji, *The Struggle for Meaning*

South: OFIRDI seeks to assert the right of Africans to speak in their own language and metaphors. We must reclaim our right to cognitive freedom, by evolving our own research method-ologies *geared towards African epistemological emancipation.*

East: iSRA involves a *rebirthing of the Prophet's Journey of Ascension* from Trans-migration to Transformation through a journey involving 4P's (Philosophy, Principles, Practices, Paradigm) thereby CARE-ing for our society.

North: via RAiSE – A new Research Academy in Integral Semiotic Economics, in Liverpool, UK, is acting as a research-to-innovation hub, to *understand the meaning systems underpinning alternative economic models* and establish innovative enterprises that reflect these (identifying alternative economic objects, archetypes, signs and ventures).

West: In a Mode 2 university as per Da Vinci Institute (SA) knowledge is intended to be useful whether in industry, government, or society overall. As such, *knowledge production is spread throughout society, thereby resulting in socially distributed knowledge.*

9.1. INTRODUCTION: GROUNDING INSTITUTIONALISED RESEARCH IN THE SOUTH

9.1.1. Pax Scientia: OFIRDI as a Research Academy

A Fight against the Coloniality of Knowledge and Epistemicide

We start this chapter on the practical application of a research academy in the Nigerian 'south', as we have done so far in each communiversity case, albeit with a broader view to CARE-ing for society. This is because, under co-author Adodo's (1) auspices, the most advanced of our communiversity cases is lodged there. His research academy is termed Ofure Integral Research and Development Initiative (OFIRDI).

The backdrop to it is that for centuries, according to Adodo, Africans were a people spoken about, spoken for and spoken against by foreigners.

> *"We read about who we are from what others said and wrote about us. OFIRDI seeks to assert the right of Africans to speak in their own language and metaphors. We must reclaim our right to cognitive freedom, if we truly seek to be free."*

Africa, for Adodo, must be aware of and fight against the coloniality of knowledge and epistemicide (which are modern forms of colonisation), by evolving and educing its own research methods and research methodologies suited to and geared towards African epistemological emancipation. To this effect, OFIRDI is on the way to becoming a serious and genuine research academy that will set new models for an Afrocentric education, in partnership with local communities, Ibadan University Institute for African Studies and Pax Herbals itself, via their Transformation Studies masters programme and other integral research communities across Africa.

Communitalism: Reconnecting with Original African Cosmologies

The journey to genuine freedom only begins, says Adodo, when Africa takes control of its epistemological and economic destiny. Communitalism, for him, is an indigenous theory of knowledge creation in Africa, embracing CARE-ing for self, community and society. The starting point is to unravel the missing depths, thereby reconnecting with, based on African cosmologies, the continent's original foundation stories.

In that context, men and women in Africa are gradually losing the ability to tell and re-tell their stories in a liberating way. *Storying is the means whereby we pass over from one life to the other and then come back to rediscover ourselves.* It is a means of self-knowledge and self-identity. In times of crisis and doubts, stories help to reconnect one with one's origin and ultimate meaning. To be alive is to have a story. Just as each of us has a story, so does the universe. Plants, animals and the entire cosmic system all have their own particular stories. Myth, in its original form of *mythos*, means a tale, a story, or a narrative. The storyteller decides the cast, arranges the scene and decides which scene to leave out or keep in.

The Most Important Freedom is Cognitive Freedom

For Africans then, economic and social freedom is not enough. Contrary to what prominent Nigerian political economist Claude Ake (2) believed, political freedom is necessary but not sufficient. The most important freedom, for Adodo as for Ndlovu-Gatsheni (see chapter 2), is cognitive freedom: *the freedom for Africans to tell their own stories based on their own experiences, so as to understand the present in light of the past.* Africans must 'own' the story they tell and take control of telling it in their own language and metaphors. They need cognitive freedom to help them resist the danger of being 'storyotyped' again, as their ancestors were. This is what OFIRDI as an institutionalised entity, a knowledge-creating research academy, is setting out to do.

Moreover, for Adodo, the path to emancipation in today's Africa is for the common people to free themselves from their own leaders. African leaders, from Zimbabwe to Uganda, from the Cameroons to Liberia, from Burundi to Togo, from Nigeria to the Ivory Coast, from Senegal to the Benin Republic, from Kenya to the Democratic Republic of Congo, to mention a few, have betrayed the trust of their people. They have succeeded in amassing state wealth to their own private pockets, lacking the will, skill and sincerity to govern and transform their countries. It is therefore obvious that Africans should not expect much from their leaders and must seek cognitive freedom, first and foremost, as a precondition for genuine political and economic freedom.

As such, civil wars or violent protests, as we recently saw in the so-called Tunisian and Egyptian uprisings, or indeed in the recent Zimbabwean opposition protests, cannot make this happen. A more systematic approach needs to evolve from the ground up or originate from one or more learning communities, emerging naturally and culturally, navigating scientifically and technologically and effecting economy and enterprise within a functional polity immediately within, in Adodo's case, Ewu, Edo State, Nigeria. Such overall transformation altogether through the integral Communitalism/Communi-versity/CARE model, is a more efficient and sustainable way to transform Africa than can be achieved through conventional political (electoral democracy) and economic (capitalism or socialism), thereby setting an example for the rest of the world.

9.1.2. Communitalism and the Four Pax's

Overall then, Adodo proposes the theory of communitalism as a more indigenous, sustainable and integral approach to tackling the social, political, economic and developmental challenges of today's Africa. Such a communitalist perspective, also called Pax Africana, builds on what he terms the 'Four Pax's (4P's)', addressing the four key dimensions of development. He terms these, duly aligned with Trans4m's integral worlds: Pax Communis (nature/community), Pax Spiritus (spirit/pilgrimium), Pax Scientia (science/academy) and Pax Economia (economy/laboratory), altogether woven into a cultural compatible African polity: Communitalism. These 4P's are expressed concretely in Ewu rural community of Edo State, Nigeria, through four corresponding local institutions, namely: EDEMCS in Ewo Community for Pax Communis; St Benedict Monastery for Pax Spiritus; OFIRDI together with Ibadan University Institute for African Studies for Pax Scientia and Pax Herbals for Pax Economia.

We now turn from 'south' to 'east', from OFIRDI to iSRA (integral Soulidarity Research Academy) and, societally, from Nigeria in West Africa to Pakistan in South-East Asia.

9.2. EMERGENT INSTITUTIONALISED RESEARCH IN THE EAST

9.2.1. Knowledge and Islam

Cognition Involves the Illumination of the Mind by the Active Intellect

Aneeqa Malik (3), co author with Amjad Saqib of *Integral Finance – Akhuwat – A Case Study of a Solidarity Economy*, initially asks "What is intuitive knowledge?" According to Persian polymath Ibn Sina, also known as Avicenna, every act of cognition involves the illumination of the mind by the active intellect, which bestows upon the mind the form whose knowledge is the knowledge of the subject in question. We can see therein the difference of natural-cultural emphasis between 'south' and 'east'.

The power of creative imagination then, for Saqib and Malik, which is only perfected in the Universal Man (*al-insan al-kamil* in Arabic), is able to create forms in the imaginal world and knows these forms ontologically, thereby duly embodied in iSRA. As maintained by Iranian Islamic philosopher Mulla Sadra, the very existence of these forms is the knowledge of them in the same way that according to Persian philosopher and founder of the Iranian school of Illuminationism, Shabab al-Din Suhrawardi, God's knowledge of the world is the very reality of the world.

Tasawwuf: Spiritual Science – Three Knowledge Domains Informing iSRA

Tasawwuf (spiritual science) is a branch of Islamic knowledge which focuses on the spiritual development of the Muslim. Thereby it disciplines the Self to act in accordance with its authenticated intentions by becoming an empty vessel receiving direct divine guidance. The subject of *tasawwuf* can be summarised as three knowledge domains as follows:

• Salvation from ignorance and attainment of gnosis *(ma'arifah)*.

264

- Refinement and purification of the Self (*tazkiyah al-nafs*) as the *existential knowledge domain*.
- Cleansing of the spiritual heart (*tasfiyah al-qalb*) and the enlightenment of the soul (*tajliyah al-ruh*) as the *active knowledge domain*.
- Sincerity and devotion to the Creator (*ikhlas*) and detachment from material and worldly concerns (*zuhd*), as well as commitment to the service of all the creatures of God as the *social knowledge domain*.

Soulidarity Economy: Spiritual, Social, Economic

As Aneeqa immersed herself more deeply into Akhuwat's philosophy of *mawakhat* (see chapter 5) and as it is professed by Amjad Saqib, a Sufi, she sensed that Akhuwat had the potential for defining a new model of economics and finance which was so unique that there might not be a single definition for it. Rather, it encompassed a combination of many disciplines and cultures in its spiritual, economic and social approach to development. It was therefore altogether distinctive in its *integral* approach, as few institutions, if any, (certainly no financially based institutions), had hitherto dared to incorporate as many human dimensions.

As such, Akhuwat is fully conscious of the various societal challenges faced by the Pakistani society and has thereby set out to provide solutions (and a societal framework) to assuage the social consequences of abject poverty. While providing interest-free micro-loans, it does not function or operate merely as a microfinance organisation; it also educates the masses by raising their awareness of 'reciprocal endowment' (Akhuwat's principles of volunteerism on the one hand and borrowers becoming donors on the other), thereby instilling a communal spirit of *mawakhat* (solidarity). Yet there is more to it than that.

Circumambulating the Ka'bah: Ishq – Ilm – Amal – Akhuwat

Fundamentally, in an Islamic setting, the four rounds of the rhythmic circumambulation of the Ka'bah (the God-GEN*E*), manifests itself through *ishq* (divine love), *ilm* (universal knowledge), *amal* (communal action and/or good deeds) and finally, *akhuwat* (universal soulidarity).

Amal, moreover, is underpinned by *ihsan*, an Arabic term meaning 'perfection' or 'excellence' (root word: *husn*). It is a matter of taking one's inner faith (*iman*) and showing it in both deeds and action (*amal*), a sense of social responsibility borne of religious convictions. It involves attaining perfection in performance through righteous deeds on Earth, doing good to people and advocating for the oppressed and vulnerable. So what, in light of the above, is iSRA?

9.2.2. Towards an Integral Soulidarity Research Academy (iSRA)

iSRA as a Research Academy, for Malik:

- spans in particular the UK and Pakistan, *contextualised with a particular learning Community* (Akhuwat has 800 such branches in Pakistan) within each;
- builds upon an *ummah-wide pilgrimium*, that is, the rebirthing of the prophet's Journey of Ascension from Trans-migration (from one land to another) to a transformation journey of 4 P's: Philosophy, Paradigm, Principles, Practices;
- thereby establishing *ways and means of CAREing for society* through iSRA's 4 E's: Epistemology, Economics, Enterprise and Ethics;
- ultimately leading, in conjunction with Akhuwat as a socioeconomic laboratory, to a new kind of 'communiversity', within which a Research Academy is key.

We now turn from 'east' to 'north', from Asia to Europe and more specifically to the developing RAiSE (Research Academy in Semiotic Economics) in Liverpool, UK, based at Hope University and the Communiversity Liverpool. In fact, it is our integral academies that undergird our overall approach to an *integral* communiversity, OFIRDI and iSRA forming a part of that whole, on the 'south' and 'east' respectively. As we shall see, our 'northern' centre based in the UK is more overtly 'social scientific' than our naturally 'southern' Nigerian and spiritually 'eastern' Pakistani counterparts.

9.3. *RAISE*: NAVIGATING INSTITUTIONALISED RESEARCH IN THE NORTH

When we turn 'north' we enter into the world of systems, models, science, technology and navigational processes. As such, it is to be expected that in this world we focus on institutionalising theories of knowledge that have been used to interpret meaning, values and culture, picking up from the 'east' and thence facilitating a transformation of neighbourhoods through 'sustainable regeneration', navigating towards the 'west'. This is the task of the evolving RAiSE academy and Communiversity Liverpool in the North of England.

9.3.1. Liverpool's post-Capital of Culture – Looking Forward and Back

It is far too simplistic to see Liverpool as rising like a phoenix from the ashes as a result of the cultural changes that took place in the city in the 1990s and the first decade of the new century. That said, it is clear that a new sense of vitality and purpose emerged in Liverpool, after the dark days of disruption that characterised the city during the 1970s and 80s. It was the fastest declining city in Western Europe, following decades of job losses, with the port losing out to competitors, strikes and political turmoil. But when the city, somewhat surprisingly, was successful in winning a bid to host the European Capital of Culture 2008 in 2003, it kick-started a *raising* of confidence in the city, looking to its future, based on its cultural history.

As far back as the early 18th century, Liverpool had always been one of the global centres of human cultural consciousness. Part of this resulted from the sickening evil of the 18th–19th century slave trade, which funded much of Liverpool's mercantilist and colonial prosperity. Even after abolition—and Liverpool and Manchester's port and mill workers had been officially thanked by US President Abraham Lincoln, for refusing to work for 'King Cotton' during the American Civil War—cotton remained king on the quaysides of Liverpool docks. Equally, with cotton, came a musical fusion of West African and Caribbean rhythms, spirituals, English folk tunes and street poetry. The great salvationist anthem, *Amazing Grace*, was penned by John Newton, a former slave-ship captain from Liverpool. A century and a half later it was sung at the Presidential inauguration of Barack Obama.

In the early 20th century, arts and culture movements were spawned in Liverpool on the back of worker militancy, police strikes, gunboats being sent by government down the Mersey River and the influence of visiting anarchist and Bolshevik leaders. Throughout the 20th century, Liverpool was famed for its entertainers, actors, film stars, comedians and, of course, musicians. By the 1960s 'Merseybeat' Liverpool had become one of the world's most important centres for popular music, nurturing not only The Beatles, but more than 300 rock-and-roll and R&B bands that changed pop culture forever.

Arguably, this legacy contributed to the city winning the bid to host the European Capital of Culture 2008. Alongside other celebrated sporting cultural products—such as the city's two top tier English football clubs and the staging of The Grand National—Liverpool's World Heritage Site waterfront, museums, galleries, theatres, historic buildings and two cathedrals, offered an unmistakable backdrop to displaying the meaning of a cultural city. These were icons of community, which challenged many of the darker aspects of Liverpool's culture of dependency and deprivation. They reflected an activated consciousness of what it was to be 'Scouse', with a unique identity, more so than in most cities. But, equally, they could be seen to reflect the deep divisions between cultural tribes across the city, often based in religious identity.

9.3.2. A meaningful culture-economy nexus?

Nevertheless, the Capital of Culture (CoC) helped to replace Liverpool on the cultural map as an outward-looking city, with significant impact in terms of attracting millions to its visitor economy, largely because of the city's cultural production. The Culture Company claimed that more than £1bn of direct benefits had accrued to the city from the CoC year (4). Moreover, there was widespread discussion of a 'Liverpool model' having been created.

Subsequently, other commentators (5, 6) have identified that the 'official model' of a cultural planning framework for urban renewal has been replaced by a more sober and realistic assessment of the limited potential for cultural events to transform a city's economic fortunes. This is partly because the definition of 'cultural production' had become so overarching as to become meaningless. At the same time, the capacity of the cultural industries sector, especially in an age of austerity, simply could not bear the burden of major city regeneration.

Kokosolakis et al. (7) argues that the branding of the city was imbalanced between the 'Livercool CoC' and the blight in vast parts of the city's urban landscape and severe poverty felt by a significant minority of the local population. An imbalance exists between culture and economy, in the way in which Liverpool tells its official story, of spatial representation, compared to the representational space experienced by the city's ordinary people. Nevertheless, in looking towards creating a new communiversity research academy, we argue that Liverpool's economic fortunes have been inextricably linked to the city's cultural consciousness and productive outputs for centuries.

Liverpool displays a culture-economy nexus. It has remained either the 5th or 6th most visited destination in the UK over the decade since the CoC year (8). As such, it is possible to extract very strong economic benefit trends from the data for Liverpool's recent expansion since 2008. However, much of these benefits accrue to businesses that appeal to those from outside the region, with only limited evidence that the impact is felt, in a balanced way, by those inside the city's local area. The challenge, therefore, is to work in partnership across the city, through a communiversity, to GEN*E*rate a more inclusive and transformation social and solidarity economy (SSE), for the Liverpool City Region. That is the prospective purpose for the development of Communiversity Liverpool and its RAiSE research academy.

9.3.3. RAiSEing the standard – steps towards the Communiversity Liverpool

Liverpool is a major port city. Indeed, it remained the world's second most important port after London well into the second decade of the 20th century. As such, it is used to receiving large ships and container vessels, each of which can be identified by the ensign or standard flag that it flies. The flag indicates the significance of the ship as it arrives at or leaves the port. The Port of Liverpool underwent a major decline during the latter part of the 21st century. However, it has been rejuvenated by the creation of Liverpool2 – The Superport, which is one of very few worldwide maritime centres that is capable of receiving the new post-Panamax super-containers. These will transport goods and materials to Europe's western coast through the newly constructed next generation Panama Canal.

This is both a reality and also a metaphor for the current transformative stage of Liverpool, albeit one which is yet to impact, in any substantial way, the city's many deprived neighbourhoods. In consequence, a team has been working on several complementary projects to develop Communiversity Liverpool, housing a new research academy, which is seeking to ground itself within the city's community, emerging a pilgrimium journey, utilising a particular 'northern' methodology, to navigate the co-creation of innovative enterprises, to develop the city's SSE.

Its grounding is within three communities:

• Liverpool Hope University's Business School (LHBS). Currently, the main research centre within this Mode 1 university is SEARCH (Social and Economic Applied Research Centre, at Hope). Within that centre two of the main projects developed by Tony Bradley are: (1) the investigation of how ecological economics is influencing changing patterns of business and politics in the UK; and, (2) working paper case studies in alternative economics, using the new methodology of semiotic economics. Over time, this facet of SEARCH is migrating to become the theoretical focus of a new, applied, research academy in semiotic economics: RAiSE. This reflects a play on words, to 'raise the flag' or a sign of the meaning and values bases that undergird many of the alternative economic systems that are emerging to challenge mono-cultural neo-liberal capitalism, as we enter deeper into the 21st century. Some of the methodological approaches of RAiSE were introduced in the Pilgrimium Theory chapter above.

• The Fabric District is an important enclave close to the city centre, which has been seriously neglected and run-down in recent decades. It abuts the city's Knowledge Quarter and Liverpool's three Mode 1 universities and is minutes from the city's main theatres, shopping centres, (Lime Street) railway station and historic museums and galleries. It is largely disregarded and unknown to the city's millions of visitors and most of its own population. Even so, as its name suggests, it has historical significance as the neighbourhood where fabrics and materials from across the world were made into garments and textiles for Liverpool's gentry.

Liverpool's Fabric District, looking North

Liverpool's Fabric District, looking East, Victorian buildings
(Photos courtesy Richard Jennions & Fabric District Team)

• Whilst some of the original fabric manufacturers continue to occupy sites in the district, it has become more associated with low-grade market stalls and a thoroughfare without any particular distinction. Even so, it contains a number of iconic Victorian buildings, some of which have been empty for decades, which are part of the renovation and regeneration process associated with Communiversity Liverpool. A significant aspect of the communiversity is to connect the current indigenous population of the district, some 15,000 students who live on its edge and the thousands of visitors who come to the city to the historic 'fabric' of the neighbourhood, as well as regenerating towards becoming the 'Fashion' District for the city. This involves a multi-million pound regeneration process, including the physical location of Communiversity Liverpool and the RAiSE research academy within the district's iconic buildings. The methods for engaging these communities will be through auto-ethnography, interpreting the district's historiography, semiotic economics methods and the generation of new research-to-innovation social enterprises.

• Liverpool City Region's (LCR) Social and Solidarity Economy. SSE is an increasingly understood phrase to reflect the changing pattern of many urban systems. As the local state retrenches under conditions of fiscal crisis and 'austerity', many third sector organisations such as social enterprises, co-operatives, charitable foundations and voluntary organisations have taken on the service functions that were traditionally associated with local and central government. The LCR has a thriving third sector. However, whilst several oversight bodies existed to connect the sector, these have largely disintegrated, as there has been a shift from third sector co-ordination to the formation of Impact Hubs, linking all sectors together. Communiversity Liverpool is developing that range of linkages, both physically and virtually, whilst offering a 'home' for the city-region's third sector to gather, study, learn and share. At this early stage the CL team is working with a wide range of stakeholders who have a role in the third sector. It is a matter of co-creative working to develop the research-to-innovation enterprises which will formally deliver this work over the coming years, to increasingly coalesce the SSE in Liverpool. This has been a very successful strategy in other UK cities, such as Brighton, Bristol, Manchester, parts of North and East London and Edinburgh, inter alia.

Within Communiversity Liverpool we are utilising a specific research methodology, as outlined in this book. It follows the pattern:

- Community activism
- Participatory action research
- Semiotic economic analysis
- Community building

That said, what is distinctive, in comparison with other examples included in this chapter, is the focus on infrastructural development, a formal process of planned regeneration and connecting the communiversity to urban design and heritage. This latter aspect is vital within the UK context and, specifically, in respect of Liverpool's culture-economy nexus. We see that transitioning from the Fabric to the Fashion District, as from materials to culture, is a vital feature of 21st century regeneration.

Equally, the significance of sustainable working, in the sense of following a de-carbonising process agenda, greening the city and offering a model case for how to create the environmentally conscious future city, are all aspects of communiversity's working. At this early stage we have placed far less emphasis on developing any formal curriculum for study. Rather, Communiversity Liverpool, as might be expected from a 'northern' perspective, is centred on RAiSE, understanding, interpreting and acting on the alternative economic meaning-systems that will help the city take its place in a world where culture, economy and a sustainable environment intersect at every level.

We now turn from 'south', 'east' and 'north' to a 'western' style research academy that is the Mode 2 University on which our South African partner institution, the Da Vinci Institute in South Africa, has modelled itself, duly inspired by recent developments primarily in the UK and first introduced in chapter 2.

9.4. MODE 2 UNIVERSITY: EFFECT INSTITUTIONALISED RESEARCH IN THE WEST

9.4.1. Towards the New Production of Knowledge

The Cast of Knowledge-Producing Characters

In the 1990s lead author Michael Gibbons (9), when the concept of the Mode 2 University was launched through *The New Production of Knowledge,* was Director of the Science Policy Research Unit at the University of Sussex in the UK. His countryman Peter Scott was Professor of Education at the University of Leeds and Martin Trow was Professor (Emeritus), Graduate School of Public Policy, at the University of California, Berkeley. All three were 'western' Anglo-Saxons by background and orientation, albeit supported by continental European and Canadian counterparts.

Mode 1 versus Mode 2 University

'Mode 2' knowledge production for them, as for our partner university, Da Vinci Institute in South Africa—co-founded by Nelson Mandela (10) in the 1990s, who also co-evolved the 'Robben Island University' (see chapter 2) while in prison for 27 years, in Mode 2 guise—is different from the approach of a Mode 1 university in nearly every respect. To begin with, it is *trans-disciplinary rather than mono or multi-disciplinary.* Secondly, it is carried out in *non-hierarchical, heterogeneously organised forms which are essentially transient, rather than being institutionalised primarily within conventional university structures.*

Mode 2 thereby involves the close interaction of many actors throughout the process of knowledge production, as is the case for ourselves, Trans4m, in conjunction with Da Vinci and our wider Trans4m Community. This means that knowledge production is becoming more broadly socially accountable. Thereby, Mode 2 makes use of a wider range of academic criteria in judging quality control than the conventional Mode 1 university. Overall, the process of Mode 2 knowledge production involves becoming more reflexive and affects at the deepest levels what shall count as 'good science', whether natural or social science, or indeed the humanities.

9.4.2. Towards Managing Socially Distributed Knowledge

The Challenge to Universities

The transformation of knowledge production, in the sense described above, is one of the central processes characterising the societies of the advanced industrial world. Knowledge production is less and less a self-contained activity. It is neither the science of the universities nor the technology of industry, to use an older classification for illustrative purposes. Knowledge production, not only in its theories or models but also in its methods and techniques, has spread from academia into all those institutions that seek social legitimation through recognisable competence and beyond. Science is less the preserve of a special type of institution, from which it is expected to spill over or spin off to the benefit of other sectors.

Knowledge production is thus an increasingly socially distributed process. Moreover its locus, for Gibbons, is global—or soon will be. At its base lies the expansion of numbers of sites which form the sources for a continual combination and recombination of knowledge resources; the multiplication of the nerve centres of knowledge. It is then in the adaptation of their research function to this distributed character of knowledge production that universities are most challenged. The university must enlarge its view of its role in knowledge production from that of being a monopoly supplier to becoming a national and international partner.

9.5. CONCLUSION

We have now run the full course of research academies, emerging in and around Trans4m, ranging from OFIRDI, locally in Nigeria, to iSRA, locally-globally in Pakistan–UK, to Liverpool Communiversity's RAiSE in the north of England, to the Mode 2 Da Vinci Institute globally-locally in the UK–South Africa, whereby through:

- INTEGRAL RESEARCH: OFIRDI as a 'southern' Institute dedicated to Integral Research and Development *seeks to assert the right of Africans to speak in their own language and metaphors* geared towards African **epistemological emancipation.**
- INTEGRAL ECONOMY: iSRA, an 'eastern' Soulidarity Research Academy involves a *rebirthing of the Prophet's Journey of Ascension* from **trans-migration to transformation** involving 4 E's: Epistemology, Ethics, Economy and Enterprise.
- INTEGRAL DEVELOPMENT: via 'northern' RAiSE – Research Academy for Integral Semiotic Economics, *a whole economic region is being developed through the prospective regeneration of Liverpool* into a knowledge based, **social and solidarity economy.**
- INTEGRAL ENTERPRISE: In a MODE 2 university as per Da Vinci Institute (SA) *knowledge production is spread throughout community, economy and society,* thereby resulting in **socially distributed knowledge.**

We now turn from research academy to socioeconomic laboratory.

277

9.6. REFERENCES

1 Adodo A (2017) *Community Enterprise in Africa: Communitalism as an Alternative to Capitalism.* Abingdon. Routledge.

2 Ake C (1996) *Democracy and Development in Africa.* Washington DC. Brookings Institute

3 Saqib M.A. and Malik A (2018) *Akhuwat - Islamic Finance: A Case Study in Solidarity Economy.* Abingdon. Routledge

4 Liverpool Culture Company (2008) *Liverpool 2008 European Capital of Culture. The Impact of a Year Like No Other.* Liverpool: Liverpool Culture Company.

5 Connolly, M.G. (2013) The Liverpool Model(s): cultural planning, Liverpool and Capital of Culture 2008. *International Journal of Cultural Policy*, 19, 2, 162-81.

6 Garcia, B, Melville, R and Cox, T (2010) Creating an Impact: Liverpool's experience as European Capital of Culture. Report to *Impacts 08 – European Capital of Culture Research Programme.* Liverpool: University/ John Moores. [Available at: http:// iccliverpool.ac.uk/].

7 Kokosalakis, C, Bagnall, G, Selby, M and Burns, S. (2006) Place image and urban regeneration in Liverpool. *International Journal of Consumer Studies*, 30, 4, 389-397. June.

8 Liverpool LEP (2015) Tourism Data Summary, June 2015. Liverpool: LLEP. [Available at: https://www.liverpoollep.org/wp-content/uploads/2015/07/Tourism-Data-Summary-June-2015.pdf.

9 Gibbons M, Limoges C, Nowotny H, Schwartzman S, Scott P, Trow M (1994) *The New Production of Knowledge: The Dynamics of Science and Research in Contemporary Societies.* London. Sage

10 Mandela N (1994) *The Long Walk to Freedom.* London. Abacus

WEST

PART 4: SOCIOECONOMIC LABORATORY

Chapter 10

Socio-Economic Laboratory in Theory

LEARNING/EXPERIMENTATION/INNOVATION

Epochal historical events have determined that the laboratory will continue to dominate the life of learning. Other late-twentieth century trends, like the democratisation and commercialisation of knowledge, are now pressuring existing institutions to meet the needs of the 'knowledge society'. Above all, the ascendancy of the laboratory is reshaping the basic missions of other institutions, pushing some toward obsolescence and giving others a new lease of life.

Wolverton and McNeely, *The Reinvention of Knowledge*

Integral Research/Action Research: In action research, *scientific research is inseparable from democratic social action.* Scientific knowing, like all other forms of knowledge, for individual and enterprise, is a product of continuous cycles of action and reflection.

Integral Development/Cultural Topography: There is a *rupture between the institutional design of a private enterprise and the cultural philosophy within most societies.* This needs to be surfaced, making such a rupture conscious prior to re-constructing enterprises.

Integral Enterprise/Sustainable Development: Capital stocks are constituted of natural and human, as well as manu-

281

factured and financial capital. The resulting *multifaceted flow forms enable companies and communities to engage in sustainable development.*

Integral Economy/A Genuine Well-being Assessment is analogous to a corporate annual report to shareholders, in this case revealing the economic, social and environmental conditions of well-being *using indicators that actually matter to people.*

10.1. PAX HERBALS AS A *SOCIO-ECONOMIC LABORATORY* IN THE SOUTH

10.1.1 Action Research, Social Experimentation and the Laboratory School

Dewey's University Laboratory School

We now turn from research academy to socioeconomic laboratory, our final 'western' port of communiversity call, firstly now in theory. The origins of action research (1), as we have already seen in chapter 8, underlying our laboratory, can be traced back to American pragmatic philosopher John Dewey (2) and his Euro-American compatriot Kurt Lewin (3). John Dewey moved to the University of Chicago at the turn of the 19th century to head the Department of Philosophy, Psychology and Pedagogy. It was at this time that he began to consider the philosophy of education in a serious and systematic way. In 1896, he therefore founded the University Laboratory School, now better known as the 'Dewey School'. It was a place for educational experiments in the genuine etymological sense of experiment—that is, to make a trial of something.

Theories and practices were developed, tested, criticised, refined and tried again. Experimentalism became increasingly important as Dewey's philosophy matured. For him, not only were these experiments falsifiable, but in a contingent evolving world, their generalisability was always subject to revision. There was no end of inquiry for Dewey; he believed it the best way to render human experience intelligent. For us then, the knowledge creating company, or other similar enterprise, becomes such a socioeconomic laboratory, especially when aligned with integral research and development, enterprise and ultimately, such an integral economy.

Hull-House Laboratory: John Dewey to Jane Addams

The Laboratory School was not the only site for educational research in Chicago at that time. Jane Addams and her work at Hull-House, for which she eventually received the Nobel Prize, greatly influenced Dewey. For Dewey, Hull-House was a laboratory and an example of what he was trying to accomplish in education. There he met some of the most influential early feminists whose involvement in the political issues of the day caused by massive immigration, the social and economic effects of urbanisation and rapid technological advance, exercised considerable influence. He also mixed with workers, trade unionists and political radicals.

Some of his most influential educational works emerged out of both these laboratories. These works not only set out Dewey's practical pedagogy, but they also outlined the psychological and philosophical principles upon which it relied. These principles devolved from the trial and error experiments that occurred within and without the walls of the Laboratory School. As we can see, then, they carried both a masculine (John Dewey) and feminine (Jane Addams) impulse. For us, they served to combine academy and laboratory in one and indeed their missionary zeal has pilgrimium-like connotations. What, then, are the specific tenets of the action research that both Dewey and Addams espoused?

10.1.2. Undertaking Action Research

Experimental Knowledge Creation

Dewey believed that all humans are capable of scientific judgment and that organisations specifically and society generally, could both be improved to the extent that these capacities are increased among all their members. Consistent with this, he strongly opposed the division of public education into vocational and academic tracks, seeing this as the preservation of inequality and ultimately the weakening of democracy as a whole. Everyone could be a capable participant in experimental knowledge creation. He believed that *limiting the learning of any individual ultimately limited society as a whole.*

For Dewey, scientific research was not a process separate from democratic social action. *Scientific knowing,* like all other forms of knowledge, for individual and enterprise, *was a product of continuous cycles of action and reflection.* The centre of gravity was always the learner's active pursuit of understanding through puzzle-solving activities with the materials at hand. The solutions achieved were only the best possible ones at that moment; hence, the denomination of his philosophy as pragmatism. At the same time he believed it was necessary to challenge prevailing, hierarchical power relations.

You Challenge Power Relations

Action research then, from the outset, has always had a political dimension to it. Overlapping with both feminism and critical theory, action and participatory research are closely interconnected. To listen to people is to empower them. Before you can expect to hear anything worth hearing, you have to examine—with a view to challenge—the power dynamics of the space and the social actors.

Social Research for Social Change

For American contemporary social researchers Greenwood and Levin (4), as such, *action research is a set of self-consciously collaborative and democratic strategies for generating knowledge and designing action, in which both trained experts in social and other forms of research and local stakeholders work together.* The research focus is chosen collaboratively among the local stakeholders and the action researchers and relationships amongst the participants are organised as joint learning processes. Action research (AR) centres engaged in doing 'with' rather than doing 'for' stakeholders, credit these with the richness of experience and reflective possibilities that experience with living in complex situations brings with it.

AR promotes broad participation in the research process and supports action leading to a more just, sustainable or satisfying situation for the stakeholders, thereby all too often challenging existing power relations.

Action Research Incorporates Action Learning

Finally, for the renowned English management philosopher Reg Revans, as the originator of 'action learning' (5), also hitherto mentor to Ronnie, the salvation of individual countries and their enterprises is not to be found by observers scouring the world in the hope of uncovering some miracle there. Their salvation, their 'Kingdom of God', is rather to be found within their own shores, their local sources and within the wills of their own people. At the level of individual enterprise, he further argues, it is not unreasonable to suggest that an essential part of any research and development policy is the study of the human effort, out of which the saleable products of the enterprise are largely created. Such a study involved 'scientific method' (survey, hypothesis, test, audit and control—the core elements of the action learning cycle).

Figure 2 Action Learning Cycle

Learning, moreover, must demand not only research and analysis; it must demand power to gain the knowledge needed to see one's part in what is going on. In particular, one needs to know the effect of one's behaviour upon those with whom one works. For Revans, this is best achieved within small 'action learning' groups. In the Japanese context, he referred particularly to the establishment of such work groups, not only with a high degree of autonomy, but organised in a way that gives people a continuing opportunity to develop. You learn with and from each other, in small groups or 'learning sets', by supportive attacks upon real and menacing problems, through:

- An exchange of information: ideas, advice, contacts, hunches, concepts.
- Interaction between set members, offering each other support/challenge.
- Behavioural change resulting more often from the re-interpretation of past experience than the acquisition of fresh knowledge.

Ultimately, for Revans, through the action learning process, *you learn more from comrades in adversity than from a teacher on high*. We now turn from action research to enterprise development—from the individual and interpersonal, if not also societal, to the specifically institutional—altogether underlying, initially in this micro enterprise guise, the

286

socio-economic laboratory. The transformative emphasis shifts, as such, from the individual and the group, to the enterprise in its environment.

10.2. INTEGRAL DEVELOPMENT, SOCIOECONOMIC LABORATORY

10.2.1. Ultimate Western Means: Tapping into Your Developmental Topography

The Four I's: Images, Ideas, Institutions, Inclinations

We now turn from action research to what we term our developmental topography (6). Our development topography distinguishes between four layers—images, ideologies, institutions and inclinations—with which a socioeconomic laboratory needs to be concerned and which we playfully dubbed 'the four I's'. In the following table we sketch out the characteristics of each layer and we also illustrate how the four layers are roughly related to our four integral worldviews or realities, all of which, for us, are required for a 'western' socioeconomic laboratory that builds integrally on what has come before.

Understanding the Developmental Topography

For thoroughgoing development to occur then, all four levels need to become dynamically interconnected. We begin with the images at the deepest level of our or enterprise self. They form the source of individual or institutional creativity and imagination.

Images – Touching the Core

The deepest source of individual and organisational—and indeed societal—development are archetypal images drawn from ancient stories (such as creation myths), the humanities and from the cultural depths of religion and spirituality, inclusive of language in its original context. They inform our imagination. They are the subject of what, in semiotic economics vein, co-author Tony Bradley refers to as 'archetypes of signification'. The uncovering of these represents the 'Eastern' second stage of the semiotic economics methodology, as an example of how an action research socioeconomic lab, connected to the RAiSE research academy can be involved in innovation-based knowledge creation.

Table14: Development Topography			
Topography	*Developmental Layers*	*Expressions*	*Integral Realities*
Top-Soil	Inclinations	Visible attitudes and behaviours/Outer practice	West
Sub-Soil	Institutions	The institutional frameworks that organise and direct our attitudes and behaviours, as well as the scientific disciplines underlying them	West North
Bedrock	Ideologies	The philosophies and worldviews that inform our way of thinking/ This layer includes ontology and epistemology, defining what counts as valid knowledge and how new knowledge is to be created	North East
Core	Images	The deep rooted images, beliefs and archetypal structures that inform, often unconsciously, our lives and that are directly related to our physical, psychological and spiritual existence ('human infrastructure')/ These root images provide in turn the foundation for philosophies and worldviews, as well as for institutional and conceptual frameworks	East South

Ideologies – The Bedrock on Which We Stand

At the bedrock level, we are dealing with philosophies and ideologies that lie well below the everyday surface. All too often, such a bedrock is globally imported from elsewhere—as was the case for both Russia and China in relation to communism—without being aligned with the local cultural and societal core. This always serves to distort whatever processes of renewal take place, unless such dis-integration is consciously addressed. Often, outer ideological imprints fall upon stony ground if they are not embedded or creatively assimilated in the individual, organisational and societal consciousness. In the RAiSE Liverpool case these relate to the ideologies of 'northernness', which differentiate the north of England from London and the south-east, in UK terms.

Institutions – Built up from our Collective Intelligence

Institutional and conceptual frameworks are the object of concern on this next layer. It includes legal systems, political and economic structures and predominating forms of public, private or civic enterprise. Here we are called to carefully distinguish whether we deal with a Spanish cooperative, a Zimbabwean integral *kumusha*, or an American corporation or a Japanese *kereitsu* (a Japanese style business group). Also included in this subsoil layer of depersonalised systems are management models, albeit conventionally restricted to 'western' ones that we study at Business Schools and that inform the design of much of our business institutions. Whereas it is individuals who characteristically get things going, with their personal and formative and idiosyncratic inclinations, institutions keep things going over the long haul, with their standardising rules and procedures. The power of the system is something that everyone who deals with institutional change recognises immediately. Within Liverpool, these institutions surround the port, the culture-economy nexus and the legal-insurance industrial sectors for which that city is second only to London, in the UK. They represent the *signs* of the semiotic process, pointing towards the ways in which that social economy is navigating its way through the choppy waters of capitalism.

Inclinations – The Visible Surface

We finally come to the practice of our individual inclinations, including attitudes and behaviours. Engaging with diverse development contexts, here we learn and discover how to exchange business cards in

Japan, whether or not to shake hands with Arab women, how formal or informal we should be with the French and what your attitude to time is in Harare or Hamburg. Many of our everyday conversations and dealings with different people and cultures tend to be conducted in these almost instinctive 'topsoil' terms and are thus focused on individual traits and identities. So far as Liverpool is concerned there is a very distinctive Scouse culture, with its own lingo, accent, music, sporting culture and ways of life.

What is then crucial, for our socioeconomic laboratory, is that it taps into and stays connected with all layers. In many individuals, organisations and societies—in particular in the so-called developing world—we will discover ruptures in between the four layers. We will notice that often ideologies (bedrock) are imported and not sufficiently home-grown or assimilated on the level of the core. Equally, in particular in the business world, we see a lack of connectedness with the institutional design of a private enterprise in Anglo-Saxon style (institutional layer), with the guiding cultural philosophy (bedrock) within many societies and so on. The development topography can help us to surface these ruptures, make them conscious and subsequently engage in re-constructing our enterprises, enabling them to become more authentic.

10.3. INTEGRAL ENTERPRISE TO SUSTAINABLE DEVELOPMENT

10.3.1. Community to Laboratory

In terms of this book, the culminating socio-economic laboratory, lodged inter/institutionally within the overall communiversity, builds purposefully on what has come before, though ultimately embodied in the practicality of the archetypal 'west'. However, it is a 'western-ness' that is able to take into account all that has come experientially (learning community), imaginatively (developmental pilgrimium) and conceptually (research academy) before it.

10.3.2. The Next Industrial Revolution

Capital Stocks: Financial to Human

At an enterprise level, America's Paul Hawken (7), together with his compatriots Amory and L. Hunter Lovins (economist, sociologist and physicist in turn) are seasoned environmental campaigners in America. They have, as such, reconceptualised business in an ecological light with a view to promoting sustainable development. *What is required,* Hawken suggests, *is the diligence to understand when and where Western style markets are dysfunctional and misapplied and to choose the correct targeted actions to help them operate more holistically* while retaining their pragmatic vigour and efficiency.

Hawken and his colleagues then seek to ensure, at an enterprise level, that what for them are four distinct capital stockholdings—financial and manufactured, natural and human—are as prudently stewarded as money is by the corporate finance director. This would lead to what we term not a purely financially-oriented free market, but ultimately a more holistically-based market integration of all the capital stockholdings, as outlined above.

The next industrial revolution after the digital revolution, as a result, has a particular structural as well as processal base to it. Within it, four kinds of 'capital stock' (structural) would be recognised, each one manifesting itself in four types of interconnected 'capital flows' (processal). These capital stocks are constituted of natural and human, as well as manufactured and financial capital. The flow forms enable companies and communities to engage in sustainable development. This means technically productive, biologically integrative, economically facilitative and ecologically restorative development.

291

Capital Flows: Productive to Restorative

- **Enhancing Productivity:** Hawken believes, as far as the flow of capital is concerned, that *radically increased resource productivity is required to 'kick-start' what he terms 'natural capitalism'*. Indeed, using resources more effectively has three major benefits: it slows resource depletion at one end of the value chain, lowers pollution at the other end and provides a basis for increasing worldwide employment.
- **Promoting Bio-mimicry:** Reducing the wasteful throughput of materials—thereby eliminating the very idea of waste—can be accomplished by redesigning industrial or utility-based systems along biological lines. This serves to change the nature of industrial processes and materials, enabling the newly sustainable company to maintain and develop a constant use of materials in continuous closed circles. *A knowledge-creating ecology needs to be uncovered and promoted, so as to recast knowledge management in a contemporary, biodynamic light.* This idea has been strongly developed by Ellen MacArthur and her foundation for the circular economy.
- **Service and Flow:** In calling for a fundamental change in the link between production and consumption, Hawken advocates a third *shift from an economy of goods and purchases to one of service and flow.* This entails a new perception of value, a shift from the acquisition of goods to the purchase of services, whereby quality, utility and performance is continually sought to promote natural and social well-being.
- **Restorative Economics:** Finally, a reversal of worldwide planetary destruction is required, through *reinvestments in sustaining, restoring and expanding stocks of natural and social capital.* As a result, the biosphere will be able to produce more abundant ecosystem services and natural resources.

Towards an Integral Perspective on Capital

Hawken's concept of natural stock comes very close to a 'four world' perspective, both being ultimately encompassed by our socioeconomic laboratory. In his capital stocks, then, Hawken distinguishes between a natural (southern), human (eastern), manufactured (northern), as well as financial (western) form of capital. His four capital flows have a strong emphasis on our south (ecologically restorative) and further include a northern (technically productive) as well as a western perspective (economically facilitative), though our 'east' gets less attention in their overall reformulation of the enterprise, as we find is so often the case. It is one of our principles of semiotic economics that there is a 'missing East', wherein the archetypes of signification, deep within the core of the economy, are ignored. We now turn from micro-enterprise to macro-economy, whereby our organisational laboratory now serves a more overtly societal purpose, starting with a review of wealth, well-being and money, in society.

10.4. WELL-BEING ECONOMY AND THE SOCIOECONOMIC LABORATORY

10.4.1. Wealth and Well-being

While the dominant meaning of wealth, for leading Canadian authority on 'well-being economics', Mark Anielski (8, 9), is associated, he says, with money, when he examines the origins of the word, he finds that the Old English term 'weal' or 'well-being' is combined with 'th' or 'condition'; that is, altogether, 'the condition of well-being'. In Greek the word for wealth is *euporeo*, which can be broken down into *eu* (well) and *poros* (a passage). In other words, wealth is a means to be well. For Anielski, then, wealth should not be defined in its narrow terms of the 'money value of material possessions', but must include the many intangible things that contribute to our quality of life including our spiritual well-being, hope, happiness and strength of our relationships.

According to the Jewish, Christian and Islamic tradition in fact, we learn that we are not owners of the earth but are at best co-stewards with

God. Jesus challenged, "What good will it be for a man if he gains the whole world, but forfeits his soul?" He taught a radical reordering of priorities, challenging us that we couldn't serve two masters—money and God—at the same time. As we saw, moreover, in our consideration of a moral economic core, many other faiths have come to similar conclusions.

For 19th century English philosopher, John Ruskin (10)—who heavily criticised laissez-faire economics for its failure to acknowledge complexities of human desires and motivation and who became a strong influence on Gandhi—real wealth is 'life', the power of living, of joy, of full life functionality. Therefore, Anielski argues, real economics should be concerned with real life issues, as opposed to a mathematical abstraction. In measuring real wealth, we should include not only monetary and worldly possessions but qualitative attributes like health (physical and mental), spiritual well-being, healthy relationships, love, respect and the well-being of nature.

10.4.2. What is Genuine Wealth?

To be genuine, for Anielski, *is to live in accordance with one's values;* to act against our values is to be disingenuous. By combining the words genuine and wealth we have 'genuine wealth', the conditions of well-being that are true to our core values in life.

Most economists today track minute changes in the production, consumption and distribution of material wealth using money-based metrics of performance like GDP, consumer price indices, stock market indices and currency exchange rates. Few are focused on measuring those conditions of well-being that households experience in their individual and collective pursuit of happiness, the virtuous or good life. John Maynard Keynes' vision of the future of economics (11) gives some hope:

> "*The day is not far off when the economic problem will take the back seat where it belongs and the arena of the heart and head will*

be occupied or reoccupied by our real problems—the problems of life and of human relations, of creation and behaviour and religion."

10.4.3. From GDP to GPI

Well-being, then, is more than making money and even more than just happiness. *Well-being means developing as a person, being fulfilled and making a meaningful contribution to the community.* GDP measures well-being purely in terms of what is bought and sold. This perspective, for Anielski, is too narrow; when searching for alternative approaches to measure well-being, he came across the GPI.

The Genuine Progress Indicator (GPI) was first developed by Cliff Cobb (12), an economist with the San Francisco Think Tank 'Redefining Progress', as an alternative measure of human well-being to the GDP. If the GDP was designed to account for the total monetary value of consumption and production in an economy, the GPI was designed to indicate genuine progress in people's quality of life and overall economic, social and environmental well-being.

The GDP's ideal economic hero for Anielski, in fact, is a chain-smoking, terminal cancer patient going through an expensive divorce whose car is involved in a 20-car pile-up, as a result of being distracted by his cell phone while munching on a fast-food hamburger—all activities that would contribute to the GNP. The inadequacy of the GDP as an indicator to measure a country's well-being, then, is highlighted by the following example: the US GPI results, for the period 1950 to 1995, showed a remarkable trend. While the GDP and the GPI rose in tandem from 1950 to 1973, the GPI reached its peak in 1973 and then declined steadily in the period from 1973 to 1995, even as the GDP continued to rise. The economists' mantra that GDP growth would be ultimately beneficial for all had been soundly repudiated.

The Genuine Progress Indicator (GPI), specifically then, addresses seven major fallacies embodied in the GDP and the national income accounts:

• GDP regards every expenditure as an addition to well-being regardless of what the expenditure is for and its effect; what economists call 'growth' is not the same as what is 'good'.

• GDP ignores the crucial economic functions that lie outside the realms of monetary exchange: unpaid housework, childcare, leisure pursuits.

• GDP does not account for natural resources required to sustain current and future economic development.

• GDP ignores overall distribution of income, social costs of inequality and poverty.

• GDP includes palliative expenditures like spending on arms, crime prevention, automobile accidents and tackling alcohol or drug abuse.

• GDP minimises the value of expenditures on education, health care, social services and environmental protection because it does not reflect returns on investment from such expenditures.

• GDP does not directly measure investment in social capital, including social institutions and democratic processes.

This leads us to the Genuine Wealth Model.

10.4.4. The Genuine Wealth Model

Genuine Wealth is Grounded in What We Value Most About Life

For Anielski, economics, as well as business, must be reoriented toward the genuine development of human well-being, in balance with the well-being of nature, not simply the pursuit of economic growth for its own sake.

Table 15	
Old Economy of Scarcity	New Economy of Well-being
Resources and money are scarce	All wealth is abundant – a gift from God
Progress driven by consumption/productivity	Progress driven by pursuit of well-being
Consumer	Citizen
Politician	Statesman
Hoarding and profit maximisation	Sharing, gifting, reciprocity
Fear of not enough	Joy in sufficiency
More growth is good and necessary	Sustainability and flourishing is sought

For him, Genuine Wealth is grounded in what he believes we value most about life: love, meaningful relationships, happiness, joy, freedom, sufficiency, justice and peace. Hence, *the ultimate goal is an economy and society dedicated to well-being.* Built on the principles and tools of the 500-year-old accounting model developed by Luca Pacioli, Genuine Wealth, for Anielski, takes into account all the conditions of life that contribute to our individual and collective well-being.

The Five Capitals of Genuine Wealth

As such, a socioeconomic laboratory may seek to contribute to, on a macro-societal level, five categories of wealth or capital which collectively contribute to the good life and form the basis for an economy of well-being. These are:

1. Human Capital: Human capital means people: the sum of our individual minds, bodies, spirit, soul, dreams, visions, knowledge, experience, skills and competencies.

2. Social Capital: Social capital refers to the strength of our relationships.

3. Natural Capital: Natural capital includes the free gifts from nature.

4. Built Capital: Built capital includes all things that have been made or manufactured with both human and natural capital, including equipment, factories, tools and buildings.

5. Financial Capital: Financial capital is essentially money or anything denominated in monetary terms including cash, savings and investments.

Concerning the accounting for the five capitals, one thing can be said: no matter how carefully we measure 'objectively', something is still missing; softer, intangible attributes of a thing or experience or what we feel in our hearts. Measuring subjectively means getting in touch with what we feel about a thing.

We finally turn to the Genuine Wealth Assessment Life-Cycle.

Genuine Wealth Assessment Life-Cycle

Like a medical check up, Genuine Wealth Assessment (GWA) is a comprehensive well-being check up for a household, business or community or nation.

1. Self-Examination: The first step in the GWA involves self-examination of our own quality of life.

2. Value Assessment: The second step is value assessment; we address the fundamental question: is life, individually or collectively, worthwhile?

3. Identifying Indicators of Well-being: The next step is to identify indicators of well-being, quality of life and sustainability. We are trying to identify measures that align with our values.

4. Genuine Wealth Inventory and Assessment: As Luca Pacioli reminded Venetian business people, keeping a good inventory of one's assets is important in running a flourishing business. Taking a Genuine Wealth inventory is more comprehensive: it involves assessing the conditions of all five forms of capital.

5. Developing the Genuine Wealth Balance Sheet: Once the inventory of community assets and liabilities is complete, we prepare a Genuine Wealth Balance Sheet, which reveals the conditions of the community's five forms of capital.

6. Well-being Visioning: Looking at our community, households or organisation, it is now possible to ask ourselves: "Given this reality, what future do we want for ourselves, our children and their children?" Visioning defines a desirable future state of well-being based on reflections in the mirror of current reality.

7. Backcasting: Comparing current conditions of well-being with our vision of the future. We must ensure that all wealth is conserved and that the integrity of all forms of capital is maintained—even improved—so that services may flow to future generations. This is at the heart of sustainability.

8. Creating a Future Well-being Report: A Genuine Well-being Report is analogous to a corporate annual report, here revealing the economic, social and environmental conditions of well-being using indicators that actually matter to people.

9. Genuine Wealth Development Projects: Reflecting on the results of the Genuine Well-being Assessment, households, businesses and decision makers can then plan to invest their time, money and other resources in actions and projects that sustain or improve the genuine wealth of the community. The Genuine Wealth process is a life cycle of designing–building–operating communities focused on improving their overall well-being.

10.5. CONCLUSION: ACTION RESEARCH TO GENUINE WELL-BEING

We have now completed our 'western' journey from action research to genuine well-being, altogether underlying our socio-economic laboratory. As such and in this duly western guise, within and across socio-economic laboratories, altogether with a view to realising a transformative effect:

• Via INTEGRAL RESEARCH you undertake **Action Research,** whereby *scientific research is inseparable from democratic social action.* Scientific knowing as such, for individual and enterprise, is a product of continuous cycles of action and reflection.

• Through INTEGRAL DEVELOPMENT you build a **Socio-Economic Laboratory**, thereby bridging the gap between underlying societal philosophies and surface business inclination, with a view to *re-constructing your enterprises, to become more authentic.*

• Through INTEGRAL ENTERPRISE, specifically turning finance into **Sustainable Development**, *capital stocks are now constituted of natural and human, as well as manufactured and financial capital.*

• Via an INTEGRAL ECONOMY, finally, you undertake a **Genuine Well-being Assessment** revealing the economic, social and environmental conditions of well-being *using indicators that actually matter to people.*

We now turn from theory to practice.

10.6. REFERENCES

1 Lessem R and Schieffer A (2010) *Integral Research and Innovation: Transforming Enterprise and Society.* Abingdon. Routledge.

2 Dewey J (2008) *Experience and Education.* New York. Free Press.

3 Lewin K (1997) *Field Theory in Social Science.* Washington DC. American Psychological Association.

4 Greenwood and Levin M eds (2007) *Introduction to Action Research.* London. Sage

5 Revans R. (2011) *The ABC of Action Learning.* Abingdon. Routledge

6 Schieffer A and Lessem R (2014) *Integral Development: Transforming Individual, Organisational and Societal Potential.* Abingdon. Routledge

7 Hawken P et al (2000) *Natural Capital: The Next Industrial Revolution.*

8 Anielski M (2007) *The Economics of Happiness: Building Genuine Wealth. Gabriola Island.* British Columbia. New Society Publishers.

9 Anielski M (2018) *An Economy of Well-being.* Gabriola Island. British Columbia. New Society Publishers.

10 Ruskin J (2007) *Unto this Last.* Milton Keynes. Filiquarian.

11 Keynes J.M. (1963) *Essays in Persuasion.* New York. W.W. Norton

12 Talberth, John, Cobb, C. and Slattery, N (2007). *The Genuine Progress Indicator 2006: A Tool for Sustainable Development.* Oakland, CA: Redefining Progress.

Chapter 11

Socio-Economic Laboratory in Practice

PAX HERBALS IN NIGERIA/AKHUWAT FINANCE IN PAKISTAN/MONDRAGON COOPERATIVES IN SPAIN/INTERFACE CARPETS IN AMERICA

The American economy bears in itself the sources of vital cultural and spiritual reality, because it is rooted in the unique American talent to use generously the gifts of great Mother Nature. Assimilating the best that European and Asian cultures can offer, it uses their unique capabilities to create an imaginative economy, politics and culture. Life, as such, is a perpetual process of becoming, evolution and transformation. This becomes the unique contribution of western culture to global culture.

Jessiah Ben Aharon, *America's Global Responsibility*

South – Pax Herbals' Healing Radiance: While in a clinic-oriented approach, emphasis is on scientific identification, conservation and use of medicinal plants, a community-oriented one applies simple herbal remedies to common illnesses: *the need is to harmonise the two.*

East – Akhuwat's Four I's: There is conventionally a rupture between the institutional design of an enterprise and the underlying cultural philosophy within most societies. In Akhuwat, as a socioeconomic laboratory, this rupture has surfaced and healed, *thereby constructing a solidarity based economy in Pakistan.*

North – Mondragon Cooperatives: *Linking of social, economic and technological ideas* is important not only in *shaping the internal development of each cooperative,* but in beginning the development of a network of mutually supportive ones.

West – Natural Interface: The idea of an *industrial enterprise underpinned by cyclical processes, doing no harm to the biosphere,* taking nothing from the earth that is not naturally and rapidly renewable and producing no waste, prevails.

11.1. ACTION RESEARCH TO *SOCIO-ECONOMIC LABORATORY* IN THE SOUTH

11.1.1. Monastery to Laboratory

What Sort of Man: Monk, Priest, Scholar, Herbalist

There had been a full-page write up in the country's *Guardian* in January 2003, one of Nigeria's elite newspapers and arguably the most respected Nigerian daily. The article was titled: 'Monk who heals with herbs'. The paper featured the picture of a man dressed in traditional and Western attire, looking like a traditional native doctor and Western physician at the same time. The caption said: "What sort of man is this?"

The article was about a Catholic priest who was also a herbalist, Christian theologian and a social scientist. It was a tribute to the uniqueness of what Anselm (Father Adodo) was doing: creating synergy, so to speak, between 'south' (nature), 'east' (spirit), 'north' (truth) and 'west' (enterprise). It also hinted at the paradox of a Catholic priest belonging to a highly conservative order who dedicated himself to the promotion of traditional medicine. It was the paradox of a man engaged in fusing indigenous with exogenous knowledge and the editor of the newspaper must have wondered, like many other observers, what sort of a man this is? Combining both the indigenous and the exogenous is certainly a challenging task.

His Goal was to Change the Face of African Traditional Medicine

Anselm had returned from America seven years earlier in 1996, armed with a bachelor's degree in Religious Studies and a master's in Systematic Theology from Duquesne University of the Holy Ghost, Pittsburgh, USA. He was immediately recruited to teach the phenomenology of religion, theology and sociology of religion, as well as comparative religion, in a nearby Catholic seminary where priests were trained. At the same time he was given the post of the monastery's bursar. The burning issue for the monastery then was how to become economically self-sufficient and stop depending on aid from the parent house in Ireland for its survival.

At the same time in Edo State, traditional healers and traditional shrines could be sighted in many corners of the village. There was a mission hospital and a government hospital in the village, but the majority of people also patronised traditional healers. Yet for a religious figure, especially a Catholic priest like Father Anselm, to be openly propagating traditional medicine was seen as a taboo of the highest order. His goal was to change the face of African traditional medicine and in fact, four years later in 2000, Anselm Adodo's book titled *Nature Power: A Christian Approach to Herbal Medicine* (1) was published.

11.1.2. Clinic versus Community-Oriented Approaches to Herbal Medicine

Clinic-Oriented Approach

For co-author Adodo (2), there were two approaches to herbal medicine practice, namely the clinic-oriented approach and community-oriented approach. In a clinic-oriented approach, emphasis is placed on scientific identification, conservation and use of medicinal plants. Laboratory research and screening is done to determine the chemical composition and biological activities of plants. Great interest is shown in quality control of raw materials and finished products and development of methods for large-scale production of labelled herbal drugs. The herbal drugs are labelled and packaged in the same way as modern drugs and distributed through similar channels; that is, through recognised health officials in hospitals, health centres or pharmaceutical supply chains. Huge sums of money are invested by the government, private companies and non-governmental organisations to promote further research in herbal medicine. Minimal interest is shown in the socio-cultural use of the plants.

Community-Oriented Approach

In the community-oriented approach, the emphasis is on the crude and local production of herbs used for common illnesses. Knowledge of the medicinal uses of herbs is spread to promote self-reliance. Information is freely given on disease prevention and origin of diseases. This approach aims at applying simple but effective herbal remedies to common illnesses. The target is the local community. No interest is shown in mass production of drugs for transportation to other parts of the country or exportation to other countries. The cultural context of the plants used is taken into account and local perception of health and healing often takes precedence over modern diagnostic technology. Simple herbal recipes are used for the treatment of such illnesses as coughs, colds, malaria and typhoid. Yet the two approaches analysed above are two extremes; there was a need to harmonise these two extremes to complement each other. Pax Herbals was thus established in 1996. It was registered as a private liability company in 2002, described then as a Catholic research centre for scientific identification, conservation, utilisation and development of African medicinal plants.

11.1.3. To Produce One Must Innovate

At Pax Herbals, Dr Father Anselm with his 150 co-producers, supported by some 1,000 distributors around Nigeria, today cultivate their own herbs directly and also through accredited local outgrowers. Pax Herbals is the only herbal manufacturing company left in Nigeria that is locally producing its herbal medicines, despite the harsh economic climate which makes it easier and more profitable to be an importer rather than a manufacturer. It is no wonder that the Nigerian market is flooded with herbal products imported from foreign countries.

Pax Herbals then believes that the only way to sustainable development is for Africa to produce what it consumes and consume what it produces. But to produce, one must innovate. Pax Herbals is determined to continue to champion the preservation of Africa indigenous knowledge for the sake of posterity of African medicine. We now turn from our practical grounding in Africa to further emergence in Asia, while still being focused on our socioeconomic laboratory. As such, we turn from Pax Herbals to Akhuwat.

11.2. CULTURAL TOPOGRAPHY TO *SOCIO-ECONOMIC LABORATORY* IN THE EAST

11.2.1. The Akhuwat Solidarity Model: *Mawakhat* and *Qard-e-Hasan*

Akhuwat's message of *mawakhat*—solidarity—and its approach to alleviate poverty, as we have described throughout this book, according to Saqib and Malik (3), is known as 'the Akhuwat Model', of, in our terms here, a 'socioeconomic laboratory' in Pakistan. Through various interactions and interventions, representatives of the organisation educate their people and their affiliates, as well as speak about their model with all relevant and interested stakeholders so as to promote its replication and also to promote better understanding of the Islamic principles involved.

The benefits are twofold: firstly, it helps to broaden the Islamic microfinance (*Qard-e-Hasan*) industry within the country, which helps immensely to reach more beneficiaries so as to enhance economic efficiency and create more jobs. Secondly, it creates a parallel microfinance industry that produces a *shari'ah* (Islamic law) compliant social and economic system tailored to the religious and cultural practices of the region. Akhuwat also supports all organisations engaging in this endeavour and makes resources available for interested stakeholders in order to facilitate their transition into this field.

Their support for replications is purely based on Amjad's dream of building an interest-free *mawakhat* community throughout Pakistan and ultimately the world. Thus, without any interest in capitalising on market shares, they invest their energy and resources into helping develop other organisations without detracting from their own Akhuwat objective. It contributes to Amjad's ultimate vision of a poverty-free society. In a period of over a decade, several organisations have implemented 'The Akhuwat Model' and added *Qard-e-Hasan* as one of the means towards their communal economic end.

11.2.2. A Virtuous Circle of Caring for Society

Akhuwat, then, is a beacon of hope, a virtuous cycle of caring for society and sharing happiness with others, which in turn takes people out of isolation and engages them to think about others too. It binds them with a sense of ownership and solidarity within their particular communities. More specifically, the overall Akhuwat model is underpinned by four principled activities:

Qard-e-Hasan: Interest-Free Loans

Microfinance is the provision of capital in small amounts to those who do not offer physical capital as a security for the return of borrower capital. Conventional microfinance is the circulation of that capital in such a way that it earns a financial return for the lender. Islamic microfinance is a form of non-conventional microfinance that is in keeping with the principles of Islam, i.e., interest is not involved. Akhuwat is a practitioner of the latter and is based on the principle of *Qard-e-Hasan*, the provision of interest-free loans to those in need.

Mawakhat: Compassion and Social Justice

The earliest illustration of *mawakhat* was seen in the network formed by the citizens of Medina and the *muhajir* (or Meccans who had migrated to Medina to escape persecution). Inspired by the idea which induced the Medinites (*ansar*) to share half of their wealth with outsiders, with the two groups declared brethren by the Holy Prophet (peace be upon him), Akhuwat seeks to diffuse this brotherly spirit through its operations.

Central Role of Religious Spaces

For Muslims, the mosque occupies a central place in the social, political and economic activities of the community. Most certainly, the mosque is first and foremost a place for remembering and worshipping the Almighty. The fact that Akhuwat has been able to achieve awe-inspiring success in meeting its goals is the natural consequence of the earnest application of its policy of abolishing *riba* (interest) and honourably helping the poor. As such, it gives houses of worship a significant role in the implementation of its objectives, i.e., the loans are always disbursed from the premises of the mosque (the church in the case of Christians and temples for Hindus).

The disbursement event symbolises the communal harmony which Akhuwat propagates and is attended by both borrowers and guarantors, where they become members of the Akhuwat family and its torchbearers. The mosque, church or temple is transformed into a centre of social and economic development.

Khidmet-e-khalq – Role of Volunteerism

One very important contributor to the success of Akhuwat is volunteerism. According to Amjad Saqib, as cited by Aneeqa Malik:

> *"We expect people to give their time and their abilities in the spirit of* Khidmet-e-Khalq *(community service); the spirit of the entire organisation is based on volunteerism. This is also derived from our faith, in which the principle of volunteerism is the most important part of our tradition. Every prophet is a volunteer, right from Abraham, Moses, Jesus and the Holy Prophet. The Prophets always looked beyond themselves to help the community socially, morally, economically and politically. We wanted to follow the footsteps of these great prophets and adopt their methods of bringing change to the community through participation."*

Altogether some 3,500 people are involved as volunteers and the senior executives of Akhuwat are themselves 'volunteers', thereby earning their daily living through other sources.

The 4 I's of Akhuwat Paradigm: Ikhlas, Ihsan, Iman, Ikhuwah

In more conceptual as well as spiritual terms, as a socioeconomic laboratory, for Amjad and Malik, the Akhuwat paradigm involves 4 I's:

- **Deploying Interest-Free Loans** *(Qard-e-Hasan)* – *Ikhlas* – Sincerity: a derivative of *tawhid* (Oneness of God).
- **Transforming Borrowers into Donors** – *Ihsan* – (Spreading) Excellence: the multiplier effect of virtue/*barakah*, further forming a solidarity bond amongst the community of Akhuwateers.
- **Activating Religious Spaces** – *Iman* – Faith: being a higher degree of Islam, *Iman* covers all faiths on a non-discriminatory basis as per Akhuwat's policy of non-discrimination by religion, race, class and gender.
- **Promoting Volunteerism** – *Ikhuwah* – Brotherhood: the eventual effect of the solidarity—transforming the spirit of solidarity into SOUL-idarity.

We now turn from Africa in the 'south' and Asia in the 'east' to Europe in the 'north', specifically to *Co-operativo Mondragon* in the Basque country in the Iberian peninsula, which Madrid would describe as part of Spain, also inspired—as has been the case for Father Anselm and Amjad Saqib—by a spiritual mission, in this case that of Catholic Father Arizmendi.

11.3. INTEGRAL ENTERPRISE TO *SOCIO-ECONOMIC LABORATORY* IN THE NORTH

11.3.1. Industrial Cooperatives as the Basic Building Blocks

The formative years in the history of the Mondragon complex (4) began with their projects in community health, the building of a sports programme and a campaign to establish a school in the Spanish Basque country in the middle of the last century. In the continuing dialogues with its originator, Father Don Jose Maria Arizmendi, the founders learnt the importance of integrating into their social vision a high level of competence in technical and economic affairs. This linking of social, economic and technological ideas was important not only in shaping the internal development of each cooperative, but in beginning the development of a network of mutually supportive ones, altogether set, for us, in the context of the Basque people's socioeconomic laboratory.

The development of the Mondragon cooperatives then falls into two phases: the establishment of the Ulgor steel foundry and the many cooperatives that followed over the course of the next 35 years, as well as the more closely integrated Mondragon Cooperative Corporation (MCC) in 1991. The basic building blocks of MCC are its industrial cooperatives owned and operated by its workers. They share in the profits or losses of the business according to the work value of their jobs and have an equal say in its governance. That they are able to do this is due to the unique structures and systems of governance that the Mondragon cooperatives have developed.

11.3.2. The Development of Unique Mondragon Structure and Systems

The General Assembly is the highest authority. The Governing Council conducts the affairs of the cooperative. Council meetings are held before the working day begins. The manager may attend in an advisory capacity, but has no vote. There is a separate Management Council where the top executives meet, so governance and operations are clearly separated. The final body, the annually selected Social Council, primarily represents the workers.

The earnings of the Mondragon cooperative are the property of its members. In place of wages, members are paid monthly advances—known as *anticipos*—against the income their cooperative expects to receive. The basis for advancement, except for the most senior members, is the labour value ratings assigned by a committee made up of the HR director and seven chosen members of the Social Council. Factors taken into account are decision-making responsibility, level of experience, skills or training required and health and safety considerations such as exposure to noise.

A further share of the cooperative's earnings is credited to the members as capital. The capital structure has been designed to produce the greatest possible consciousness on the part of members that they are stakeholders in their cooperative. An entry fee stands at $12,500 based on a 25% initial contribution, subsequently paid in monthly instalments. The cooperative then established individual capital accounts, which earn interest at an agreed rate and are credited each year with 45% of the cooperative's surplus, apportioned according to salary grades. A further 45% gets paid into reserves and 10% is set aside for social and educational purposes. How, then, has Mondragon evolved, economically as well as socially, over the years since its establishment in the 1950s?

11.3.3. The Advent of Consumer Cooperatives

Mondragon's initial focus on industrial cooperatives has expanded in recent years to include a major presence in consumer cooperation. In 1968, after a study of Swiss and French consumer cooperatives, Eroski was created, bringing together the existing consumer cooperatives in a single family. These cooperatives incorporate both workers and consumers as members. Consumer members are charged a $75 annual subscription, receive a 5% discount on all purchases and have access to consumer education courses. In 1992, Eroski was joined within MCC by the independent Valencian consumer cooperative, Consum. Hypermarkets, supermarkets, as well as shopping malls have since been established. However, the real key to Mondragon's growth and development lies elsewhere.

11.3.4. The Caja Laboral Credit Union

Stakeholding and democratic governance apart, the success of the Mondragon cooperatives is also largely due to the *unique system of secondary or support cooperatives from which the primary cooperatives (manufacturing and retailing) source key specialist services.* Arizmendi realised at a very early stage in the life of the cooperatives that expanding the existing businesses and creating new ones would require reliable access to capital on affordable terms. "A cooperative," he wrote, "must not condemn itself to the sole alternative of self-financing." His insight led, in 1959, to the establishment of the Caja in order to mobilise capital from the local and regional communities. It was to become not only the financer but also the driving force in shaping development and in holding the cooperatives together. Indeed, this expression of cooperative 'brotherhood', drawing on finance as a vehicle for such, is not unlike the mission of Akhuwat.

The slogan used by the Caja in the early stages was 'savings or suitcases'. Its real attraction to the local population was that they knew the money would be working on their behalf, to bring about development

313

from which they could directly benefit. The Caja in its original form was also the means whereby the cooperatives managed the capital held in their permanent reserves. They were able to borrow, moreover, at interest rates 3 to 4 per cent below the conventional market rate, freeing themselves from capital constraints which would have drastically curbed their development. From functioning purely as a source of capital for the cooperatives, the Caja then moved on to become the mechanism through which their association with one another—as another form of solidarity—was formalised and their activities integrated. Each cooperative was required to invest in the Caja, including holdings on behalf of the members, such as pension funds and workers' share capital. Each one was also required to adopt a five-year budget and report on it at monthly intervals.

11.3.5. The Financial Caja as a Socioeconomic Laboratory

As such, the Caja played a key role in developing new cooperatives and advising and helping existing cooperatives that were experiencing difficulties. These latter services were performed by the 'Empreserial Division' as 'factory factory'. The division consisted of 7 departments: advice and consultation; feasibility studies; agricultural and food promotion; industrial promotion; intervention; urban planning and building; auditing and information.

Together with the Caja Laboral Popular as a whole, it is the prototype of a new kind of economic development organisation, indeed a veritable socioeconomic laboratory, which further institutionalises the initial functioning of the small business enterprise. Where new cooperatives are concerned, a group of workers who were interested in establishing a new venture had first to find a product or service for which they believed there was a market, along with a manager. They were then in a position to approach the so-called Empreserial Division of the Caja. If the division believed the proposal was sound they assigned an advisor or 'godfather' to the group.

The group in turn registered as a cooperative and accepted a loan to cover the manager's salary while feasibility studies were being undertaken. These studies lasted up to two years, during which time a new product might emerge from the Division's 'ideas bank' and after which, design, production and marketing issues would be addressed. The completed study would be presented to the Operations Committee of the Banking Division of the Caja, which determined whether the venture should be approved. If approved, the 'godfather' continued to be seconded until a break-even point was reached. The Division then continued to remain in touch through the monthly reporting.

Moreover, when an existing cooperative experienced difficulty, there were various categories of intervention in place. Overall, no more than a handful of the more than 100 cooperatives have gone out of business to date. In all other instances of cooperatives finding themselves at risk, the Intervention Department was successful in putting them back on their feet. Just as the systematised innovation of the modern scientific research laboratory represented a major advance over the garage inventor, so the institutionalisation of entrepreneurship in the Empreserial Division represented a quantum leap over the isolated small business enterprises of the capitalist world. Further to such, indeed, is the institutionalisation of knowledge.

11.3.6. Knowledge Creation and R&D Are Key

For José Maria Aldecoa, President of Mondragon's 'consejo general', its knowledge orientation, with its own university, is what makes it stand out as a business group. The knowledge industry in which it operates, is, next to finance, industry and distribution, the fourth product area of the Group. The Mondragon University offers engineering and management degrees, alongside studies of humanities and education, including teacher training and psycho-pedagogy. It is worth noting that the research model which the university is pursuing is a collaborative one, carried out with the collaboration of three main agents—universities, technology centres and companies—thereby, in our terms, linking research academy and socioeconomic laboratory.

According to conventional wisdom, even if worker cooperatives can overcome the problems of democratic management and save or borrow the funds to expand or survive during recession, they are doomed to fail in the long run because they are small and lack the capacity for R&D (Research and Development). The solution in Mondragon was to create an applied research cooperative, to be supported by the industrial cooperatives. Initially, the purpose of the research at Ikerlan, which emerged out of Mondragon's Polytechnica, was to observe technology and production processes of the cooperatives to strengthen the teaching programme of the school. After several months, however, the vision was expanded to include research that would contribute to increasing the efficiency of the cooperative.

We now finally turn, laboratory-wise, from 'north' to 'west', to Interface Carpets.

11.4. WELL-BEING ECONOMY TO *SOCIO-ECONOMIC LABORATORY* IN THE WEST

11.4.1. Interface's Mid-Course Correction: Becoming Economically Restorative

Triggered by Engaging with Progressive Economic and Ecological Theorists

Interface Carpets in the U.S., upon the initiative of its founder Ray Anderson (5) in his late fifties, duly if inadvertently inspired by environmentalist Paul Hawken's *Ecology of Commerce* (6), started its drastic 'mid-course' transformation in the new millennium. Thereby, it incorporated life-enhancing principles into its organisational design. What is furthermore of interest (7), is that Anderson's initiative was *triggered by engaging with progressive economic and ecological theorists,* including the work of Paul Hawken, Al Gore, Donella Meadows, Rachel Carson and others.

Preparing to Provide 'Cradle-to-Cradle' Service

Anderson then challenged his 7,000 employees in the latter part of the 1990s to make Interface Carpets the first industrial company in the world to attain environmental sustainability and thereby to become restorative. To him, to be 'restorative' means to put back more than we take and to do good to the earth, not just avoid harm. Interface was preparing to provide cyclical, 'cradle-to-cradle' service to its customers, to be involved with them beyond the life of the company's products, into the next product reincarnation and the next. The distribution system would, through reverse logistics, become a collection and recycling system, keeping those precious carpet molecules moving through successive product lifecycles. Such a transformation did not come about by accident, but rather, as Anderson puts it, through a 'mid-course' correction in his life and enterprise. What led to it?

Anderson Was Talking About His Ultimate Purpose

As Anderson was coming to terms with his own midlife and maturity, with the sense of 'legacy' that comes with it, some of the people in Interface Research Corporation, the company's research arm, received questions from customers about what the company was doing for the environment. At that stage Anderson had no environmental vision whatsoever. Then, through sheer serendipity, someone sent him Paul Hawken's above book. He read it and it changed his life. It was an epiphany; a spear in the chest. A powerful sense of urgency emerged. A child prodigy in its youth, Interface would now become a virtuoso. Anderson was talking about his ultimate purpose: in our terms, his calling aligned with what the planet was ultimately calling for.

What was that?

11.4.2. Business Must Take the Environmental Lead: Exercising Ecosense

In making his first environmentally based speech, at the time Anderson borrowed Hawken's ideas shamelessly. He agreed completely with the latter's central thesis: *that business and industry must take the lead in directing the Earth away from the route it is on toward the abyss of man-made collapse.* Anderson then offered his vision: Interface, the first name in industrial ecology. His mission was to convert Interface into a Restorative Enterprise, first to reach sustainability, then to become restorative—to put back more than it takes out from the Earth. And he suggested a strategy: reduce, reuse, reclaim, recycle—later, 'redesign' was added. Anderson gave this effort the name 'Ecosense', hoping to involve all 7,000 people in the company.

There was much for him to learn that year. He continued to read, going back to Carson's seminal *Silent Spring* (8), then US Vice President Gore's *Earth in Balance* (9) and Meadows' *Beyond the Limits* (10). He devoured Daly and Cobb's *For the Common Good* (11), trying to get to grips with the economics of sustainability. Their books sought to turn traditional economics on its head by suggesting that enlightened self-interest, which, it was argued, guided the individual, should be replaced by an understanding of the place of persons within the community. It was then that Interface developed for the first time in history the perpetual lease carpet. It was called the 'Evergreen Lease'.

11.4.3. Evergreen Release

Orientation to Recycling

In the Evergreen Lease, Interface not only made the carpet with state-of-the-art recycled content, but also took responsibility for installing the carpet and maintaining it. Not only did the company clean it regularly, but also replaced damaged carpet squares. Interface implemented a rolling, progressive continuous facelift, recycling the carpet tiles that came up for replacement. Specifically, it recycled used fibre into new face fibre to be made into new carpet tiles. The Evergreen Lease is a manifestation of the future, for a wide range of durable manufacturing goods. It is one example of how commerce can be redesigned for the 21st century to use abundant labour and reduce dependence on diminishing virgin resources as well as increase efficiency in resource usage by forcing manufacturers to think cradle-to-cradle. What, then, was the company's vision and mission?

Vision and Mission

Vision: Becoming Restorative

"To be the first company that, by its deeds, shows the entire industrial world what sustainability is in all its dimensions: people, process, product, place and profits—by 2020—and in doing so we will become restorative through the power of influence."

Mission: Become the First Name in Industrial Ecology

"Interface will become the first name in commercial and institutional interiors worldwide through its commitment to people, process, product, place and profits. *We will strive to create an organisation wherein all people are accorded unconditional respect and dignity; one that allows each person to continuously learn and develop. We will focus on product (which includes service) through constant emphasis on process quality and engineering, which we will combine with careful attention to our customers' needs so as always to deliver superior value to our customers, thereby maximising all stakeholders' satisfaction. We will honour the places where we do business by endeavouring to become the first name in industrial ecology,* a corporation that cherishes nature and restores the environment. *Interface will lead by example and validate by results, including profits, leaving the world a better place than when*

we began and we will be restorative through the power of our influence in the world."

There was no blueprint for this kind of organisation in business; however, there was in nature. If nature designed an industrial process, what might it look like? How could Interface translate the operations of nature into a model for a business?

11.4.4. Interface Following Nature's Design Principles

Nature, for Anderson, has a set of *fundamental operating principles* (12): it runs on sunlight and other renewable energy sources, it fits form to function, it recycles everything and is extremely efficient—never creating excess or wasting—and, finally, it rewards cooperation. Interface's job was to translate these principles into a new model for business. To begin with, it meant that it would become a business that runs on renewable energy. The company would carefully eliminate waste from all areas of its operations and recycle and then reuse the materials from its products and those that support its business. It would find a use for everything it used and waste nothing. And finally, it, too, would reward cooperation—with suppliers, customers, investors and with communities.

Anderson told a group of his people at a design workshop: "Go and see how nature would design a floor covering. And don't come back with leaf designs—that's not what I mean. Come back with design principles. What are nature's design principles?" His people subsequently spent a day in the forest, looking at the forest floor, looking at the streambed and finally it dawned on them: there are no two things alike on the forest floor. Each stick and every leaf is different. Yet, there is a uniformity to that chaos; a sort of organised chaos. "You can pick up a stick here and drop it there and you can't tell you've changed anything."

Nature's design principle is basically organised chaos and total diversity. Thus, they designed a carpet tile where no two were alike. Aside from being a very pleasant aesthetic that emulated the forest floor, it turned out to be practically waste-free in the production process. Interface was becoming a natural, as well as a socioeconomic, laboratory.

11.4.5. Inspired by Biomimicry

The head of product development then read Janine Benyus's famous book, *Biomimicry*, (13) and he was inspired. He came to the chapter on the industrial organisation and how a company could be organised to simulate nature. As he read it, he envisaged a new Interface. Benyus did not know Interface when she wrote the book, but what she described as the industrial enterprise that is modelled after nature was Interface: the idea of cyclical processes, doing no harm to the biosphere, taking nothing from the earth that is not naturally and rapidly renewable and producing no waste (c.f. MacArthur's circular economy).

Anderson (14) wanted to drive the whole company with sunlight, renewable energy, closing the loop on material flows so that one has not only the basic organic cycle—the dust to dust cycle—but in an analogous way, a technical cycle that takes used-up products and gives them life-after-life through the recycling process, so that no molecules are lost; everything stays in the material loop. All of this is basically emulating nature in an industrial system and that remains the company goal. This represents a total transformation.

11.5. CONCLUSION

Interweaving the theory of a socioeconomic laboratory—from integral research and development to enterprise and economy, with now the practice—spanning south (Pax Herbals) and east (Akhuwat), north (Mondragon) and west (Interface), we transformatively and effectively involve here, as in the previous practical cases:

- INTEGRAL RESEARCH: Through **Action Research** an analytically based *scientifically-oriented approach* is harmonised with a communally oriented, participative one.

• INTEGRAL DEVELOPMENT: *Overcoming the rupture between overarching institutional design and underlying cultural philosophy,* a **Socioeconomic Laboratory** serves ultimately to heal this divide.

• INTEGRAL ENTERPRISE: Linking of social, economic and technological ideas is important not only in *shaping the internal development of each enterprise,* but in promoting **Sustainable Development** as a whole.

• INTEGRAL ECONOMY: Promoting **Economic and Natural Well-being** via an *industrial enterprise underpinned by cyclical processes* takes nothing from the earth that is not naturally and rapidly renewable and produces no waste.

In this respect the Socioeconomic Laboratory, as illustrated in each of the four above cases, serves as the culmination of our communiversity, building respectively on the Learning Community, Re-GEN*E*-rative pilgrimium and Research Academy that came before. To illustrate this, now as an integral whole, we turn to the concluding chapter on our communiversity in Nigeria and the communitalism with which it is associated, before finally introducing the next stage of our institutional journey: Trans4m Communiversity Associates (TCA).

11.6. REFERENCES

1 Adodo A (2012) *Nature Power: A Christian Approach to Herbal Medicine. New Edition.* Edo State. Benedictine Publications

2 Adodo A (2003) *Healing Radiance of the Soul: A Guide to Holistic Healing.* Edo State. Agelex Publications

3 Saqib A and Malik A (2018) *Integral Finance – Akhuwat: A Case Study in Economic Solidarity.* Abingdon. Routledge

4 Lessem R and Schieffer A (2010) *Integral Economics: Releasing the Economic Genus of your Society.* Abingdon. Routledge

5 Anderson, R (1998). *Mid-Course Correction: Toward a Sustainable Enterprise: The Interface Model.* Vermont: Chelsea Green.

6 Hawken, P (1994) *The Ecology of Commerce: A Declaration of Sustainability.* New York: HarperBusiness.

7 Lessem R and Schieffer A (2010) *op cit*

8 Carson, R. (2002) *Silent Spring.* Boston: Mariner.

9 Gore, A. (2006) *Earth in the Balance: Ecology and the Human Spirit.* Emmaus: Rodale.

10 Meadows, D (1993) *Beyond the Limits: Confronting Global Collapse, Envisioning a Sustainable.* Vermont: Chelsea Green.

11 Daly, H & Cobb, J (1994) *For the Common Good: Redirecting the Economy toward Community, the Environment and a Sustainable Future.* Boston: Beacon.

12 Anderson, R (Spring 2004) Nature and the Industrial Enterprise. In: *Engineering Enterprise.* Alumnae Magazine for IsyE. Atlanta: Georgia Institute of Technology.

13 Benyus, J (2002) *Biomimicry: Innovation Inspired by Nature.* New York. Harper Perennial.

14 Anderson, R (2009) *Confessions of a Radical Industrialist – Profit, People Purpose. Doing Business by Respecting the Earth.* New York: St. Martin's Press.

CONCLUSION

Chapter 12

Communitalism to Communiversity

FROM GLOBAL IDEALS TO LOCAL RELEVANCE

Until the Lion learns to write, every story will glorify the hunter.

African Proverb

12.1. INTRODUCTION

12.1.1. Communitalism and Communiversity

In this concluding chapter, co-author Anselm Adodo carries on from where he left off in his book, *Integral Community Enterprise in Africa* (1), with his theory of communitalism, which is resonant with our overall orientation towards a communiversity, before our final consideration of an association to take this story onto its next phase. The basis of the theory of communitalism, generally, as for our communiversity, specifically, is that we cannot separate community from spirituality, science from economics, research from teaching and ecology from politics. In that guise we are also in tune with the arguments underlying de-coloniality (chapter 2). Moreover, the reason this culminating chapter is based in Africa is that it is the African continent which is giving birth in practice to the idea of the communiversity.

Communitalism demonstrates the critical role of African voices, or southern theories, in the global intellectual space. Thomas Sankara (2) once said that there could be no true liberation for Africa without the true liberation of women. In the same vein, there can be no integral development in the world without the contribution of the southern voice, precisely Africa. Former French president Nicolas Sarkozy, during an address in Dakar, Senegal in 2012, infamously and cynically said, "The tragedy of Africa is that the African has not fully entered into history... They have never really launched themselves into the future."

Perhaps the problem is that the Western world is too engrossed in its own concepts, theories and stereotypes to see the contributions Africa has and is making to the world. The Igbo of eastern Nigeria have a proverb that says, "When something stands, another thing will stand beside it." This proverb refers to openness to new ways of life, a new way of doing things and the fact that mono-culturalism, mono-economics, mono-politics are not only against democracy but are also against nature. We now look at the theory of communitalism in detail and how it is being applied in Africa, particularly in Nigeria.

12.1.2. Communitalism: An African Theory of Interconnectedness of Knowledge

Western theories such as Marxism, capitalism, socialism and communism, while focusing on economics, technology and enterprise, failed to build their concepts on nature and culture, thus leading to unsustainable and imbalanced development. Communitalism argues that an integral approach, which takes account of the totality of the above, set within a particular society, building up from nature and community and embracing culture, politics, economics, spirituality and enterprise, is a surer path to sustainable and integral development in Africa. What, then, is communitalism?

Communitalism, as opposed to capitalism or communism, is an integral approach to knowledge creation and development that is grounded in a particular enterprise-in-community, while ultimately affecting a whole society, emerging indigenously and exogenously as such. Such a communitalist perspective, built on the four Pax's (4 P's), addresses the four key dimensions of development, which are identified as follows: Pax Communis (community), Pax Spiritus (pilgrimium), Pax Scientia (university) and Pax Economia (laboratory). We will now look at the four Pax's in detail.

12.2. PAX COMMUNIS, PAX SPIRITUS, PAX SCIENTIA AND PAX ECONOMIA

12.2.1. The Four Pax's

The chief characteristic of conventional or Mode 1 universities, as we saw in chapter 1, is their preoccupation with fundamental research with little or no interest in the application of the knowledge, especially in the social sciences. Mode 1 universities are built on the concept of research as an objective search for truth, independent of nature, community and the environment. It is assumed that to become 'educated' and be recognised as a 'scholar', one must separate oneself from the environment and assume a 'scientific' distance from the object under observation. Schools become places set apart from one's natural habits, a place where one goes to acquire knowledge. The question then is not whether such an approach to knowledge creation is valid or not. The problem is that such an approach, which reflects the attitude and tendency of a small part of the world, has been universalised, globalised and imposed on most of the world. The educational system has become so structured and rigid and the means of knowledge creation so regimented, that no other mode of knowledge creation can survive. So pervasive is this control of the tools of knowledge production that most people do not realise that the current system of education is recent. One hundred years ago, education was carried out mainly in homes and the emphasis on paper certificates was non-existent.

For Ivan Illich, a deschooling of the society is urgently needed, both in the Western world and in Africa (4). According to him, schools and universities are structured to serve only as recruiting grounds for workers in the consumer society. University students look forward to their graduation day when they will receive their certificates and be qualified to be employed in the civil service or in corporations. In post-colonial Africa, the emergent universities were built on Western concepts of schooling and had nothing to do with indigenous institutions. The structure, arrangement and orientation of the universities were based on 19th century German educational models. Universities were located away from communities and characterised by gated high walls and foreign-style architecture. Clear boundaries were drawn between the administrators, academic communities and fee-paying students. The different groups were also characterised by peculiar dress codes, inspired by their Western counterparts.

The tragedy of education in Africa is that the university system, which was inherited from the colonial rulers, has become an effective tool of re-colonisation. The African university system is so deeply entrenched in the Western worldview that it is unable to critique its own relevance within the local, political, economic and cultural settings. Students who come to the university are made to feel that they are being introduced to a different world from their native world and the path to progress lies in how quickly they can imbibe this new world. They are expected to adopt the dress codes and research methodology of their academic disciplines, as a mark of induction into the new academic community.

The communiversity movement, which this book has initiated, is a major contribution towards a practical and constructive critique of schooling in Africa and how African universities can re-examine their 'university-ness' and their relevance in present day Africa. Our 'communiversity' then, as intimated from the outset of this book, evolves from university, beyond pluriversity to a multiversity. One of the core ideas is that there are different types of intelligence. In the communiversity, recognition is given to the myriad of forms of intelligence and everybody can discover and develop himself or herself accordingly. To limit every student and all reality to a certain way of thinking, seeing and being, is a great disservice to human creativity and intelligence.

12.2.2. Towards a Communiversity: Locally Global and Globally Local

The four Pax dimensions, for us, are brought together as a commune, a community of knowledge, bridging the gap between community, spirit, nature and reason. It is a return not just to a 'Mode 2', or context-driven method of research, which was the dominant way of knowledge creation until the 19th century; rather, it envisions a new way of knowledge creation that consciously addresses contextual issues in every community. Such a newly African philosophy-in-practice, for Adodo, has moreover been developed in and grounded on four real, tangible and visible institutions, representing the four dimensions of our envisaged communiversity: community, culture, knowledge creation and laboratory. The emphasis is on contextualising knowledge and anchoring it in particular contexts. We now look at how this contextualisation of knowledge has been done in Nigeria.

Each of the four dimensions is anchored in a visible, living institution in a particular polity. In Table 16, the characteristics of each Pax dimension and the corresponding institution that actualise the characteristics are described. This is the unique feature of communitalism: *ideas must be translated into action*. A communiversity, then, is a laboratory, a place of action-research, philosophy-in-action, where theories and action, dream and reality, are dynamically merged. It is a place where knowledge is translated into capabilities and capabilities are translated into knowledge. Education is not something done in isolation from one's community. Rather, education takes place in full embeddedness in the real world of one's community.

12.2.3. Introducing the Four Pax's

The Four Pax Dimensions

The table below shows the structure of the Nigerian communiversity:

Table 16: THE NIGERIAN COMMUNIVERSITY CASE		
PAX DIMENSION	CHARACTERISTICS	CORRESPONDING INSTITUTIONS
PAX COMMUNIS (COMMUNITY)	- A visible, physical, identifiable community with a leadership structure, tradition and ethical codes - A physical environment with ecological features such as land, river, plants, animals and an ecological ecosystem - A group of people living in recognised locations, who trade with one another and interact with one another, operation under codes of conduct and interaction	- The Ewu Kingdom in Edo State, Nigeria
PAX SPIRITUS (SANCTUARY/ PILGRIMIUM)	-A physical location set aside for spiritual exercises - A spiritual centre where people come for prayer, meditation or spiritual renewal - A church, mosque, shrine, meditation room, or even a meditation chair - A place of worship - A shared spiritual journey	- St Benedict Monastery
PAX SCIENTIA (UNIVERSITY)	- A research and learning institution with clearly defined the structure - A research academy - A polytechnic - A school for boys and girls - A scientific research institute - A village study centre - A library	- Pax Centre for Integral Research and Development - University of Ibadan Institute of African Studies - African Action Research Community
PAX ECONOMIA (LABORATORY)	- A functioning enterprise with leadership and administrative structure - A business centre with a clear organogram - A sole entrepreneurship - A production factory - A laboratory where codified knowledge is declassified and converted into products and services	-Pax Herbals

Figure 3 Decoding the Four Pax's

12.2.4. Pax Communis: Natural and Human Learning Communities

The Power of Place

For the African, the community is a place of creativity, healing and relationship. Even though the community embraces both the visible and invisible, the natural and supernatural world, like the world of spirits, it should be noted that the point of interaction is always the visible community. The earth is where we live, relate, procreate and discover our creativity. As a person, I am born into a certain place, on a certain date, at a certain time, into a certain family. These facts play a key role in determining my destiny, my orientation and my sense of self. I am not just a vague entity. I belong to a place. No one becomes a global citizen at birth. Each person is a local entity, a local person.

The Christian religion maintains that Jesus Christ is the Son of God, a universal king and ruler of the world. However, Jesus Christ was born into a local community; he was utterly local. In fact, the Bible goes to great lengths to establish the genealogy of Jesus. In the Gospel of Luke, the author went further back to Adam, regarded as the father of humanity in Christian Tradition: the first man. Luke identified 42 generations from David to Joseph. In the book of Matthew, his roots were traced to several generations, starting with Abraham. According to Matthew, there were 27 generations from David to Joseph. Matthew's account (Matthew, 1:1–17) goes thus:

"An account of the genealogy of Jesus the Messiah, the son of David, the son of Abraham. Abraham was the father of Isaac and Isaac the father of Jacob and Jacob the father of Judah and his brothers and Judah the father of Perez and Zerah by Tamar and Perez the father of Heron and Heron the father of Aram and Aram the father of Aminadab and Aminadab the father of Nahshon and Nahshon the father of Salmon and Salmon the father of Boaz by Rahab and Boaz the father of Obed by Ruth and Obed the father of Jesse and Jesse the father of King David.

And David was the father of Solomon by the wife of Uriah and Solomon the father of Rehoboam and Rehoboam the father of Abijah and Abijah the father of Asaph and Asaph the father of Jehoshaphat and Jehoshaphat the father of Joram and Joram the father of Uzziah and Uzziah the father of Jotham and Jotham the father of Ahaz and Ahaz the father of Hezekiah and Hezekiah the father of Manasseh and Manasseh the father of Amos and Amos* the father of Josiah and Josiah the father of Jechoniah and his brothers, at the time of the deportation to Babylon.

And after the deportation to Babylon: Jechoniah was the father of Salathiel and Salathiel the father of Zerubbabel and Zerubbabel the father of Abiud and Abiud the father of Eliakim and Eliakim the father of Azor and Azor the father of Zadok and Zadok the father of Achim and Achim the father of Eliud and Eliud the father of Eleazar and Eleazar the father of Matthan and Matthan the father of Jacob and Jacob the father of Joseph the husband of Mary, of whom Jesus was born, who is called the Messiah."

Each person, then, is a product of a community. We must recognise, embrace and identify with our local origin. Jesus was not a faceless global citizen. He is Jesus of Nazareth. Mohammed is not a global citizen; he was an Arabian preacher. The Pope is primarily referred to by Catholics as the Bishop of Rome, not the Bishop of the world. Each person must accept his or her local identity and recognise the local identity of others so that they can see how humanity is connected. All education, all learning, must begin with this consciousness; that we are products of our environment, through the physical and social, biological and cultural.

Communis: A Symbiotic Community

As Adodo (5) has claimed, there is in fact a very close link between plants and animals. Their names often describe their relationship with animals, for example, catnip, horsetail, goat weed, bird's eye, cat eye and pigweed, among many others. There are over 400,000 species of plants on this planet. Human beings in different continents use about 100,000 of these plants for medicinal purposes. Of these, only 10,000 have been clinically analysed and thus recommended for human consumption.

Biology studies the human bodily system and how it works. Botany studies the similarities and dissimilarities of different species of plants and their usefulness. Taxonomy studies the varieties of plants and how to identify them. Pharmacognosy analyses the chemical composition of different plants. Through these disciplines, our knowledge of plants has increased and the usefulness of plants is now better appreciated. In fact, science is discovering that we have not yet even begun to explore the deep mysteries of life. Every day, every hour, new species of plants are created, unnoticed to our human eyes.

Every plant has a reason for existing. Plants grow for a particular purpose. Every plant is a manifestation of the energy field of the universe. Some plants exist to nourish the earth; some exist to give support to other plants; some grow to help regulate the exchange of oxygen and carbon dioxide between human beings and plants; some give information about events.

It has been demonstrated that plants feel the vibration of human thought (6). This is because both plants and animals have their own particular energy field, each vibrating at different frequencies. To a greater or lesser degree, the different energy fields interpenetrate and affect one another. A plant growing in a compound that is inhabited by unhappy and envious people will appear unhealthy, dull and lifeless, no matter how much attention is given to it. The plant is simply reflecting the negative radiation produced by the inhabitants of the house.

For one who has eyes to see and ears to hear, plants speak many languages. They are mirrors reflecting the intensity and nature of the energy field of the environment in which they grow. There are some plants that signal the coming of a drought; others sprout to signal the coming of rain or an epidemic. On entering a new place, experienced herbalists and mystics know the prevalent sickness and mood simply by observing the kinds of plants growing nearby. A plant growing in a house of happy and fulfilled people is radiant, attractive and healthy, even when little attention is given to it.

Trees are a good source of information about the past. Our thoughts send out vibrations which stay behind after we have left the place. Whatever we come into contact with absorbs part of our thought-forms. Every tree picks up the vibration of those who stayed under it. When a great, kind and knowledgeable man or woman sits under a tree, the tree becomes enriched; conversely, when people with negative thought-forms pass under a tree, the tree diminishes. However, the influence does not last. When a holy and enlightened person passes under a tree, the vibration remains with the tree for a longer time. A sensitive person who passes under the tree years later would be able to feel this vibration and even know that a great person passed by the tree. Whatever is said or done under the tree is never a secret. The tree hears everything, sees everything and absorbs everything.

Expanding Our Sense of Communis: The Soil and Oceans

While we often focus on the world of plants and animals, there are other parts of our communis that we tend to overlook. Scientists have

336

reminded us that the oceanic world is a universe of its own which is yet to be adequately studied. There are millions of species of marine animals that are yet unknown and modern science is just beginning to discover this amazing world. It is said that one third of all living organisms reside in the world's oceans. The soil of the world's ocean is one of the largest reservoirs of biodiversity in our ecosystem (7).

However, there is still another part of our ecosystem, our communis, that has been almost totally neglected until recently: the soil under our feet. There is much activity going on in the soil under our feet; the microbes, fungi, nematodes, mites and even gophers that make up a complex web of interrelationships.

A teaspoon of soil may have billions of microbes divided among 5,000 different types, thousands of species of fungi and protozoa, nematodes, mites and a few termite species (8). Scientists still marvel at how these intricate and complex webs of interactions, organisations and interrelationships are woven together to maintain a balance in our ecosystem. Without this balance, the world would not be able to feed itself. We are far more dependent on the soil than we can ever imagine or are willing to admit (9). For Leonardo da Vinci, humans have devoted more time to the study of the movement of celestial bodies than they have to the study of the soil beneath their feet (10). The biological world under our toes is often unexplored and unappreciated, yet it teems with life. In one square metre of earth, there live trillions of bacteria, millions of nematodes, hundreds of thousands of mites, thousands of insects and worms and hundreds of snails and slugs. However, because of their location and size, many of these creatures are as unfamiliar to us as anything found at the bottom of the ocean (11).

We live in a symbiotic community, but the problem is that we have little knowledge of other members of our ecosystem, our communis. Pax Communis is an invitation to immerse ourselves in our immediate life-world and rediscover a sense of community; a community comprising of humans, animals, plants and unseen entities. We now turn from nature and community to culture and spirituality.

12.2.5. Pax Spiritus: The Sanctuary and Pilgrimage of Life

Pax Spiritus is Not About Going to Church

The spiritual, within the context of Pax Spiritus, is not about going to church, the mosque or the temple, or partaking in external religious rituals. Such religiosity shares all the features of secularism, with an added slant of hypocrisy to it. The Nigerian political, economic and social space is occupied by such religiosity, which is often bereft of morality or good character. Once religion (spiritus) loses touch with the community (communis) and with reason (scientia), the result can be disastrous.

There is a new form of witchcraft flourishing in African societies, in which witches and wizards are the so-called spiritual and political leaders. It is witchcraft based on systematic and subtle brainwashing of the ignorant worshippers and followers and is known as 'priestcraft'. Unlike witchcraft, which is associated with the night and can be detected by the suffering patient, priestcraft operates in broad daylight. The victims' blood is sucked before their very eyes, yet they rejoice in this fact. They are told that their reward will be in heaven, even as they wallow in suffering and desperation. While their 'spiritual' leaders revel in opulence, the followers struggle to eat a single meal in a day. Priestcraft pollutes the victims with the poison of ignorance and religiosity, weakens their critical intellectual questioning and turns them into people who are more dead than alive. Moreover, while their blood is being drained, they thank God and ask for God's blessing on their exploiters.

Modern Africa has become a battleground for bitter wars and disunity fuelled by religion. It is in Africa that you often find the bitterest and most violent forms of religious violence. Until this problem is solved, Africa will know little or no peace and there will be no genuine and sustainable economic progress, social transformation and development.

However, things have not always been like this. Traditional African religion was not a perfect religion; however, it promoted peace and harmonious living among people because it was well-entrenched in their culture and worldview.

Africa and Ineffective Religiosity

The arrival of foreign religions in Africa came in tandem with capitalism and materialism. Africa did not convert to Christianity or Islam. Rather, these religions were imposed along with trade and globalisation. Over time, these religions were distorted and modified by the local population in a bizarre form of indigenisation and a shallow form of spirituality, beginning the era of capitalist Christianity and political Islam in Africa. How can Africa rediscover her authentic spirituality to gain true religious freedom?

The big challenge is, how do you free a slave who is happy being a slave? How do you open the eyes of the oppressed to see and accept that they are in bondage so that they can fight to free themselves? If you are a human rights activist, or a social critic, or an ardent defender of the poor and oppressed in Africa, know this: nothing is more difficult and risky than fighting to rescue a slave who is happy to remain a slave or an oppressed person who is content with his or her oppressor. It is in the poorest and most illiterate parts of Africa that you also find the most fervent religious fanatics who worship at the altar of rich 'leaders'. The leaders are able to maintain their hold on power through the support of the very people whom they exploit and subjugate. This is what makes priestcraft so dangerous.

We live in a world where greed, injustice, materialism and racial prejudice are rampant. Religion, which is meant to be an instrument of our reunion with the Divine (religion comes from *re-ligare*: to bind, reunite, link together), has also become an instrument of disunity and violence. Millions are dying of hunger in Somalia and Malawi in a world where American and European companies spend millions of dollars to destroy thousands of tons of excess food. A man may be sick but many pass him by because he does not speak their language. A woman may die in an accident and some people are happy simply because she does not practise their religion. African churches are overflowing every Sunday, but how many are Christians at heart? How many Muslims know what Islam is really about?

Spirituality: Beyond Piety

Perhaps the time has come for us to drop the Bible and the Qur'an and look each other in the face. We need to share our common humanness. We need to experience our human fragility together and acknowledge our inherent flaws, so that we can reach out to one another.

Our modern society deifies religion and trivialises spirituality. What we have, then, is a lifeless religion, for religion without spirituality leads to ignorance, fanaticism, brainwashing and deceit. Religion without spirituality allows evil leaders to deceive and manipulate their subjects to their selfish advantage. Religion without spirituality leads to spiritual stagnation and immature and unbalanced personalities. Religion without spirituality leads to vain religiosity. Religion without spirituality leads to a dead conscience. Spirituality is the soul of religion. Spirituality is your life, your fundamental decision for God, your inner resolve to live a creative and morally sound life. Spirituality is what makes you religious or not. Religion is a way of expressing spiritual experiences. Much of religious practice today is devoid of sound spirituality, which can lead to acts of sheer inhumanness.

The millions of immigrants from the plundered, poor countries who sit at the gates of rich nations is a reminder that there will be no peace in the world unless there is equity, fairness and justice. We are either happy together or unhappy together. The choice is ours. Pax Spiritus calls for a new approach to religion; hence our combined notion of Sanctuary and Pilgrimium. A sanctuary is a place where we put into practice the ideals and principles of religion—a place where spirituality expresses itself in love and care for fellow human beings, for nature, for the environment and the entire ecosystem.

In the context of Pax Spiritus, the St Benedict Monastery in Edo State, Nigeria, is the real-life actualisation of Sanctuary. For others, it could be a mosque, a shrine or a place set aside for religious activities. The important factor is that it is a physical place in time and space. Pax Spiritus goes beyond mental abstractions of religious piety or an imaginary spiritual journey into the soul. The Sanctuary, within Pax Spiritus, is a real place, a public space, a place where human solidarity and human love is expressed. At the same time the co-spiritual journey is also a real experience of learning how to live together, sharing and reciprocally giving and receiving life. We now turn from Pax Spiritus to Pax Scientia.

12.2.6. Pax Scientia: Research Academy

Africa's Knowledge Deficit

It is said that humanity is going through the most fertile, creative, productive and fruitful period of history. Contemporary civilisation is the greatest producer of wealth, affluence, prosperity and development. Ironically, it is also the producer of the greatest pollution, destruction, poverty, hunger, violence, hatred and inequality between humans. Many 'developed' countries are underdeveloped in many ways, while many 'developing' countries are not actually developing. While the global north is struggling with the negative effects of overdevelopment, mis-development or mal-development, Africa is struggling with the negative effects of slow or no development. The north is excessively rich; Africa is excessively poor.

Both poverty and wealth put pressure on the resource bases of the world. The rich contribute to damaging the earth through excessive greed, consumerism and unsustainable lifestyles. The poor also damage the earth through bush burning, cutting down valuable trees without any plans to replace them and selling rare animal parts—all in a bid to raise money to feed themselves and their families. Poverty can be as damaging as excessive wealth and both over-development and under-development are incompatible with sustainable development.

Looking at Africa, what is obvious is not the growth of basic and mature engineering, automation, post-harvest preservation, food processing and packaging technologies, infrastructural developments, social amenities, oil management technology and water technology—all of which are vital for poverty eradication. Rather, what is evident is the spread of religious dogma, extraordinary sprouting of churches, Pentecostalism and piety, which demands unquestioning submission to revealed 'truths' and discourages reason, dissidence and logic. Excessive religionism and spiritualism may be one of the greatest obstacles to the progress of African nations. Moreover, the greatest challenge facing Africa today may well be her ability to cultivate a mindset that is steeped in chemistry, economics, mathematics and physics while still maintaining a reasonable and balanced approach to religion (12). Development here refers to the ability of nations to order society in such a way that there is stability and security and basic amenities such as water, housing and energy. In this sense, it is true that many African countries are yet to see 'development' or modernity.

Africa and a Deficient Education System

Young people in Nigeria and Africa know all the latest news on the English Premier League. They can tell you when Manchester United is playing Chelsea and can even predict who will win and by how many goals. Due to cable, internet and satellite TV, young people also know how many soldiers are killed in war zones daily, how many suicide bombings take place and how many people are kidnapped by militants. They know which countries have the most relaxed immigration rules. However, ask them about the health benefits of bananas, or how bush burning affects soil productivity, or what a balanced diet is and you will be surprised at their level of ignorance.

Young Nigerians are readily acquiring information about other lands, while rapidly losing knowledge of their own land, their environment, their culture and their people. This is a problem because no nation can genuinely develop until it has a deposit of local knowledge which it preserves and nurtures. Real and lasting development is not imported from other countries—it is home-grown. The art of development is the ability to convert and exploit local knowledge to create relevant, sustainable and affordable technology. The best solutions to a nation's problems are those which come from within. However, because this is not recognised, indigenous knowledge is not adequately valued and as such is being lost at an alarming rate.

In many indigenous societies, when a knowledge-bearer dies, his knowledge dies with him. Today we speak of protecting the environment and our rare species of plants and animals. However, equally important is the need for national and international efforts to protect and preserve indigenous knowledge. At a national level, the education system in Africa has a vital role to play in ensuring that indigenous knowledge is shared, preserved and used for our country's development. However, today, education is too preoccupied with other interests and goals. Most students in Africa are conditioned to think that the reason they go to school is to acquire paper certificates in order to get a career. Society prides acquisition of degrees over holistic and integral personal development.

Africa: To Glocalise or to Globalise?

How relevant is university education to our society's development? If the educational system in Nigeria and Africa is useful, why is unemployment increasing, the poverty level rising and growth still a pipe dream? Why do people still go to school? Many students are not stimulated by the curriculum; however, they are made to believe that it will launch them into a better world: the corporate world of white-collar jobs, away from the poverty of their parents. They are expected to adopt the dress codes and research methodology of their academic disciplines as a mark of induction into the new academic community; that of the Ivory Tower.

The teachers in many African schools are still teaching students of today using methodologies that were developed to solve the problems of 50 years ago. They copy from lecture notes which they have inherited from their teachers, who inherited them from their own teachers and who in turn inherited them from their own teachers. How did we get here? What went wrong? How do we solve the problem? Why is the African educational system not built on our indigenous knowledge, worldview and culture? We have inherited a faulty educational system, but why can't we change it?

That is the crux of the problem. One cannot change what one does not understand. First, one must understand, then re-interpret and then change. To change a world, one must first re-interpret it. The tragedy of education in Africa is that the university system, which was inherited from the colonial rulers, is so deeply entrenched in the Western worldview and epistemology that it is unable to critique its own relevance within the local, political, economic and cultural settings of Africa. In Nigeria, we have indigenised the education system; however, we have not decolonised it.

Therefore, while the university system critiques different aspects of the current social system like governance, economics, health policies and other social issues, it lacks the ability to critique itself and question its own existence, methodology and the relevance of its 'university-ness'.

Can We Return to the Universitas?

The word 'university' derives from the Latin: *'Universitas magistrorum et scholarium'*, which means 'community of teachers and scholars'. In the past, a university did not refer to physical structures and buildings, but to a community of people who gathered to reflect and share ideas. Its origin can be traced back to the monastic communities in Europe. Universities started in the monasteries, from where they evolved into public institutions. The very first scholars were monks and clergymen.

What was the focus of the 'universitas', the 'community of teachers and scholars'? They discussed issues that affected their daily life. They reflected on day-to-day realities and proffered solutions. Their concerns were local issues; issues that affected themselves and their community. They philosophised, theologised and moralised on practical matters of daily life.

Every institution, every university, is a local entity; they exist to solve local issues. Why? Because every person is a product of a community. In Nigeria, when new universities are created, their focus is immediately global. They want to go to the moon with ladders and ropes. Their websites are filled with outlandish goals, such as: 'to be a world-renowned centre of learning', 'to be among the top ten universities in the world' and 'to train students who will compete with the best brains in the world'.

Thus, local universities in villages in Western or Eastern or Northern Nigeria for example, where there are no developed roads, no regular electricity and no water, now want to train students who will compete with world-class entrepreneurs like Bill Gates, Mark Zuckerberg and Steve Jobs (none of whom are university graduates). Some Nigerian universities want to train students who will be more brilliant than Albert Einstein, Richard Dawkins and Stephen Hawking. But, pray, why not teach them to be as bright as Nigerian heroes such as Wole Soyinka, Chinua Achebe and Uthman dan Fodio? Why not teach our students how to think critically about the problems of Africa: hunger, political instability, inadequate infrastructure, outdated agricultural practices, religious fanaticism, etc.? To do this, we need to cultivate a mental outlook that thinks locally, looks inwardly and acts locally. Of course, we must be open to the world and learn from the rest of the world. We must tap into the global knowledge system.

However, openness to the world is not the issue. The issue is that what Africa is learning from the world is not technological innovation, theory building, scientific innovation and agricultural technology. What Africa is learning from the global world are things that encourage consumption of Western products and destruction of our tradition and culture: we learn to wear Western dress and use Western tools of violence like guns and bombs to kill. We practise democracy, the principles of which we neither understand nor believe in.

The idea of the communiversity, then, is a move towards glocalisation of education and development rather than globalisation.

Re-shaping Education in Nigeria and Africa

The goal of education should not be mastery of a subject matter, but the mastery of one's person. The goal of education should not be to cram facts, techniques, methods and information into students' minds, but rather to teach them how to use ideas and knowledge to develop their personhood. Rather than seeing education as a means of personal development, most students tend to see it as a step towards a career, as something that will launch them into a so-called 'successful' life. Proper education should help students to find a decent calling or vocation, not just a career. A career is a job, a way to earn one's daily bread. A calling is about life, personhood, values and one's vocation and gift to the world. It comes out of one's inner convictions. A career can always be found in a calling, but it rarely happens the other way around (13).

For centuries, human beings lived under the illusion that with enough knowledge and technology, we could manage and control the Earth. As new factories and industries produced more computers, electronics and machines, we thought we had succeeded in mastering our planet. We thought that a rapid increase in data, words, paper and technical details was equivalent to an increase in knowledge and wisdom. The truth, however, is that as we grew in technical knowledge—in 'know-how'— we lost other kinds of knowledge: intelligence, which is characterised by an ability to foresee the consequences of one's actions; wisdom; and 'know-why'. Our students graduate from universities with a distorted view of reality, of nature and the cosmos. Some of these students score highly in their examinations and are then regarded as 'experts'. They are brilliant and bright. They have the technical know-how, but they cannot ask the more profound questions of life. University education provides students with answers—without them even knowing what the questions are.

It is worth noting that the people whose work and ideas have led to the destruction of the ecosystem, disturbance of climate stability and depreciation of biological diversity, are not ignorant people; indeed, most of these people have letters after their names. For humanity to survive, we must give up the misleading conception that Western culture represents the pinnacle of human achievement. Modern capitalist culture does not nourish that which is best and noblest in the human person. It does not cultivate vision, imagination, a sense of wonder and spiritual sensitivity. It encourages pride instead of humility, violence instead of gentleness, greed instead of generosity, individualism instead of commonality, selfishness instead of selflessness, monoculture instead of cultural diversity.

University education has three aspects: *form, process* and *content.* Form—which is the focus of almost all discussions about university education in Nigeria and most parts of Africa—refers to a university's physical structures, bureaucratic systems, salary, finance systems and organogram. Process refers to the relationships between vice chancellors and lecturers, between students and lecturers and between the university and the host community as well as the society at large. The third aspect is content, which refers to the curriculum and the literature used in teaching. A look at the content of Nigeria's university curricula indicates that colonialism is still very much alive and active and true independence is still far off. University education is the most colonised aspect of African life. Each year we churn out graduates who lack knowledge of their history, have no appreciation for their tradition and who see reality through the prism of Western reality. In my view, the decolonisation

347

of our university curricula and literature is the most urgent reform of education that is needed in Nigeria and Africa. One looks forward to the days when strikes by university lecturers will not just concern money and finance (form), but also about morality (process) and the quality of the curricula (content).

It is not enough to engage in education. The structure of the education itself must be examined and challenged. It is not enough to study scientific truths; how science arrived at such 'truths' has to be questioned. Science does not exist independently of its cultural context, despite its pretence to undiluted objectivity. While education can bring liberation, it can also be a means of keeping people in bondage. Moreover, lest we forget, education is no guarantee of decency, prudence or wisdom. Learning in itself will not make us better people. The worth of education must be measured against the standards of decency and human survival. It is therefore unrealistic to think that education in itself will save humanity. Our survival in the next century depends on education, but not education as we have conceived it for over 60 years. We need a new kind of education.

Transformation Studies in Africa: Towards Educational Reform in Nigeria

Higher technical education is increasingly recognised as critical to development, especially with growing awareness of the role of science, technology and innovation in economic growth. Universities and research institutions are well placed to aid development through their involvement with the local business industry and society. Universities and institutions in developing countries can aid development by focusing some of their technical training on specific development needs. Nigerian polytechnics were established precisely to meet the need for technical training in various fields of expertise, in order to hasten development. Unfortunately, the trend of acquiring university degrees and the prestige of being labelled a university graduate often makes polytechnic graduates feel inferior and less valued.

It is very important that universities in Africa focus on encouraging innovation and concentrate on building entrepreneurial skills among students to help them develop the capacity to transform ideas into business proposals and actual products and services; otherwise, these universities remain mere ivory towers with no impact on societal transformation. University education, as it is presently constituted in Nigeria and Africa, is geared toward producing graduates who are job seekers rather than job creators. Universities also need to integrate with their local communities and help to promote local economic transformation. The aim of such a new movement of the formal education system, which we call a communiversity, is to produce enterprising graduates who are likely to generate jobs in their communities while adding to the growth of the economy. Such communiversities consciously recognise and transcend the embedded dichotomies in the conventional mode of knowledge creation. How, then, is this working out in practice, within a Nigerian research academy?

From African to Transformation Studies

In 2017, after a series of meetings and engagements with the relevant authorities, a new curriculum on Transformation Studies in Africa was approved by the Senate of the University of Ibadan, Nigeria's premier university, rated among the best in Africa. The curriculum was designed by co-authors Anselm Adodo and Ronald Lessem, together with Trans4m co-founder, Alexander Schieffer. A year earlier in 2016, Anselm Adodo founded the Africa Centre for Integral Research and Development, later renamed Ofure (Pax) Integral Research and Development Initiative (OFIRDI).

The aim of OFIRDI was to establish new templates for carrying out research *in* and *for* Africa. For centuries, Africans were a people spoken about, spoken for and spoken against by foreigners. We read about who we are from what others have said and written about us. OFIRDI asserts the right of Africans to speak in their own language and metaphors. It affirms that Africans must reclaim their right to cognitive freedom if they genuinely seek to be free. Africa must be aware of and fight against the *coloniality of knowledge* and *epistemicide*, which are modern forms of colonisation, by evolving its own research methods, research methodologies and critical theory *suited to* and *geared towards* African epistemological emancipation (14). OFIRDI asserts that research in Africa must not end in lecture halls but must lead to innovation. The aims and objectives of OFIRDI are:

- To develop and institutionalise distinct Afrocentric research methods and research methodology interdependent with, rather than dependent upon, the dominant Eurocentric system.
- To research and develop the theory of communitalism, at both macro and micro levels, as the African antidote to the imbalances of rampant capitalism, relevant to particular societies and enterprises both within Africa and without.
- To give voice to the oft-neglected voices from the peripheries, which account for 80% of the world population.
- Charting an individual, communal and institutional path through research to a sustainable socio-economic and political liberation of Africa, duly documented and disseminated, operating at both micro and macro levels.
- Developing the concept of cognitive justice as the key to social, economic, political, mental and moral liberation of Africa.
- Development and institutionalisation, within a newly contextualised African university context, an ongoing evolution of the theory of communitalism.
- Disseminating integral research knowledge through the local book series on Innovation and Transformation as well an Integral Green Economies and Societies.
- Hosting international conferences on African knowledge systems.
- Postgraduate degree programmes on integral research and development.
- Research and teaching partnership with universities worldwide.

OFIRDI and the Emerging Field of Transformation Studies in Africa (TSA)

The first set of students of Transformation Studies in Africa hereafter referred to as TSA, were admitted at the Institute of African Studies, University of Ibadan, in January 2018. This set of 10 pioneer students came from different academic backgrounds and were fully inducted as students of Transformation after a series of interactions and class work, to ensure that they were truly grounded in integral research methodology. The Institute of African Studies, University of Ibadan, the pioneer of such institutes on the African continent, was established by an Act of the Senate of the University of Ibadan in July 1962. As a postgraduate institute conceived as an interdisciplinary research centre, it offers courses in the core disciplines of African Studies, spanning Anthropology, African History, African Law, African Music, African Visual Arts, Cultural and Media Studies, Diaspora and Transnational Studies, Gender Studies, Traditional African Medicine and Belief Systems.

It aims to build a body of knowledge and to construct an attitude of intellection that will not take for granted the heritage of African peoples, their experiences in the present and their aspirations for the future. The concerns for this heritage, these experiences and aspirations, have led it to adopt a multidisciplinary approach to scholarship in order to sharpen the Africa-centredness of its vision.

TSA: The Integral Approach to Research and Innovation

The TSA course contents at master's level are structured around four key terms, based on the Integral Research model developed by Lessem and Schieffer (15), which also serves to provide the underlying, integral architecture for our book:

1. The Four Pax's: Communis, Spiritus, Scientia, Economia
2. The Four C's: Calling, Context, Co-creation, Contribution
3. The Four Worlds: South, East, North, West
4. The Fourfold Rhythm: Grounding, Emergence, Navigation, *Effect*

It is essential that we deal—interactively—with all four realms as we engage with given transformational issues. Also, we must work closely with competent others; individual researchers cannot provide integrated solutions to the complex problems we face today.

From TSA to AARC: Philosophy in Action

The African Action Research Community (AARC) is the most recent evolution of TSA. While TSA focuses on developing masters and PhD students in integral action-research guise, AARC is an open community of scholars from across Africa, Europe, Asia and the Americas. Membership is by invitation or recommendation by existing members.

AARC is a voluntary association of scholars, academics, intellectuals, social entrepreneurs and activists who believe that a new world is possible—a new Africa that thrives on its own inner and outer resources. AARC members mainly comprise of university lecturers, independent scholars, political activists, thinkers, policymakers and students from across Africa, Europe, Asia and America. What binds the members together goes beyond race or colour. Instead, they are united by a belief in the power of action-based ideas to change the African narrative.

For many decades, the mantra of neo-liberal and capitalist policies in the global north/west was that there is no alternative to capitalism, globalism and the Western university system. Such a mantra projects a one-sided, Euro-American, monocultural worldview and neglects the perspectives of the other parts of the world. In the past ten years there has been a renewed interest in transcultural, transdisciplinary and transformational approaches to research, which embraces the four corners of the world: South, East, North and West. AARC members approach research from such transdisciplinary perspectives. For AARC, action research is research that not only examines, analyses and criticises, but also proposes concrete solutions and goes ahead to act, along with others, on the proposed solutions.

AARC is an open community for all interested in African Transformation and in exploring other ways to development in Africa. The group spans all corners of the globe. While the focus of research is Africa, members comprise people from every part of the world who are interested in Africa and the challenges of development it faces today. At the time of writing this book, there are over 100 serious minded members of AARC: heads of departments in universities, rectors of polytechnics, university vice-chancellors, professors in different disciplines, government officials, research institutes, policymakers, politicians and independent researchers. AARC is historic, as this is the first time such a diverse group of interdisciplinary and diverse group of specialist have come together under one umbrella with a clear vision—to be a 'think-tank' and a 'do-thank'; to translate theory into practice. It is also impressive that all the current students of TSA are committed to both.

The mission of AARC is to actively work towards a better Africa that thrives based on its ingenuity and resourcefulness; an Africa that evolves its own educational, technological, political and economic models based on African worldview, culture, spirituality and humanism. AARC provides practical answers and solutions to government policymakers based on research, thereby bridging the gap between academic research and practical application, between theory and practice, between being and doing. We now turn finally, in relation to the Four Pax's to Pax Economia.

12.2.7. Pax Economia: Integral Enterprise and Wellness

The Birth and Growth of Pax Herbals

In 1996, as a young student interested in the ethnography of development, Anselm Adodo travelled around the length and breadth of rural Nigeria, a country of 356,700 square miles, about 3.75 times larger than the UK, or 3 times the size of Germany, with a population of 120 million who speak over 250,000 dialects. He was amazed at the amount of knowledge, mostly tacit, which was available among the local communities. German pharmacist, Martin Hirt and his African counterpart, Bindanda M'pia (16), observed that the waste of knowledge is indeed the saddest feature of African life, especially in rural communities. There is evidence of waste everywhere. For example, after eating oranges, the peels are thrown away, not knowing that the peels of fruits are in fact more nourishing than the fruits themselves. High-quality cattle are taken to the city to be sold and the money used to buy poor-quality imported corned beef. A poor woman in the village sells her nutritious cassava flour so as to buy biscuits for her child attending secondary school. Precious beeswax is thrown away after honey is harvested while importing shoe polish containing poor, artificial wax. To buy a bottle of Coke, a mother sells oranges rich in vitamin C to quench her child's thirst. Africans export cheap but high-quality palm oil to Europe, where an expensive soap is made from it and then exported back to Africa and sold at unaffordable prices.

From Pax Herbals to Pax Economia

Through the utilisation of common plants and weeds, Pax Herbals was able to develop science-based herbal recipes that have been of help to the local community and to millions of Nigerians. It also has a home-grown business model that puts the interest of the local community as its central focus point. Rather than practise capitalism, which encourages the individual to acquire as much for himself as possible, Pax Herbals operates the business model of communitalism. The term communitalism is distinct from communalism. Communitalism is a business concept that makes up for the imbalance of capitalism. It affirms that some aspects of capitalism, such as individual inventiveness, is beneficial, but such inventiveness must be put at the service of the community so that both the individual and the community prosper. The key philosophy of communitalism is 'we are either happy together as a prosperous community or unhappy together'. For communitalism, the health and prosperity of the individual cannot be separated from the health and prosperity of the local community. Global health must start from local health, not the other way around. In the process, the link between individual, community and enterprise, between health and wholeness and making the integral will be made.

Pax Herbals is the registered business trademark for Pax Herbal Clinic & Research Laboratories. Although Pax Herbals was established in 1996, it was not registered as a private liability company until 2002. Pax Herbals is officially described as a centre for scientific identification, conservation, utilisation and development of African medicinal plants. Some of its stated objectives are:

- To serve as a centre for genuine African holistic healing that blends the physical and the spiritual aspects of the human person.
- To become a model comprehensive health care centre where the Western (North, West) and traditional (South, East) systems of healing are creatively blended.
- To be an example of how proper utilisation of traditional medicine can promote grassroots primary healthcare systems that are culturally acceptable, affordable and relevant.
- To disseminate knowledge of the health benefits of African medicinal plants through documentation, publications, seminars and workshops.
- To carry out research into ancient African healing systems with a view to modernising them and making them available to the wider world through education.
- To demystify African traditional medicine and purge it of elements of occultism, fetishism and superstition and promote its rational use so as to make it a globally acceptable enterprise.
- To be a truly indigenous herbal Phyto-medicine Centre that combines respect for nature and community with wealth creation.

In this vein, Pax Herbals has become a model profit-making enterprise that strives on putting nature, community and people at the heart of its existence.

Nature Power, Economics, Ecology

From the virgin soil in the Monastery of St Benedict sprouted the Pax Herbals tree, which has grown into a giant tree in the rural community of Ewu village, Edo State, with roots spreading out beyond Edo State to the whole of Nigeria and beyond. The concept of Pax Herbals, among others, is firstly to locate health, medicine and healthcare within the social context of the local community and secondly, to correct the distorted educational curricula in the local schools in Ewu, Edo State and Nigeria, which do not allow young people to understand the language of the earth, the trees, the soil and the streams.

In 1995, on a virgin piece of land in the monastery garden, populated by seemingly useless common weeds, there sprouted life-giving herbs. On a piece of land in an African bush in Ewu village, Edo State, Nigeria, within the precincts of a monastery (our sanctuary), there came an inspiration that a new way of life, a new source of livelihood, could sprout from the earth. After all, the earth is our home. We were made from the earth and the secret of our health and well-being lies in the earth. It is not a surprise that the more alienated we become from the earth, the sicker we become.

Pax Herbals is one of the few herbal manufacturing companies left in Nigeria that locally produces their herbal medicines, despite the harsh economic climate which makes it easier and more profitable to be an importer rather than a manufacturer. It is no wonder that the Nigerian market is flooded with herbal products from other countries. By so doing, Nigeria is creating wealth abroad and promoting poverty at home. At Pax Herbals, we believe that the only way to sustainable development is for Africa to produce what it consumes and consume what it produces. But to produce, one must innovate. Africa must innovate or perish.

At Pax Herbals, the herbs are cultivated directly and through accredited local outgrowers. We know the herbs, where they live, where they grow and how they grow. We know their names, their families and their stories. We journey with the herbs from the farm, to the collection and verification rooms, to the washing room, drying room, the processing factory, to the final product, through the quality control and to the market. We continue the journey by monitoring how the finished products interact with society, the reactions as well as the counter-reaction. To this effect, we have Pax pharmaco-vigilance centres in different parts of Nigeria. We ensure that we maintain this connection with the soil, with nature, the community, the environment, with people and with science. The inability to maintain this connection is the main reason behind the crisis rocking the modern world today.

It is no accident that the golden age of modern medicine and drug discovery, from 1900 to 1950, was the period when science was not yet disconnected from nature, when scientists tilled the soil, sharpened their gifts of observation of nature and the human body and were in touch with the natural environment. After many years of wandering in the wilderness of genetic engineering, genetic screening and gene therapy costing billions of dollars in research with little or nothing to show for it, modern science is now looking back towards the African bush. After billions of dollars in cancer research with no sign of a solution in sight, science is beginning to wonder if the solution is not actually in the African bush. As the 19th century priest and healer, Sebastian Kneipp, once said: "Many people die, while herbs that could cure them grow on their graves."

Gradually, the modern world is beginning to recover the true meaning of research. Re-search: to search for something that was once known but forgotten, to look again for what is missing. In fact, there is a connection between re-search and religion, from the Latin word *re-ligare* (to re-bind, re-unite, re-connect with a higher power). True scientists are spiritual by nature. Science does not and cannot create. Science only tries to re-discover, to re-fine, to re-interpret, re-design, re-confirm and re-search what is already there in nature. Call it what you wish, describe it as you like: chemistry, physics, agronomy, botany, microbiology, medical science, biology, anatomy, engineering, biochemistry etc., it still boils down to the same thing: *nature*.

12.3. CONCLUSION: COMMUNIVERSITY/COMMUNITALISM ALTOGETHER

12.3.1. The Four Pax's Come Alive

We—Adodo, Lessem and Bradley—began this concluding chapter by looking at the four Pax's in detail. We described them as dimensions of human realities in particular contexts, in this case within Africa, but with implications world-wide. Each dimension represents a visible and existing entity, an institutional entity, through which the realities are expressed and experienced. This is the key characteristic of the four Communiversity Pax's: that each reality is expressed in concrete institutions.

Pax Communis is expressed in the Ewu village community of Edo State, Western Nigeria, West Africa. *Pax Spiritus,* sanctuary or pilgrimium, is expressed in the existence of St Benedict Monastery, a monastic community located within Ewu local community in Nigeria. *Pax Scientia* is expressed through the Pax Centre for Integral Research and Development (OFIRDI), which has recently given a birth to a research Academy called African Action Research Community (AARC). *Pax Economia* is expressed through the existence of Pax Herbals, an indigenous laboratory that promotes physical, material and economic well-being. The staff strength of Pax Herbals is over 120. Even though Pax Herbals is located within a Catholic monastery (Our Spiritus) and operates based on Christian principles, only 20% of its staff is Catholic. Over 50% of the staff is non-Catholic, belonging to other Christian denominations, while over 30% of the staff is Muslim.

Nevertheless, the staff work together as a family. On Christian feasts and solemnities, the Muslims join the Christians for celebrations. On Muslim feasts, the Christians join the Muslims to celebrate, united by a belief in our common humanity which we all share. *'Pax'* is a Latin word which means peace. True healing requires peace. Religion without love is evil. When people fight because of religion, they are not fighting because they love God, or because they are spiritual. They are not merely hiding under the cloak of religion to fight for their own selfish interests.

12.3.2. Trans4m Communiversity Associates

As we approach the end of describing our journey around the stages of the communiversity we have arrived at the point of introducing the future organisational engine, to drive forward the communiversity movement, locally and globally. In 2019, Trans4m has arrived at an exciting new moment. Its former work is to become divided between two complementary organisational 'wings'. These are 'Trans4m Home for Humanity', with a particular focus on the re-GEN*E*-ration of self in the context of organisation and society and 'Trans4m Communiversity Associates' (TCA), with a particular orientation towards the re-GEN*E*-ration of contextualised knowledge-and-value, hence social innovation, in the context of self, organisation and society. This will be led by a local and global team and key associates, locally, from the four worlds-and-centre.

TCA's Core Work

TCA will operate in four spheres of work, which reflect the GEN*E*alogical pattern of the Trans4m philosophy. These are:

> **1. (Grounding) TCA Learning Community:** Shared Experience and Context Setting. An extension of the CLAD process—Communal Learning and Development—that has been initiated, in association with the prolific civic institution Akhuwat, focused on promoting economic SOUL-idarity, in Pakistan. The focus therein is on contextualising socioeconomic development in a particular community and society, through an individual and communal program and process, aligned with a significant 'model' organisation. Such Communiversity grounding and

contextualisation will take place in locations as diverse as Lagos and Lahore; Ljubliana and Liverpool; Amman and Alexandria; Harare and Hendala, invariably combining internal communal learning with external TCA catalysation. In subsequent years such context setting will turn into further co-evolution to wider global-to-local effect.

2. (Emergence) TCA Re-GENE-rative Pilgrimium: Imaginative Co-Evolution. One of the main planks of Trans4m's work, over the past two decades, has been its Mode 2 doctoral programme, validated by Da Vinci Institute of Technology, Johannesburg, South Africa. The TCA Doctoral programme will continue to operate but with some key differences. Firstly, in the future, it will be aimed at groups of doctoral students, working locally as well as globally together, in a Mode 2 way, to co-create their communiversities as such from the outset. It will have a mix of entry requirements, including those based on the standard master's academic route but, also, welcoming PHD (Process of Holistic Development) students with significant post-experience (rather than postgraduate) qualification. Thirdly and most importantly given the overall re-GENE-rative orientation of the TCA Pigrimium, the primary emphasis will be upon internalising the communiversal journey towards social innovation: from community through pilgrimium on to academy and laboratory, underpinned by our recursive GENE.

3. (Navigation) TCA Research Academies: Conceptual Innovation. For many people the way they know about Trans4m is through the many books that their co-workers have produced over the years. The flow of books, articles and research monographs will not abate under the new pattern of TCA. If anything, it is likely to expand to draw in a wider range of researchers, authors and students, in association with new publishing houses in Nigeria, Zimbabwe, the UK, Pakistan and elsewhere that TCA will be working with. However and now critical to this emancipatory phase of navigation, will be the research academies, serving to align theory and practice, in each particular cultural context, building on what is now emerging in Zimbabwe (Nhakanomics), Nigeria (Communitalism), Jordan (Tanweer), Pakistan (Soulidarity Economy) and Liverpool (Semiotic Economics), serving to re-GEN*E*-rate Integral Economics and Enterprise as a whole.

4. (Effect) TCA Socioeconomic Laboratory: Practical Experimentation. Through the work of Trans4m a vast range of expertise has been developed, facilitating local groups to develop grounding-to-effect social innovations, utilising the unique Trans4m Four Worlds/GEN*E* dynamic methodology, both in relation to developing integral enterprises (e.g. Sekem in Egypt, Medlabs in Jordan, PHC in Zimbabwe, Pax Herbals in Nigeria) and an integral economy (e.g. Slovenia) Such work to build up socioeconomic laboratories will continue, though now with a more concerted focus on the process of social innovation that underlies such, fostering integral research and innovation. To that end, work has already started on explicitly developing the southern, east and northern paths of research and innovation, as a process and in substance, so that relational, renewal and reasoned approaches to social innovation ensue, locally-globally, having a renewed focus on more tightly-defined facilitations with specific groups of leaders and transformation agents, both in locales that Trans4m is familiar with and new arenas for social innovation, GEN*E*rating a range of communiversities.

The communiversity, then, first intimated by us in 2013 (18), is a place, ultimately a laboratory, where communitalism is practised and expressed in real life, with identifiable impact. The acquisition of Western knowledge has been and is still invaluable to all, but on its own it has been incapable of responding adequately in the face of massive, intensifying disparities, uncontrolled exploitation of pharmacological and other genetic resources and rapid depletion of the earth's natural resources.

The same could be said of the communiversities we are co-evolving around the world. In a divided world such as ours, we do not necessarily

361

need more billionaires, more consumers and more powerful men. The world is in dire need of more healers, more peacemakers, more artists and more storytellers and this is where our communiversities comes in. We hope you and your community will join us on this ongoing journey.

12.4. REFERENCES

1 Adodo, A (2017) *Integral Community Enterprise in Africa. Communitalism as An Alternative to Capitalism.* London. Routledge.

2 Adodo, A (2017) *op cit*

3 Ba, Diadie. (2007) 'Africans still seething over Sarkozy Speech'. [online]. Reuters.com. Availableat:https://uk.reuters.com/article/uk-africa-sarkozy-idUKL0513034620070905

4 Illich, I. (1995) *Deschooling Society.* London. Marian Boyars Publishers

5 Adodo, A. (2000). *Nature Power. A Christian Approach to Herbal Medicine*: Akure. Don Bosco press.

6 Buhner, S (2002) *The Lost Language of Plants.* London. Chelsea Green Publishing: VT

7 Rose, P and Laking, A (2008) *Oceans: Exploring the Hidden Depths of the Underwater World.* London. BCC Books.

8 Nardi, J (2007) *Life in the soil: A Guide for Naturalists and Gardeners.* Chicago.University of Chicago Press

9 Taylor, B (2017) *An Altar in The World: Finding the Sacred Beneath Our Feet.* London. Canterbury Press

10 Nardi, J (2003) *The World Beneath our Feet: A Guide to Life In the Soil.* London. Oxford University Press

11 Nicholl, C (2005) *Leonardo Da Vinci: Flights of The Mind.* London. Penguin.

12 Adodo, A (2017) *op cit*

13 Orr, D. (1994) *Earth in Mind. New York.* Island Press.

14 Ndlovu-Gatsheni, S (2013) *Coloniality of Power in Postcolonial Africa Myths of Decolonization.* Dakar. CODESRIA.

15 Lessem R and Schieffer A (2010) *Integral research and Innovation: Transforming Enterprise and Society.* Abingdon. Routledge

16 Hirt, M, & M'pia, B (1997) *Natural Medicine in the tropics.* Frankfurt. Anamed.

17 Adodo, A (2000). *op cit*

18 Lessem, R., Schieffer, A, Tong, J, Rima S (2013) *Integral Dynamics: Political Economy, Cultural Dynamics & the Future University*. Abingdon. Routledge

Index

Lightning Source UK Ltd.
Milton Keynes UK
UKHW031819090919
349465UK00001B/1/P